MAGISTERIAL IMAGINATION

MAGISTERIAL IMAGINATION

Six Masters of the Human Sciences

Max Lerner

Edited and with an introduction
by Robert Schmuhl

Transaction Publishers
New Brunswick (U.S.A.) and London (U.K.)

Library of Congress Catalog Number: 93–39856
ISBN: 1–56000–168–2 (cloth)
Printed in the United States of America

Library of Congress Cataloging-in-Publication Data

Lerner, Max, 1902–
    Magisterial Imagination: six masters of the human sciences / Max
Lerner : edited and with an introduction by Robert Schmuhl.
        p.   cm.
    Includes index.
    ISBN 1-56000-168-2 (cloth)
    1. Philosophy—History.   I. Schnuhl, Robert.   II. Title.
B73.L47   1994
190--DC20   93-39856
                                                                  CIP

Contents

Preface and Acknowledgments

Shortly before Max Lerner died on June 5, 1992, he asked me to gather these essays together in a single volume. Professor Irving Louis Horowitz, president of Transaction Publishers, immediately saw the value of such a work. I am deeply grateful to him for his counsel and encouragement. Thanks to Professor Horowitz and Transaction, several of Lerner's books are back in print, and I am delighted that this collection will take its place at their side.

In most cases, these essays appear exactly as they were originally published. In a few instances, phrases that refer to subsequent passages in the books in which they first appear have been deleted. Some footnotes, too, have been either dropped or changed to function more appropriately with the existing essay.

Edna Albers Lerner and Stephen Lerner offered valuable advice. I am grateful to them and other members of the Lerner family for many kindnesses.

Thomas J. Stritch, professor emeritus of American Studies at the University of Notre Dame and the former editor of *The Review of Politics*, kindly offered his wise advice as the introduction was being written.

Evelyn Irsay, Max Lerner's long-time and ever-efficient assistant, always knew the answers to an editor's questions. Nancy Kegler, equally efficient assistant in the Department of American Studies at the University of Notre Dame, worked her magic on the computer to come up with the finished manuscript.

Judith Roberts Schmuhl and Michael Robert Schmuhl, once again, created the right environment to produce a book, and I appreciate their thoughtful avoidance of a certain room in the house as it came into being.

—R.S.

Introduction

Robert Schmuhl

As Max Lerner grew older, working on book projects assumed an urgency bordering on obsession. Columns and other essays were written, university classes taught, and public lectures delivered, but publishing new books or up-dated editions of earlier ones occupied much of his time. He charted the future by composing lists of titles for volumes to be completed. At the time of his death (in 1992 at the age of eighty-nine), Lerner was looking forward to finishing thirty—yes, thirty—more books or new editions, including *Magisterial Imagination*.

A public intellectual engaged in America's actions and passions for much of the twentieth century, Lerner always possessed big ideas—and they possessed him. Although possibly wide-eyed about what he could personally accomplish, he had a steady, penetrating vision of the destiny of his adopted country and other civilizations. Indeed, for the last few years of the long life (forty-nine years) of his syndicated newspaper column, he called it "Civilization Watch," describing himself as a "civilization watcher."

Lerner's analytical commentary, especially his essays for newspapers and magazines, exemplified what is called the "higher journalism." Concerned as much with ideas and their impact as men and events, this type of writing, common in Europe, is notably uncommon in the United States. The steady flow of insightful interpretation by the likes of G. K. Chesterton, Raymond Aron, Bertrand de Jouvenal, Karl Kraus, and Walter Benjamin set standards for this "higher journalism" that continue to be an influential dimension of the serious press in

England and on the continent. In America, one thinks of Walter Lippmann, H. L. Mencken, Russell Kirk, and Garry Wills—along with Lerner—as writers engaged in exploring ideas for a popular reading audience. Yet such work, always relatively rare, is nowadays increasingly crowded out by chatter and gossip, usually about shooting-star celebrities.

Anyone who enjoyed the pleasures of his company knows the range and depth of Lerner's intellectual concerns. All was grist to his mill. No thinker, from Aristotle to Allan Bloom, escaped his notice; no science, from Pythagorean geometry to contemporary oncology, failed to engage him. No original idea was alien to him. Although Lerner's voluminous output of commentary, both journalistic and academic, was decidedly his own, he anchored his work and gave it even greater depth by drawing on the writings of classic representatives of Western thought.

In one of the essays that follows, Lerner characterizes Thorstein Veblen as "the last man who knew everything." But, in fact, Veblen's powerful analysis was just one more framework to enrich Lerner's own writing. Lerner's knowledge encompassed philosophy, history, literature, psychology, economics, law, and sociology, plus some nameless provinces of the mind. His years of work on the *Encyclopedia of the Social Sciences* (from 1927 until 1932) and the essays he composed and collected for *Ideas Are Weapons* (1939) and *Ideas for the Ice Age* (1941) were more than an apprenticeship.[1] These early-career experiences established a foundation of learning on which he built a succession of sturdy interpretations of critical ideas, their creators, and their consequences.

To a certain extent, Lerner (like Veblen) was a representative of an earlier intellectual tradition, one that believed in the adventurous and fulfilling possibility of linking different realms of inquiry into a meaningful whole. The rise of specialization in the academy, so marked during the second half of the twentieth century, made such boundary-breaking scholars an endangered species—and also suspect in many rarefied quarters of higher learning. Lerner submitted his work to this charge of attempting too much joyously. He was suspicious of narrow expertise. He remained committed to wholeness, to gestalts, to unity. He eagerly tackled new subjects he thought might illumine both the past and the present. In this sense, he was a rebel, fiercely clinging to a prior tradition despite rushing currents that tried to keep "disciplines" distinct and separate through the narrowing of specialization.

In the foreword to *The Unfinished Country*, a collection of newspaper columns about the 1950s, Lerner praises the much-maligned "generalist," laboring during a time of ever-growing specialization in the academy and elsewhere. "In an era of the specialist, I make an appeal for the vocation of the generalist," he writes, noting later the danger of being too narrowly focused: "Unfortunately life itself is not divided into these specialized patches, but comes to us whole and asks to be grasped whole."[2] Arriving at "A Sense of the Whole"—the title of one of Lerner's never completed books—required exploration of as many different facets of human experience as possible. Of Veblen, he remarks: "Veblen was notable for breaking down the fences that separated the disciplines, and roaming under whatever intellectual sky and among whatever cultural pastures he chose." Statements of comparable meaning appear about the other figures discussed in the essays that follow as tributes to their scope and breadth. Of course, writers with such range can be accused today of sacrificing the specialist's unswerving consideration of a specific subject. However, their powers of intellectual penetration more than compensate for singular attention to a particular topic.

Lerner's own biography reflects intellectual wanderlust, a conscious effort to visit any area of human inquiry offering insight for answering a question or resolving a problem. He earned a doctorate from the Robert Brookings Graduate School of Economics and Government in 1927 and later held academic appointments in government at Harvard University and in political science at Williams College before becoming a professor of American civilization and later a professor of American civilization and world politics at Brandeis University, where he taught for thirty-five years. From 1974 until shortly before his death, he was Distinguished Professor of Human Behavior at United States International University in California. His literary work reflects both his expanding concerns and his effort to bridge the academy and the wider world at large. As he told one interviewer, "In Jefferson's day, it was possible to have the sense of encompassing what was known and thought, but it is very hard now. For that reason I feel if any writer, any thinker, has the urge to broaden out and try to do the overarching, synthesizing work, it is all to the good."[3]

Although his range was wide and his reading omnivorous, Lerner returned to certain thinkers repeatedly to help shape his own thought. These "masters of the human sciences"—one Greek (Aristotle), one Italian (Niccolò Machiavelli), one French (Alexis de Tocqueville), one English (John Stuart Mill), and two American (Thorstein Veblen and Oliver Wendell Holmes, Jr.)—had in common what Lerner liked to call a "magisterial imagination." They saw life steadily and saw it whole. Although they all broke new ground, some, like Tocqueville and Veblen with astonishing originality, none was anarchistic. All were synthesists, bringing together ideas old and new, re-arranging knowledge and systems of knowledge into patterns the intellectual world recognizes as unmistakably their own. They wrote with authority and creativity in ways Lerner found both powerful and illuminating. Indeed, in all cases their works moved him to publish new editions of their enduring books and essays.

These six figures share with Lerner a deeply rooted sense of the world as it is. Assigning shorthand labels to describe such thinkers is a difficult task, but collectively they might be viewed as "philosophical realists" or, if you prefer, "realistic philosophers." They understood what it means to be human and the various forces that affect thought and action. In all cases, the political dimension of life occupies a central, animating place, with the dynamics of power (what it means? who gains it? how to use it?) of critical importance. Throughout their work, a reader sees the validity and significance of Aristotle's observation that "man is by nature a political animal." Times, circumstances, and systems of governing change, but questions about what constitutes a polity and where people operate within the particular political structures they find themselves remain relevant. Each of the six figures discussed in this book deserves the designation of philosopher—as does Lerner himself. But these philosophers—unlike, say, René Descartes, Immanuel Kant, Sören Kierkegaard, or even Bertrand Russell—rooted their abstractions and theories of politics in the rich soil of reality, as they came to understand it through their direct experience, close study, and individual analysis. The vaporous realms of *cogito ergo sum* and of being and nothingness were less attractive than the more down-to-earth human condition they confronted and could philosophize about.

Lerner mastered these "masters" by probing to the core the meaning of their thought and its significance. He also offered biographical portraits of these figures as well as explanations of their times. This text-context approach yields rounded assessments, but Lerner did not stop there. He used each thinker as a point of departure for articulating aspects of his own thought, and for providing commentary on his time. Some references may seem dated today, but they reflect Lerner's abiding effort to write concretely and accessibly for a general reader. Lerner was above all shrewd. Even among his masters he noted weaknesses, flights of fancy, puncturing prejudice and provincialism.

Lerner described his method in a memoir he wrote covering the years between his birth in Russia in 1902 and his adventures as a foreign correspondent during the Second World War:

> In writing about a thinker I tried to understand how his life-journey came out of his time, class, family and circumstances, and how his thinking in turn came out of the ways he saw the world, his society and himself. For me he was, in Emerson's term, "man thinking," grappling with the bramble-bush of man's cosmos and his mind, bloodying himself in the process, yet driven by a powerful force to penetrate the thicket. I didn't have much truck with the weary arguments over idealism, realism, positivism, intuitionism, which have filled the methodology of the history of ideas. They struck me as the bloodless battles of the categories. What moved me more was why a thinker chose the intellectual encounters he did, where he found help and light, what bedevilments of thought and living he hoped to untangle, how he felt about himself and his work, to what uses his thought was put by those who followed him. On the last of these I felt that if a thinker had been distorted by his "school" it was because their needs were not his and because he had left them something to distort, but that he was not therefore responsible. Plato has to be disengaged from the Platonists, Machiavelli from the Machiavellians, Marx from the Marxists, Freud from the Freudians.[4]

Very much his own man intellectually, Lerner worked hard to avoid the simplistic stereotyping so common in journalism and academic circles. His articles for *The New Republic* and *The Nation* during the 1930s as well as the publication of his first book, *It Is Later Than You Think: The Need for a Militant Democracy*, in 1938 led to the label of "liberal" that followed Lerner the rest of his life.[5] In its June 15, 1992 obituary, *Newsweek* referred to him as "an unabashed liberal"; however, such pigeonholing wasn't accurate because through the years his political and social thinking had become not only more complicated but individualistic. He was always alert to new patterns of thought and how they functioned vis-à-vis earlier, "classic" models and systems.

The six figures discussed in the essays collected in this book occupied the place they did in Lerner's personal pantheon because they approached whatever they wrote about in ways he admired and tried to emulate. He saw each of them—and himself—as what he called "a working thinker," someone in a continuing search for answers to the larger questions. Lerner remarked about Mill: "Primarily he was a working thinker, intent on finding the best sources and conditions for his thought, reading books and conversing with their writers for the light they might shed on whatever problem he was tussling with." In Mill's case, you see the work of a mind evolving and developing over time—from his early work in logic through his vast output of political and social philosophy to his posthumously-published essays about religion and the existence of God. Such probing requires intellectual stretching and the building of an encompassing system of thought.

For Lerner, resolving "whatever problem" that arose involved an *agon*, a struggle not only to find the most appropriate solution but the most arresting, stylish explanation of it. Unlike Mill, who found in his refinement of utilitarianism a philosophy he and others could follow, Lerner steered clear of such "isms" or intellectual movements. Democracy, however, in all its unruliness and contradictions always absorbed his attention and drove him to explore its political, social, and economic possibilities. Tocqueville, Veblen, and Holmes loom large in this context because they explicitly deal with democratic questions in the American setting. Aristotle, Machiavelli, and Mill tend to concern themselves with democracy and discontents related to it in somewhat more general terms—of indisputable value yet removed, of course, from Lerner's abiding interest, from the late 1940s on, of explaining America as a distinct civilization.

Besides being working thinkers, all of these figures have a broad gauge. Lerner says of Aristotle, "There was nothing alien to his consuming curiosity, and no items of experience which he did not seek to digest and relate in the form of general propositions." A similar sentence could be written about the other masters—and also about the person analyzing them. Aristotle, for example, was as much scientist as philosopher. His efforts to collect, consider, and classify whatever gained his attention made his work less metaphysical than that of Plato or the disciples of Platonism. But by staying tethered to the world around him, Aristotle approached subjects as they were, with a stunningly uncommon common sense. Transcendent models were for other thinkers, given to soaring flights of speculation. Aristotle, like the other figures discussed in this book, wrestled with real concerns and circumstances within the larger context of ultimate meaning and consequence. In each case, too, there's the centrality of the political nature of human experience.

Like Lerner himself, his masters are very much their own thinkers, strikingly independent in providing explanations and interpretations. As Tocqueville (in Lerner's phrase) "accustomed himself to the search for the relation between the concrete fact and the frame of the universe," so too did the other figures strive to present their singular visions. These visions, however, were based on realities embedded in human experience across time. What Lerner writes about Holmes could also apply to the other thinkers, not to mention to their commentator:

> To lay violent siege to history was as little in his temperament as to shake his fist at the cosmos. He accepted the limits both of history and of nature and within those limits he found his freedom in a free world. He was part of no movement. What he said and wrote did not grow out of the current social experience or the emerging cultural forces. They were rather the reaping of past experience and the extraction of its full implications by a man who was content enough with life, but who did not feel God enough to hem in those whose passion for change was greater than his.

Being of independent mind for Lerner did not mean there were no influences on his thinking. Indeed, these six masters helped form what became Lerner's core beliefs, the concepts and principles animating his thought. He saw all aspects of life organically. From an individual or an institution to a civilization, there are stages of birth, maturation, decline, and ultimately death. Watching a civilization, as far as Lerner was concerned, involved trying to figure out which stage of life most accurately described the civilization at a given time. In the essays that follow, the phrases "organic whole," "organic unity," or "organic concept of society" appear frequently. Moreover, there is a related refrain of the need to consider subjects in their totality. He applauds Veblen for his "study of cultures-as-wholes," and makes similar statements about Tocqueville and Holmes.

A critical principle common to these six figures is the need for "equilibrium" and "balance" for a polity, society, or civilization to confront problems and to make progress. Discussing Aristotle, Lerner observes: "Just as his basic ethical concept was that of virtue achieved through the mean, so his basic political concept was that of health achieved through equilibrium." In writing about Holmes, Lerner describes the great jurist and philosopher's "equilibrium of life" whose "critical mind sought always to balance the excesses he saw around him." A working thinker surveys the spectrum of human thought and action before rendering a verdict involving meaning, significance, or morality. The mind establishes the mean of fruitful existence and pursuit.

Throughout his career, Lerner was fascinated by revolutions in thinking or behavior. In fact, *Ideas for the Ice Age* carries the subtitle *Studies in a Revolutionary Era,* and one of his collections of newspaper columns, *Actions and Passions*, is subtitled *Notes on the Multiple Revolution of Our Time.*[6] Two decades later, he contributed an essay, "Six Revolutions in American Life," to a book titled *The Revolutionary Theme in Contemporary America.*[7] The treatment of Tocqueville and Veblen in the essays included in this collection also reflects Lerner's shrewd, tough-minded understanding of political and social convulsions.

But study and analysis of revolutions past, present, and to come did not distract Lerner from his core belief that equilibrium was essential for welfare and growth. In the long "Afterword" chapter for the thirtieth-anniversary edition of *America as a Civilization*, he notes that the 1980s, with their "decelerations of change," helped quiet the revolutions of the 1960s and 1970s: "Once again [as in the 1950s when Lerner first wrote *America as a Civilization*], even with deep divisions and scarring scandals, the civilization is moving toward a working equilibrium which may give its watchers a chance to view it in action as a new whole, for however long it may last."[8] Later, in chronicling "The Great Tides of Change" between the 1950s and 1990s, he writes:

> I find it useful to see a civilization as a system of systems—a knowledge and information system, a sustenance system, an ecological system, a class and ethnicity system, a power and authority system, an intimacy and relational system, a system of arts and play, a values and belief system. The problem is of course to find the connective pattern that holds the systems together, with some cohesion, in a working equilibrium.[9]

Without some semblance of equilibrium, there is a lack of steadying balance. Without "cohesion," another concept Lerner discusses in these essays and stresses elsewhere, there is the possibility of fragmentation that can lead to a troubling incoherence within a polity, society, or civilization.

Lerner's use of the phrase "human sciences" to describe what these six thinkers mastered is deliberate. Although he began his career by working at the *Encyclopedia of the Social Sciences*, he subsequently found the term "social sciences" unsatisfactory, neither descriptive nor inclusive enough. As he remarked in a lecture, "One Man's Intellectual Journey," delivered at the University of Notre Dame in 1983, "The idea [of the social sciences] was to study the individual in his social setting, but there was more emphasis on the setting than on the individual, on the ground than on the figure."[10] Lerner appropriated the French designation of "sciences humaines," but defined the term his way. Later, in his lecture at Notre Dame, where he occupied the W. Harold and Martha Welch Visiting Professorship in American Studies from 1982 to 1984, he explains:

> What I have of course been trying to do is to suggest a replacement for the social sciences. My replacement is the human sciences, as integrating a concept as one could imagine. . . . To speak of the human sciences means of course to move away from society as repressive, to move away from society as the distorting element and to fix upon the individual as a human being, a human being in a social context, in a context of value changes, in a context of belonging, a context of belief, a context of attempting to travel his life journey, attempting in some way to grow by the experience of it, the human being as a whole human being, a whole person, of his connectedness and his relationships in a healthy, reasonably cohesive culture and society. And I have some sense of liberation when I think that we may be moving into an era when the human sciences can perform that kind of function for us.[11]

Although each of the following essays was originally written independently to introduce an edition or collection, there is a remarkable unity among them. In part, this comes from Lerner's emphasis on specific ideas or principles central to his thought. This connectedness isn't contrived; Lerner didn't consider bringing these essays together until late in his life. It happened naturally, one might even say organically, as his thinking about these "masters" and "the human sciences" evolved.

Lerner completed all but one of these essays before 1970; however, he kept returning to the six figures in his writing, teaching, and lecturing. In the memoir about the first half of his life, he reconsiders these masters and his approaches to them. What he says about wrestling with Machiavelli and Veblen is particularly revealing and enlightening. The essay about Machiavelli began as a faculty lecture, delivered in the fall of 1939 at Williams College, where Lerner was a professor of political science from 1938 until 1943. It had a definite, contemporary purpose and a larger philosophical point.

> I launched on the reading of my essay, whose theme was that Machiavelli had to be rescued from "Machiavellianism," that he was in his own day a liberal New Dealer but a hard-thinking, tough-minded one, that his dissection of power was like Harvey's study of the circulation of the blood and marked the transition from the normative thinking of Dante's *De Monarchia* to a detached and dense thinking of the unfooled and unclouded intelligence, and that between the realm of what must be and the realm of what is there is the third realm of what can be—that in speaking to his Prince and in writing about the lessons of Roman history Machiavelli was acting as a *possibilist*, which we must do in our time as well. . . . It was the philosophy of power as the art of carving out the possible from the imperatives, necessities, and contingencies of life, which required great leaders (with Machiavelli's quality of *virtu*, or command).[12]

Lerner published his essay about Machiavelli in 1940, and it provoked considerable commentary then and later. Jacques Maritain made several references to it in his essay, "The End of Machiavellianism," in the January 1942 issue of *The Review of Politics*.[13] Forty years later, in his book *Leaders* Richard Nixon presents two extensive quotations from what he calls Lerner's "brilliant introduction."[14] (Ironically, a few years earlier, when Nixon was president, Lerner's name was included on the White House enemies list.) Using Machiavelli as his springboard, Lerner subsequently developed his thinking about the need to search for "the possible," the realistic alternatives and solutions to whatever confronts us individually and collectively. He even devoted a "My Turn" column in *Newsweek* to the subject "On Being a Possibilist."[15] To one degree or another, each of the "six masters" is a possibilist—tough-minded about human experience, but open-minded enough to be willing to propose different approaches to the actualities of life.

As Lerner grew older and his perspective became more centered on the need for equilibrium, Veblen's strident criticism of American business and free-market capitalism in general lost much of its seductiveness. But Lerner's work on Veblen was pivotal in giving direction to future avenues of inquiry. In his memoir, he recalls that the master's thesis he wrote about Veblen at Washington University in 1925

> gave me an exploratory overview of areas I would move into—the history of ideas, the dynamics of change in history, the nature of social institutions and cultures, Marxism, the question of what makes up the health and sickness of nations, the drives that move men, the relation between thought and action. What a piece of luck it was that I had come upon Veblen when I did, and used him as the Australian native boys used their exposure to the forest, as a testing-ground for survival to enter manhood. Veblen was the testing-ground for my coming of age intellectually. My thesis was far from a disciple's acceptance of his thought. I was critical, stringent, and exacting with him. It was a way of examining the dryness of my intellectual powder.[16]

Critical he might have been; however, in ensuing years Veblen and his work continued to attract Lerner. He published *The Portable Veblen* in 1948, complete with selections that Lerner says "shook up my own thinking and left scars on it."[17] Later in his memoir, he writes: "I was to be moved by this man's life as well as his mind. It was deeply American, a dissenter's life—abrasive, cantankerous, original, very much *his*."[18] No doubt there was, to Lerner's eye, a similarity between the two. Lerner's apprenticeship at the *Encyclopedia of the Social Sciences* was matched by Veblen's editorial work at the *Journal of Political Economy*. But, more importantly, both were masterful at snthesizing, both individual, both singular, to the point of almost creating a new intellectual discipline.

Max Lerner's own life was "deeply American," "original," and "very much *his*." He provided running commentary on his times for more than half of a century, but his enduring legacy can be found in the works in which he devoted sustained attention to a specific subject or thinker. In these efforts, either whole books or contributions to books, you see not only (in Yeats's phrase) "the fascination with what's difficult" but the full measure of someone who was himself a master of the human sciences.

Notes

1. New editions of *Ideas Are Weapons: The History and Uses of Ideas* and *Ideas for the Ice Age: Studies in a Revolutionary Era*, which include Max Lerner's reflections on the books and the subjects they explore, have been published by Transaction Publishers in, respectively, 1991 and 1992.
2. Max Lerner, *The Unfinished Country: A Book of American Symbols* (New York: Simon and Schuster, 1959), xvi.
3. Clifford G. Christians, "Max Lerner," in *American Newspaper Journalists*, vol. 29 of *Dictionary of Literary Biography*, ed. Perry J. Ashley (Detroit: Gale Research Company, 1984), 172.
4. Max Lerner, unpublished and untitled memoir, 307–8.
5. A new edition of *It Is Later Than You Think* with a new preface and afterword by Max Lerner and a new foreword by James MacGregor Burns was published by Transaction Publishers in 1989.
6. Max Lerner, *Actions and Passions: Notes on the Multiple Revolution of Our Time* (New York: Simon and Schuster, 1949).
7. See *The Revolutionary Theme in Contemporary America*, ed. Thomas R. Ford (Lexington: University of Kentucky Press, 1965), 1–20.
8. Max Lerner, *America as a Civilization: Life and Thought in the United States Today* (New York: Henry Holt and Company, 1987), 954.
9. Lerner, *America as a Civilization*, 959.
10. Max Lerner, unpublished transcript, "One Man's Intellectual Journey," Department of American Studies, University of Notre Dame, March 28, 1983, p. 5.
11. Lerner, "One Man's Intellectual Journey," 20–21.
12. Max Lerner, unpublished and untitled memoir, 290–91.
13. Jacques Maritain, "The End of Machiavellianism," *The Review of Politics* 4 (January 1942): 1–33. The essay is reprinted in Jacques Maritain, *The Range of Reason* (New York: Charles Scribner's Sons, 1952), 134–64.
14. Richard Nixon, *Leaders* (New York: Warner Books, 1982), 326.
15. Max Lerner, "On Being a Possibilist," *Newsweek*, 8 October 1979, p. 21.
16. Max Lerner, unpublished and untitled memoir, 117–18.
17. Max Lerner, *The Portable Veblen* (New York: The Viking Press, 1948), 52.
18. Lerner, unpublished memoir, 119.

1

Aristotle

—1—

One of the great books embodying the Greek spirit was written by a man who was an outlander among the Greeks. Born in 384 B.C. in Stagira, Aristotle came from one of the frontier outposts of Greek settlement which faced the rising political sun of Macedon and its new "barbarian" energies. Stagira was a small city in a peninsula that had been settled by people from Chalcis. As a colony on the rim of Greek life it was for that reason all the more intensely Greek in feeling, on the same principle that makes the foreign-born in America more slavish in following the stereotypes of our culture than those whose sense of security makes them freer. Unlike Plato, who wore his aristocracy with a sure and quiet grace, Aristotle came of the upper middle class, which may serve partly to account—as it did in Machiavelli's case— for the dryness and realism of his intelligence and its lack of the more inflated and poetic values, but which sheds light also on his persistent emphasis upon the role of the middle class in a healthy equilibrium state. His father was a physician, and from him he may have derived a technical and scientific tradition which made it possible for Aristotle to deal with experience in a more matter-of-fact way than was habitual with the Greek ruling classes. We know very little of his boyhood, except that for a few years before he had reached his teens he lived in Pella, the Macedonian capital, where his father had become court physician to the king. But his parents died while he was still a boy,

Originally published as the introduction to *Aristotle's Politics,* translated by Benjamin Jowett (New York: Random House/The Modern Library, 1943), 5–27.

and he grew up with a guardian—in easy circumstances, possessed of some property.

At eighteen he turned up in Athens, drawn there by the magnetic attraction which cultural capitals have always exerted for young men of talent, whether in the Greek, Roman or American worlds. Unfortunately no Walter Pater has sought to reconstruct imaginatively, after the model set for Rome in *Marius the Epicurean,* what a shining city Athens must have been as it lay before a provincial boy like Aristotle, bent on the conquest of the Greek intellectual world. Plato had built up a brilliant school of philosophy, but he was at the moment absent in Syracuse, where he had gone on one of those missions of turning a ruler into a philosopher, which showed that the Greek thinkers were perennial optimists. The young man must have made something of a sensation at the Academy. He was an unpleasantly sardonic fellow, something of a fop and a dandy, sartorially exquisite, and there are reports that he spoke with a lisp. In part his manner and meticulousness may have been due to the affectation of a provincial, in part to a sense of order which proved to be as much a part of Aristotle's thought as of his dress.

The next twenty years, which Aristotle spent at the Academy, must have been among his happiest. With his craggy mind and his dry, severe logic, he stood out above everyone in the school but its master. He was Plato's disciple, yet without anything slavish in his discipleship. At some point during these two decades of apprentice years he discovered that his intellectual system and his philosophical salvation were his own to work out. Yet to insist on re-thinking every article of the Platonic creed was compatible with a genuine affection and regard for the master. In a very different modern context one thinks of the parallel attitude of Nehru to Gandhi—devoted and yet critically independent. During these years of unflagging study he accumulated the intellectual capital whose rewards he was later to extract in his writings. Only thus can we understand in secular terms what would otherwise be the miracle of his immense later productiveness.

When Plato died Aristotle was thirty-seven, better equipped than anyone else to carry on the work of the Academy. But that was not Plato's testament; nor could Aristotle with dignity content himself with a minor role. He therefore accepted, when it came, an invitation from Hermias, who was a big landed proprietor in Asia Minor, a political boss, and a princeling to boot, to visit with him. Hermias was interested in philosophy, and had already entertained several members of the Academy and followed their precepts in establishing a constitutional regime. He liked Aristotle and welcomed the prestige of associating with him. Aristotle lived with Hermias for three or four years, and married his niece. He had money with which to organize and carry on extensive research, and he built up a school around himself. But this too came to a close. Hermias seems to have been playing power politics on a small scale and to have had an agreement with Philip of Macedon involving the use of his cities as bridgeheads for an invasion of the Persian empire. At any rate, the Persian king thought so, destroyed Hermias's cities, captured him and—when he refused to reveal the plot of which he was accused—crucified him. Whether Aristotle was in any way caught in the tangles of conspiratorial diplomacy is not wholly clear. But here the third stage of his life ended—brief and turbulent, yet not unhappy. At forty-two Aristotle found himself again without home or occupation, a political refugee.

But now an opportunity offered whereby Aristotle could carry on his research and even play a role on the stage of world history. Philip of Macedon invited him to become tutor to his son, Alexander, already at thirteen precocious in ability and ambition. For Philip it meant having the great philosopher of the Greek world to supervise his son's training, and thus associating himself with Greek culture. For Aristotle it meant a chance to influence the most vigorous state of the time, the one that was most creative in the arts of military and political organization. Much might be done to impart a Greek quality to the Macedonian energies, and make certain that if this was to be a conquering state it would conquer with Greek ideas rather than against them. And so he went back to the Macedonian court, where he had spent several years as a boy. He is believed to have remained with Alexander until Philip's death. We know almost nothing of the relations between teacher and pupil, except from what we may infer from the disappointment which Aristotle later betrayed at the course that Alexander's ideas and personality took. It must have been a strange relationship. Everything about Alexander was exuberant and excessive, while the core of Aristotle's thinking was restraint and the mean. Here was Aristotle trying to teach the acceptance of limits to a youth who was drunk on the exploits of the Age of Heroes and who dared aspire to godhead. We must, however, avoid underestimating Aristotle's influence upon Alexander. As General de Gaulle has put it, in his

Army of the Future (1934), "There has been no illustrious captain who did not possess taste and a feeling for the heritage of the human mind. At the root of Alexander's victories one will always find Aristotle."

When his pupil was ready to assume the duties of kingship and command in the field, Aristotle went back to Athens and to the culminating period of his life work. He was just turning fifty, and was ready to communicate to others the results of his study and reflection. He came back to set up a school of his own, in the Lyceum. The young men clustered about him as he and others had once clustered about Plato; and since he walked about on the school grounds explaining and disputing, the young men asking questions and taking notes, he became known as the "peripatetic" philosopher. There was a vigor in his school which the Academy had lost with Plato's death. For twelve years he lectured and wrote. There was nothing alien to his consuming curiosity, and no items of experience which he did not seek to digest and relate in the form of general propositions. He developed a physics, a metaphysics, a biology, an astronomy, a logic, an analysis of language, an ethics, an economics and politics, an esthetics. For comprehensiveness, order and consistency as a system of thought, the world has not known the like of his system before and since.

Meanwhile, Aristotle's pupil, Alexander, had been driving deeper the rivets of empire over the Greek city-states which his father, Philip, had first established, and he had been expanding that empire over Asia and the whole known world. The reports that came back of his Asiatic exploits were glamorous enough, yet they were also puzzling and vaguely sinister to the Greeks, who felt that, in spreading his empire over Asia, Alexander was not spreading Greek culture but succumbing to the Asiatic. Their fears were reinforced by the reports of Alexander's drunken excesses, his plurality of concubines, his closeness to Asiatic advisers, and especially by a delusion he seemed to have that he was not only descended of great heroes but was himself one of the gods. Aristotle was as troubled by Alexander's behavior as were the other Greeks. Nevertheless, one of the indirect results of Alexander's conquest was that it endangered Aristotle's position in Athens. For had he not been Alexander's tutor; was not the strange young man's development attributable to him; was he not himself tied in a relationship of too close friendship with Antipater, Alexander's viceroy for Macedonia and the Greek cities?

The political climate of Athens grew unhealthy for Aristotle. His life was dragging to a melancholy close. He had few personal roots left in Greece. He was a sick, bald, thin-legged little man, suffering from acute digestive ailments. He still had his school and his lectures and his writings, but he felt it necessary to abandon them. He could not even go back to his native Stagira, since it had been burned and leveled in the troubled years of Macedonian and Greek war. Remembering what the Athenians had once done to Socrates, and fearing "lest they sin twice against philosophy," he went off into exile in Euboea, and there a year later died at the age of sixty-three.

—2—

The *Politics* is a treatise on the science and art of government which, although part of the whole body of Aristotle's work, stands on its own feet. Werner Jaeger, a great German scholar in the Aristotelian field, guesses that the book was written in two stretches: the first (including Books 2, 3, 7, and 8) dealing with the ideal state, using Plato's thought as a jumping-off point, and probably written soon after Plato's death and Aristotle's departure from Athens; the second (including Books 4, 5, and 6) being a comparative analysis of actually existing state forms, their stability, decay and overthrow, and written some time after Aristotle's students in the Lyceum had had a chance to do their research project on the contemporary constitutions. Jaeger's supposition is that these latter books were inserted by Aristotle into the middle of the original draft, and that Book I was written last, as a sort of introduction to the whole political treatise.

At any rate it is clear that Aristotle, no longer content to write on political ideals, meant to focus on political actualities. The Greek world in which he wrote was turbulent enough to throw a political thinker in either direction, depending upon his temperament. Some sought escape from this turbulence in the construction of ideal commonwealths, others were drawn to inquire into the character of shifting state forms and into the conditions of revolution and stability. Aristotle belonged with the latter.

Yet he was not unaffected by the political pessimism which his times bred. The Greeks had never discovered the principle of unification, and the price they were to pay for this failure was political suicide. Their sense of the city-state or *polis*—what would correspond to our sense of nationalism today—was so tenacious that it made them inca-

pable of thinking in terms of a Greek order—what would correspond
to a world order today. Because their economic systems were twisted
at the very start by their institution of slavery, their contempt for labor
and their exclusion of the economic virtues from the pantheon of civic
virtues, they did not undergo the industrial expansion which might
have compelled them, as it seems to be compelling us, to fashion the
image of a world order. Nor was any of them sufficiently strong in
itself to establish an imperium. Sparta, with its pride of arms, seemed
the logical city for the role. Yet Athens, whose position made it the
center of a commercial empire and whose cultural prestige dominated
the peak centuries of Greek life, would not accept Spartan hegemony.
The result was a mortal clash which left both sides too exhausted and
bitter to organize the Greek world, and left that world a ready victim
to an external imperium.

It was in this political context that Aristotle wrote his treatise—a
context in many respects parallel to that in which Machiavelli wrote
The Prince. Yet, unlike Machiavelli, there is little nationalistic feeling
in Aristotle, little of the realistic exploration of power, little receptivity
to the larger political constructions that were emerging. He clung, as a
Greek, to the exclusive sense that the Greeks had a monopoly on
culture. Not that he was attached to any particular city-state; his links
with Athens were cultural rather than political. Yet he never got far
enough to see the possibility of a Greek political order. While not
hostile to the Macedonian attempts to forge it, he could never wholly
champion them. His intellectual break with his pupil, Alexander, was
probably due to this difference between them. He had instilled into
Alexander a pride in the Greek tradition, but the Greek era Alexander
cared about was that of the early heroes; there was in him a daemonic
urge to excel them by using Macedonian power to spread Greek culture
throughout the world. But Alexander was far more of a political realist
than Aristotle. He may have understood—although Wilcken disputes
this in his biography of Alexander—the value of the divinity-myth in
holding an empire together. Even more important, he broke with
Aristotle on the question of the treatment of the conquered Asiatic
provinces. Aristotle, with his sense of Greek superiority, felt that there
could be no political health in Asiatics; they were the lowest of the
barbarians. Like those who cling to the Vansittart thesis about the
post-war treatment of Germany, he wished to crush the conquered
enemy. Alexander was convinced that the best way to keep the Asiatics

as part of his new empire was to give them a stake in it. Nothing could show more clearly that, as objective an observer as he was in the world of science, Aristotle was still caught in the taboos of the Greek political mind.

This is evident in his attitude toward slavery, which he discusses in Book I. He sees slavery as rooted in biology and psychology as well as in economics: "that some should rule and others be ruled is a thing, not only necessary, but expedient; from the hour of their birth, some are marked out for subjection, others for rule." But having made this sweeping statement, he proceeds to hedge it. "The words slavery and slave are used in two senses. There is a slave or slavery by law as well as by nature." In short, there is a natural basis to the institution, although the institution itself may be in practice unjust. What is vulnerable in this analysis is that there may actually have been no relation in Greek life between the two. Even if one grants Aristotle's *élite* theory—of the right of some men to rule others—it remains true that Greek slavery was a historical institution, growing from the helotage of conquest or the need for artisans in the urban handicraft industries. The theory of a natural aristocracy is thus stretched by Aristotle into an *apologia* for brutal subjection and coercion. What is striking is that Aristotle, who as a liberal conservative was ahead of his age in many respects, was here caught in it. His treatment of his own slaves was humane and by his will he manumitted several of them. But, like Plato and Xenophon and the other intellectuals of the fourth century B.C., his contempt for the manual occupations which the slaves plied, his pride in Greek culture and his sense of the pettiness of spirit which labor was thought to induce, all fused into an "imperfect prejudice" about slavery.

There is another sense in which Aristotle was Greek. He had the characteristic Greek sense of limits and worship of form. He broke with Plato on metaphysical grounds because the Platonic "ideas" seemed to him too misty. He developed instead a metaphysic of "forms" which was concerned with matter as the stuff on which the life processes work, and with the life process itself as the "actualization of the potential." He saw nature, essentially, as development. Yet there is still a curiously static residue in his thinking—an insistence in it upon restriction, an aversion to formlessness, a fear of what might happen once the boundaries were broken, a dread almost of anything vital or passionate. In fact, one may guess that Aristotle's encyclopedic activity was in itself something that sprung from the Greek aversion to formlessness. He had to organize the material of the natural, individual and social worlds if he was to achieve any inner peace of mind. Just as his basic ethical concept was that of virtue achieved through the mean, so his basic political concept was that of health achieved through equilibrium. In comparison with Aristotle, Plato was unstable—a brooding poetic mystic who, for all the fact that his *Republic* was meant to rationalize political reaction, burst the bounds of his own intentions and went beyond the flaming ramparts of the Greek world into untraveled areas where men have sought to follow him ever since. Plato was as much a Dionysian as an Athenian aristocrat could be. Aristotle, despite the fact that he lacked the graces of poetry and myth, was an Apollonian.

But it would be unjust to end here the analysis of Aristotle's relation to the Greek tradition. While Spengler had a truth by the tail in saying that the deep cultural pattern of the Greeks was a sense of form, it is a half-truth that misses much of the meaning of the Greek era. One may trace in world history a rough sequence: from the age of fear to the age of knowledge to the age of conquest to the age of organization. If that is true, it becomes apparent that Aristotle as a quite characteristic Greek, although of transcending intellectual ability, stood as the inheritor of the age of fear and the archetype of the age of knowledge. His function was to explain and rationalize the whole known world and man's relation to it. This he did. His achievement was to sum up the ethos of a whole civilization more completely than anyone since him has been able to do. His achievement was an architectural one.

Yet its architecture was not of the sort that went vaulting into the unknown. God was for Aristotle not the supreme mystery, but the "Unmoved Mover," the center of an orderly universe rotating about him—as Whitehead has said, so orderly as to be dramatic. He was thus, like the other Greeks, still operating in the shadow of fear, for only a people fearful of the irrational in them would thus make a fetish of order. That may have been one reason why the Greeks were so concerned to separate themselves from the "barbarians." Yet Aristotle was moving away from fear toward knowledge, which is a way of conquering fear. His knowledge was chiefly of the external world, the beginnings of science without which the human being is fear-dominated. It was also knowledge of society and of the process of thought. But while he ransacked all the storehouses of knowledge open to him at the time, the Faustian impulse was not yet in him. That was to come with the age of conquest. Knowledge was for him a way of accommodating oneself to the world rather than a way of conquering it, as it was with the scientists of the seventeenth century. It was a form of adjustment, not a form of action.

—3—

No single thinker, not even Plato, has had as much impact as Aristotle on the intellectual and institutional history of later centuries. It is true that Aristotle's doctrine lacks the winged fire which has made men Platonists or Marxians, for that there is a need of a single-minded frenzy which can only be described as possession. Yet, there were whole centuries when the civilized world lived in Aristotle's shadow—and not only the European world, but the Ottoman and African; not only the Christian world but the Jewish and Islamic—centuries when all knowledge was held to be contained in the writings of one man. Sandys, whose *History of Classical Scholarship* contains valuable although scattered material on Aristotle's influence, tells us that in the mid-fourteenth century the instructors at the University of Paris had to swear that they would not be inconsistent with the truth as revealed in Aristotle and his commentator Averroës. Unfortunately, the connected and detailed history of Aristotle's influence still remains to be written; there is nothing comparable to Paul Elmer More's book on Platonism or Lord Acton's chapter on Machiavellianism.

During the dark centuries between the Hellenistic period and the Middle Ages, the flame of Aristotle's teaching was kept alive in Constantinople, then in Arabia, North Africa, Spain, and finally to the European world. There is, in Santayana's *Dialogues in Limbo,* a delightful recapturing of the combination of reverence and sharp critical analysis which the Islamic scholars accorded Aristotle. Nor were the analytical subtleties of Jewish theology wholly unrelated to Aristotle's influence in this period.

In the eleventh and twelfth centuries the Latin translation of Aristotle was made available to European thought, and a school of commentators and glossators attached itself to him. What has been written about the aridity of this school is in the main true: there is in all commentaries an inherent tendency toward the drying up of the original creative impulse. Yet even in the Greek world, as Jaeger has pointed out, the creative possibilities in Aristotle's thought were not explored. The scientific and philosophical elements were mixed together in his work.

But the further expansion of his scientific insights was incompatible with the climate of opinion in the Hellenistic world. Farrington has suggested that the Greek ruling *elite* feared science because it might undermine the foundations of their own rule which were supported by popular superstitions and the "noble lie." For its further expansion science also required a society which gave more dignity to labor and the industrial arts than did the Greek. At any rate, Aristotle became, both for the Hellenistic world and that of the Middle Ages, a formula for elaboration rather than an avenue to wisdom.

The theologians of the Middle Ages, even including so creative a thinker as Thomas Aquinas and so creative a poet as Dante, welcomed the logical articulate structure of Aristotle's thought because it enabled them to pour into it in an orderly fashion the body of their beliefs. It was not so much his science and certainly not his politics and social science which were taken over. It was rather his logic and his metaphysics, particularly the latter. And it was in the *Metaphysics* that Aristotle sought to use the critical instrument of reason to establish and explore the realm that transcended human experience. Although the medieval Church for a time frowned upon Aristotle, his metaphysics offered a common ground to the religious philosophy of Christianity, Judaism and Islamism.

For these religious systems were philosophically uncreative, although morally creative; what they needed was a logical and critical framework, and these Aristotle made available. The thralldom of the Middle Ages to Aristotle can thus best be explained in the search of the Christian world for a logical and metaphysical structure not incompatible with its theology. The medieval world, creative in its institutional practices, had to fall back on antiquity for its intellectual universe.

So completely did the Middle Ages adopt Aristotle that when the modern centuries sought release from the bondage to the medieval tradition, they had to seek release from the symbol of Aristotle. With the rise of science in the sixteenth and seventeenth centuries, there came a sharp reaction against the scholasticism of the medieval world and against the name which stood in men's minds for that scholasticism. Actually, Aristotle as a scientist might have helped the seventeenth century to find itself; yet so intensely was he rejected that what might have been releasing in him was thrown out along with what had proved to be fettering. In one sense, the instinct of the modern man may have been right. Aristotle the scientist was not mathematician but biologist;

hence his characteristic method was classification rather than measurement. The seventeenth century moved toward the method of measurement and therefore toward its own characteristic form. The eighteenth century, the rationalism of whose outlook was as complete and as dramatic as Aristotle's own, nevertheless continued to reject him, largely because it mistook his meaning and ignored the parallelisms to its own spirit which were to be found in him. This rejection of Aristotle has continued until our own time. As late as 1848 Sir William Hamilton noted that in discarding Aristotle the English universities had neglected wholly the study and teaching of logic.

Our own times are witnessing a renaissance of Aristotelian studies and interest. There is a social logic worth mentioning here. In the turbulent times in which Aristotle wrote, the Greeks were caught between the assertion of will and the submission to law—or, as Aristotle expresses it in his *Metaphysics*, between matter and form. Hence Aristotle's method is wholly dialectical—the method that is characteristic of any age, like our own, which finds itself caught in so basic a dilemma. Aristotle's rigorous analysis by the method of division and differentiation is increasingly suited to the temper of such an age, which seeks to find amidst the welter of change some firm ground on which it can stand.

There are also universals in Aristotle's thought—in his metaphysics, his ethics, his politics—which make him attractive to any period which seeks to make itself an organic whole. That is to say, a world in danger of fragmentation, and deeply desirous of welding itself into a unity, must somehow find a philosophy which runs in universals. The nineteenth-century systems, such as those of Darwin, Marx, Nietzsche, Dostoyevsky, Mill, have been found inadequate in our own time. Such twentieth-century systems as those of Spengler and Pareto are too polemical and erratic to get common acceptance in a world which rejects their values while it cherishes some of their insights. The thinkers who may some day create a universal system of thought which will sum up the twentieth-century aspirations toward organic unity have not yet arisen. In the interval, the study of a writer who summed up the spirit of a past age is a good preparation for the coming of writers who may in their own terms sum up the inner strivings of our own age.

—4—

What are the relevant master ideas that emerge from a reading of the *Politics* in the context of today? My own inclination is to put the answer in the form of a series of propositions.

First, that the state has a natural history, and that part of its meaning must be sought in its development. I have said that Aristotle, as a scientist who is mainly absorbed with biology, saw nature as development. He was thus in a sense a forerunner of those who have seen politics as history, and especially those who have seen it as the unfolding of inner impulses within human society. If there is a trace of the doctrine of inevitability in this, it is not so much as to make the whole system rigidly deterministic. The truth that Aristotle saw was that political forms have an inner history of their own—the history of a growth toward maturity and an impulse toward decay. Thus his analysis of the basic forms of monarchy, aristocracy, polity, shows his understanding that they are not simplistic forms, but go through a series of phases. The implication is clear that at each stage there is room for human action and will. The political material contains within itself from the start the potentials to be made into actuality, but that material must none the less be acted on. If maturity can be hastened and helped, then decay can be foreseen and prevented.

Secondly, that the state has a natural basis in economics and family structure, and a natural purpose in ethics. I do not think that modern social thought has improved much upon Aristotle in this respect. While he gives us a naturalistic social theory of the organization of the state and its successive transformations, he does not fall into the trap of seeing human society in terms of biological and economic mechanism, for his conception of nature includes the ethical. It is in the nature of human beings living in society that they must work toward goals which have value. There is a far-reaching implication in this for our own age as well as for Aristotle's: that the study of politics, as well as the art, must effect a synthesis between mechanism and ethos, between survival and meaning.

Third, that there are basic state forms into which political activity falls, and that the art of politics lies in the choice among these forms and their combinations. Aristotle's itch for classification has often been noted. His most famous classification in the *Politics* is that which divides states into monarchy, aristocracy and polity, and which gives the parallel corruptions of each—tyranny, oligarchy and democracy. We need not today accept Aristotle's valuations literally, and we must see that his base of classification is wholly political and excludes the economic. Nevertheless, there is a truth here not to be ignored. Let us say that there are broad forms within which the state may be organized: one-man rule, the rule of an *élite*, the rule of the mass of people within the framework of law. What is more important is that each state form has characteristic methods and each can get out of hand. The state as a going concern must represent the best working synthesis possible. One-man rule allows for unity and decisiveness, and Aristotle's remarks are still applicable to military operations and other administrative situations. The rule of an *élite* allows for the selection of the best abilities in the state—and in this sense even a democracy must embody the *élite* principle. The rule of a polity—that is, of a constitutional democracy—allows for freedom and economic equality, and even dictatorships will not find stability until they have embodied a measure of these values. Here again what Aristotle tries to tell us is that we cannot have a simple choice. His own theory was that mixed government is the best in practice—a theory which may either be interpreted mechanically as a mixture of the basic state mechanisms, or may mean that the aim of politics is to develop a state form and state ethos which, by whatever mechanism, synthesizes the values which the basic forms embody.

Fourth, that the art of government is the art of finding a proper equilibrium for the forces in the state. In individual ethics Aristotle saw the good life in the mean; in the ethics of the state, he saw it in an equilibrium between power and liberty, between authority and its checks. In his equilibrium thinking Aristotle was a characteristic Greek—far more so than Plato, whose thinking cheerfully vaulted beyond the equilibrium toward the totalitarian. There are those who project Aristotle's theory of mixed government into the seventeenth and eighteenth centuries, and who attribute the equilibrium politics of Locke, Montesquieu, the social contract theorists and the American founders to Aristotle. There is a measure of truth in this. Despite the seventeenth-century rejection of Aristotle's logic and metaphysics, the political forms that grew out of the eighteenth-century revolutions were not very different from Aristotle's: the idea of government by poise and counterpoise, the idea of limited powers, the fear of governmental encroachment, the use of constitutional limits to set boundaries to the operation of governmental power. Yet it is probably true that the

history of equilibrium political thinking in our own world owes more
to seventeenth- and eighteenth-century science, and particularly to the
concepts of Newtonian physics, than to Aristotle.

Equilibrium thinking is today once more beginning to assert itself.
The separation of the various branches of the government, as Locke
and Montesquieu and the *Federalist Papers* had it, is being replaced
by a new type of "separation-of-powers" thinking. In this new thinking
there is an insistence on the separation of social and economic power
from political power—the idea being that a people can risk a social
and economic tyranny, or can risk a political tyranny, but it cannot
risk the joining of the two. Hence the Aristotelian theory of mixed
government has been replaced by a theory of the separation of political
control from economic functions, and by the exploration of mixed
economies. Thus we are witnessing a return to Aristotle on a plane
that has more meaning for our own age.

But what Aristotle did not see—nor perhaps his modern followers—
is that in history political equilibrium has been achieved only by the
ebb and flow of revolutionary movements. This does not, however,
prevent Aristotle from being one of the best analysts of revolution in
the political tradition. Which brings us to his *fifth* master idea. Aristotle
was interested in the rise and fall of political systems, but he did not
make the mistake of tracing that rise and fall to autonomous factors
within politics. His views on the economic basis of revolutions had to
be rediscovered, as Charles Beard has pointed out, by later thinkers—
by Harrington, Sir Thomas More, James Madison, Karl Marx.

Yet while Aristotle saw revolutions as arising from the injustices
and the blindnesses of ruling classes, he regarded revolutions themselves
with distaste. Here again he speaks for the Greek mind. From this fear
of revolution one can derive much of his characteristic political theory.
That is to say one can approach his political theory logically, from his
metaphysics, science and ethics, or one can approach it psychologically,
from the Greek mind. In psychological terms Aristotle's distaste for
the confusion caused by revolutions leads directly to much of the rest
of his political thinking: its fear of democratic rule, its stress upon
constitutional polity, upon the limits to be set to the operation of
power, upon the distrust of government, upon the rule of law. In this
context it is not surprising that sections of his treatise become a guide
book for dealing with revolution. They contain many shrewd insights
as to how revolution can be prevented, not the least shrewd of which

is the insistence that since it follows from economic injustices and from the blindness of ruling classes, it can be prevented only by the removal of their causes.

The *sixth* of Aristotle's master ideas relates to political psychology. Like Plato, Aristotle believed that much in politics depended on the image which was stamped on the young by birth and education—by nature and habit. To this theme he devotes his concluding pages. Yet the modern educator will miss the sense of concern with the individuality of the child. We must remember that personality and individuality, as we understand them, were not Greek concepts. Neither was freedom, which—like equality—did not reach its modern meaning until the Judaeo-Christian tradition, with its ideas of the sanctity of man. Since man (the Christians reasoned) is created in the image of God, it follows that he must not be subjected to indignity or curbing. And since all men are thus created, it follows that they must be equal before the law. We must be careful, despite the fact that Aristotle uses the concepts of both freedom and equality, that we do not read a content into them which is post-Greek, although Christianity itself owed much to Greek individualism and Greek ethics. Neither should we read into Aristotle's term "democracy" the egalitarian implications it has now, or the sense of the dignity of the individual.

It has been customary to think of Aristotle as the philosopher of political rationalism, in contrast with Plato's exploration of the irrational in the political myth. It is true that Aristotle used the method of reason in the analysis of politics, but that is different from saying that he saw in reason a mirror of political behavior. His analysis of revolutions shows that he understood the role of grievance and *ressentiment* in politics, just as his analysis of economic forces showed that he understood the role of class interest. His account of how political forms become corrupted shows that he understood the inner impulses in any state toward the expansion of power.

Above all, Aristotle was interested in what constituted the strength and weakness of the political community. For all his discussion of political forms, he saw that the strength of the state depends not so much upon the machinery of government as upon the moral sense of the community. And in analyzing this moral sense he saw more deeply than did the later individualistic theorists. In his famous statement that "man is by nature a political animal" and that "he who by nature and not by mere accident is without a state, is either above humanity or below it," Aristotle gave the clue to his political psychology. He meant that in their origin and in their impulses, in terms of the end toward which their development tends, men must be part of a whole that is greater than the sum of its parts. Except as he is a member of a collectivity, a man ceases to be a man and becomes either something greater or something less. We who have watched in our time the spectacle of the rise and fall of nations, and who have seen the Americans, the Russians, the Chinese, the British, perform feats of moral strength as nations which they could not have performed outside of the context of their collectivity, have come to glimpse a fresh meaning in the words of Aristotle which have been almost eroded by commentary. We have come to see that the most important element of strength in a community is the sense of greatness that it can generate, and that the most important political emotion in man is the thirst for greatness which, under pressure, stretches him beyond his everyday self so that he reaches the full outlines of his human personality.

It is here that we can best evaluate Aristotle's thought against the imagism of Plato and his stress on the irrational myth. By excusing or glorifying the Noble Lie, Plato became the forerunner of a succession of glorifiers of the irrational and the manipulative who have colored the thinking of our time. As against this tradition, Aristotle stands for the life of reason. But not in a mechanical sense, squeezed dry of intangible values; rather as a framework within which the natural irrational impulses of men—of fear and sadism and lust for power, and above all of a sense of collective greatness—can find expression without bursting the fabric of civilization.

In the light of recent history, who shall say that Aristotle was less profound in his perception than Plato? We have seen the Noble Lie end up in the desperate and cynical manipulations of the Yahoos who call themselves the master race. I, for one, prefer a theorist who taught that, because men are members of a whole, their fullest political meaning lies in helping build a working practicable state which, while it recognizes the naturalistic basis of all living, does not thereby betray the life of reason.

2

Niccolò Machiavelli

—1—

We live today in the shadow of a Florentine, the man who above all others taught the world to think in terms of cold political power. His name was Niccolò Machiavelli, and he was one of those rare intellectuals who write about politics because they have had a hand in politics and learned what it is about. His portraits show a thin-faced, pale little man, with a sharp nose, sunken cheeks, subtle lips, a discreet and enigmatic smile, and piercing black eyes that look as if they knew much more than they were willing to tell.

There is little we can say for certain about his early years. He was born in 1469, of a family that was part of the small and impoverished gentry of Florence. His father, a lawyer, tried desperately to keep his family from slipping down into the ranks of the middle class. Niccolò must have had the sort of boyhood that most children had in the homes and on the streets of Florence in the *quattrocento*. He steps onto the threshold of history in 1498, already a young man of twenty-nine, only a month after the execution of the friar-politician Savonarola, who had dominated the last decades of the dying fifteenth century in Florence. At that time Machiavelli got a minor job as secretary to the Second Chancery—an office he was to hold for fourteen years.

He was what we should call today a Braintruster and bureaucrat. He loved his job as idea-man for some of the stuffed-shirt Florentine

Originally published as the introduction to *The Prince and The Discourses,* translated by Luigi Ricci, E.R.P. Vincent, and Christian E. Detmold (New York: Random House/The Modern Library, 1940 and 1950), xxv–xlvi.

politicians. And because he was so good at it, the stuffed shirts came to regard him as someone on whose shoulders they could place the burden of administrative work—the man who got papers drawn up and orders sent out and correspondence carried on and records kept. In due time—since Florence like the other Italian city-states in an age of intrigue depended on skillful diplomacy for its survival—they broadened the scope of his work and sent him on diplomatic missions. In the course of a decade he visited as an unofficial emissary every important city-state in Italy and several of the courts outside Italy. He sent back reports which may still be read for their tough understanding of diplomatic realities. Invariably he acquitted himself well; he met the movers and shakers of the world, and the narrow horizon of the Florentine expanded into the vistas of the European state-system.

It was thus that Machiavelli was in a position to become the first modern analyst of power. Where others looked at the figureheads, he kept his eyes glued behind the scenes. He sought the ultimate propulsion of events. He wanted to know what made things tick; he wanted to take the clock of the world to pieces to find out how it worked. He went on foreign missions, organized the armies of Florence, carried through successfully the long protracted siege of Pisa. Yet always he was concerned with what these experiences could teach him about the nature of power. In an age of portraiture it was natural that he too should be a painter, but his subjects never knew they were sitting for him. He studied Pope Julius II, the secular princes, the *condottieri;* above all he studied Caesar Borgia, the Duke Valentino, who came closer to embodying the naked ideal of power than any other person Machiavelli had met. There was in Machiavelli, as in Savonarola, an intense and searing flame, but it was a secular flame, and the things it fed on were not such things as religious dreams are made of.

A man like this might have lived out his days, tasted somewhat of power, known what it was to run a state from behind the scenes as an underling, and died leaving behind him some excellent diplomatic reports, a few plays, and some polished verses in the style of the time. But Machiavelli's destiny was different.

The petty dynasties and the bourgeois merchant princes who ruled the Italian city-states played their fateful game of chessboard diplomacy all through the fifteenth century until finally in the sixteenth it led to disaster for all of them. This is not the place to review the succession of maneuvers by which France, Spain, Germany and the

Papacy vied for the supremacy over Italy. When, after the League of Cambrai, a split developed between France and the Papacy, Florence stuck to its basic alliance with France. When Julius II drove the French from Italy, Florence was lost; and not even the new citizen army that Machiavelli had trained could withstand the combined force of the Pope's prestige and his Swiss mercenaries. One of the conditions of the papal peace was the restoration of the Medici in Florence. And so Machiavelli, who had always been staunchly republican and anti-Medici, found himself in 1512 at the age of forty-three a dejected liberal without a job in a world that had come tumbling down about his ears.

He tried to make his peace with the Medici, but to no avail. There was a witch-hunting atmosphere in Florence, and everyone was suspect who had ever been identified with the liberal cause. Two ardent young republican conspirators had evidently made a list of those on whom they thought they might rely for aid, and Machiavelli's name was on the list. He was arrested, drawn by the rope, tortured. But he was plainly innocent, and finally was released. He slunk off to a small suburban farm near Florence, and for the next fourteen years until his death his letters are full of pleas to be reinstated in the favor of the Medici and the Pope, plans to recommend himself to them, strategies by which his abilities could be brought to their attention. It is, as so many commentators have pointed out, neither a pretty nor a graceful picture. Yet we must reflect that Machiavelli out of office felt himself a vessel without use. The letters he has left us during this period, for all their bitter pride and the unbreakable gaiety of their style, show that reinstatement in office spelled for him nothing less than a return to life.

Ironically, it was this period of his disgrace that represents the high point of his creative power. The enforced leisure compelled him to fall back on himself. Finding himself after fourteen years deprived of his job, he felt shut in like a bird in an iron cage. The result was his books—his solitary song. More and more he retreated to his study and his mind. From them came *The Prince,* the *Art of War, The Discourses,* the *History of Florence;* various plays, among them a first-rate comedy, *Mandragola;* poetry, stories, biographical sketches. The civil servant, the politician, the diplomat, the military organizer had become a man of letters *malgré lui.*

There remains only the final ironic act. In 1527 the papal armies

were defeated and Rome was sacked by the soldiers of Charles V. At
this the popular party in Florence overthrew the Medici and for a short
time restored democratic government. Machiavelli had hurried back to
Florence, eager to regain his post as secretary. But he never stood a
real chance. *The Prince,* circulated in manuscript, had made him enemies; the small dull men who had it in their power to dispense office
feared his brilliance and his wit. Mercifully Machiavelli fell sick and
never learned that the final vote of the Council was overwhelmingly
against him. Before the news came he was dead. And so a man who
had hoped for the ultimate glory of being restored to the Florentine
civil service died, leaving behind him nothing but the memory of a
few books he had written in his exile.

—2—

There is a famous letter from Machiavelli to his friend Vettori, the
Florentine ambassador at the Papal Court in Rome, in which he describes the tenor of his life on the farm, and the relief that he finds
among books in his study.

> On the threshold I slip off my day's clothes with their mud and dirt, put on
> my royal and curial robes, and enter, decently accoutred, the ancient courts
> of men of old, where I am welcomed kindly and fed on that fare which is
> mine alone, and for which I was born: where I am not ashamed to address
> them and ask them the reasons for their action, and they reply consider-
> ately; and for two hours I forget all my cares, I know no more trouble,
> death loses its terrors: I am utterly translated in their company. And since
> Dante says that we can never attain knowledge unless we retain what we
> hear, I have noted down the capital I have accumulated from their conver-
> sation and composed a little book, *De Principatibus,* in which I probe as
> deeply as I can the consideration of this subject, discussing what a princi-
> pality is, the variety of such states, how they are won, how they are held,
> how they are lost. . . .[1]

It was the period of the great humanist revival of ancient learning.
The books Machiavelli read were the traditional Latin authors and
(since he probably did not know Greek) the Greek authors in Latin
translation. And as he read there came crowding back into his mind
the varied experiences of his life; and out of the fusion of reading and
experience came new insights into politics, at first jotted down in the
form of notes which eventually formed themselves into a vast book.

That book was not *The Prince*. There are clear indications that Machiavelli started to write what afterward became *The Discourses,* planned on a grand scale. But as he wrote in his study, things were happening in the world outside. There was a new Pope in Rome, a new regime in Italy; the Pope was carving out a new state in Italy and placing his nephew Giuliano at its head. What more natural than to wish to influence this new prince and recommend oneself to his favor? Perhaps one could once more thus have a hand in world affairs, and— who knows?—set in motion a train of forces that might arrest the decadence of the Italian communes and free Italy from the invaders. But *The Discourses* were too vast to finish quickly, and their form was far too sprawling for the purpose. And so, carving out of *The Discourses* certain sections and ideas, Machiavelli proceeded to recast them in the form of a short treatise, *De Principatibus*. Eventually he changed the title from the Latin abstract to the Italian personal, *Il Principe*. The book was written in 1513 at an almost white heat, in what was probably only a few months. Dedicated to Lorenzo de' Medici, it was presented to him and by him neglected and forgotten. It was, however, circulated in manuscript during Machiavelli's lifetime, surreptitiously copied and corrupted, and achieved an underground fame. Since his death it has been one of the half dozen books that have done most to shape Western thought.

What gives *The Prince* its greatness? It is not a great formal treatise on politics. It is bare of any genuine insights into social organization as the basis of politics. It has very little passion in it—so little that, because the final chapter crackles and glows with Machiavelli's fervor for the unification of Italy, some commentators have suggested that it is not an organic part of the book but was added as an afterthought. It has been pretty well proved, moreover, by recent scholarship that Machiavelli's little pamphlet on princes is not even original in form. It is part of a whole traditional literature on princes that stretches back to the Middle Ages. The structure of the book, its division into chapters and even some of the chapter headings follow the conventional form of what has been called the mirror-of-princes literature: the discussion of how to rule conquered territory, what advisers a prince should rely on, how he should conduct himself among the intrigues of diplomacy, whether he should depend mainly on fortified castles or entrenched camps in warfare.

But the intellectual spirit that pervades the book is quite another matter. Here we are in the presence of something little short of a revolution in political thinking. The humanists who had written books about princes had written in the idealistic and scholastic medieval tradition; they were ridden by theology and metaphysics. Machiavelli rejected metaphysics, theology, idealism. The whole drift of his work is toward a political realism, unknown to the formal writing of his time.

I say unknown to the *formal writing*. That does not mean it was unknown to his time. Machiavelli was expressing the realism that characterized the actual politics and the popular ethos of his time. Take, for example, some sentences from the famous eighteenth chapter, "In What Way Princes Must Keep Faith." The Achilles myth of the centaur, he writes, teaches us that we are "semi-animal, semi-human" and that "a prince must know how to use both natures. . . . A prince being thus obliged to know well how to act as a beast must imitate the fox and the lion, for the lion cannot protect himself from traps, and the fox cannot defend himself from wolves. . . . A prudent ruler ought not to keep faith when by so doing it would be against his interest, and when the reasons which made him bind himself no longer exist. . . . It is not, therefore, necessary for a prince to have all the above-named qualities, but it is very necessary to seem to have them." When Machiavelli wrote thus he was not creating a new ethos, whatever we may think of it; he was expressing the ethos of the late *quattrocento* and the early *cinquecento* not only in Florence but in the whole of Italy. Machiavelli was, in short, the child of his time—neither better nor worse than the other intellectuals, politicians, diplomats and civil servants of his time.

He was able, using the traditional humanist literary forms, to pour into them a realistic political spirit which his age was acting on but which had never before been so well expressed in political thought. He had the daring to turn against the whole idealistic preoccupation of the humanists. He had the clear-eyed capacity to distinguish between man as he ought to be and man as he actually is—between the ideal form of institutions and the pragmatic conditions under which they operate.

But if we have come close to his greatness here, we have not wholly succeeded in ensnaring it. There have been other men who have expressed the consciousness of their period. They have in very few instances achieved the highest rank in the history of ideas. And while those who content themselves with seeing Machiavelli thus in the context of his time may succeed thereby in countering the charges made against him of being a sort of anti-Christ who had created a new immorality, they do not thereby get at the roots of his greatness.

To take a further step in our analysis, we must see that Machiavelli, while he expressed the ethical consciousness of his time, was also a good deal ahead of his time in other respects. He lived in a period when economic growth had gone so far as to burst the bounds of existing political forms. What gave the city-states of Italy their Renaissance grandeur was not some mysterious flowering of the humanist spirit at the time. It was the fact that with the opening of the East by the crusades, the breakup of the manorial economy and the growth of trade and handicraft manufacture, the cities of Italy found themselves strategically placed with respect to the world trade routes. There followed what amounted to a communal revolution in Italy and a reorganization of the government of the Italian city-states under democratic and guild forms. The expansion of the economic power of these cities went on apace into the end of the fifteenth century. By the time Machiavelli came to the maturity of his powers, a sharp contraction had set in. The expansion had gone as far as the political limits of the communal organization allowed.

If the Italian city-states had been able to adjust themselves to the needs of an expanding economy by resolving their rivalries and joining in a united political structure, Italy might have been spared the two and a half centuries of humiliation and cultural aridness which followed the fall of the communes. Elsewhere, however, in France, in England, in Spain, the expansion of political forms kept pace with the economic expansion. Machiavelli lived in what, with our historical perspective, we now say to have been the beginnings of the Western nation-state system. As we know it, he was himself only dimly aware of it. He was in no sense an articulate nationalist, and the fervor of his national feeling has probably been overestimated by commentators. But two elements were historically to enter into the composition of the Western nation-state. One was national unity and the idea of a common tongue, common culture and common economic limits. The second was a realistic concentration of power at the center in order to break down divisive barriers. Machiavelli only dimly foresaw nationalism, but he very clearly expressed the second element—the realistic use of power from the center, the methods by which unity could be achieved.

Therein lies the importance of *The Prince* in the subsequent history of the Western world. Machiavelli wrote a grammar of power, not only for the sixteenth century, but for the ages that have followed. Read *The Prince* today and you will be struck by the detonations which its sentences set off in the corridors of our experiences with present-day rulers. Machiavelli seen only in his historical context does become intelligible; but his greatness does not emerge until we see that when he wrote his grammar of power he came close to setting down the imperatives by which men govern and are governed in political communities, whatever the epoch and whatever the governmental structure.

The Prince has become, for better or worse, a symbol of a whole body of literature and a whole approach to politics. Just as in literature and art we must always face, under whatever names, the polar conflict of classic and romantic, so in the history of political thinking we have always to face the polar conflict between the ethical and the ruthlessly realistic. *The Prince* is part of the world's polemical literature because it places itself squarely in the ranks of realism. It brushes aside, with an impatience in which Machiavelli scarcely cares to conceal his disdain, the tender-mindedness of reformers and idealists.

There is in all of us, along with the ethical and normative strain, a strain of hard-headedness and of the acceptance of the framework of human passions and social reality within which we have to work. One can trace it back to Aristophanes and the way in which he always deflated contemporary dreams and illusions by getting back to the essential limits of the human animal. In every generation since him the young men have been divided between the pursuit of some passionate ideal and the hard-bitten inquiry into how things actually get accomplished in a real political world. It is to that pole of our political thinking that *The Prince* gravitates. As long as this strain will remain in political thinking, so long will *The Prince* be found to have expressed in undying prose its intensity and its temper.

Very few who talk of *The Prince* have ever read more than a few sentences in it. But fewer still have read the work of Machiavelli which, without having the same *éclat* in history as *The Prince,* is nevertheless the saner, the more rounded, the more comprehensive work. I refer to *The Discourses.*

It was the longer work on which Machiavelli was engaged when, because of political opportunism, he made a sudden sortie to finish *The Prince*. He came back to it later. He seems to have worked on it intermittently for the better part of a decade. It bears to *The Prince* much the same relation that Marx's *Capital* bears to the *Communist Manifesto*. It is the considered, comprehensive treatise. Outwardly a commentary (unfinished) on the first ten books of Livy's *History of Rome*, it is actually a set of *pensées*, loosely gathered together into a book— reflections on politics which use Roman history as a point of departure. It is clearly not a book which ever had a chance for real fame. The very people who have written most about *The Prince* seem to have neglected *The Discourses*, and very few seem to have read it. When we talk of Machiavellianism, it is *The Prince* we have in mind. And that is perhaps as it should be. But when we talk of Machiavelli, we must have *The Discourses* in mind as well. For if we are to judge a man it is fairer to judge him by the book into which he sought to put his whole system of politics rather than by the pamphlet which he dashed off to win a friend and influence a personage.

Scholarship has not done well by *The Discourses*. The scholars pay lip service to it as the larger frame of reference within which *The Prince* can be understood. Yet having done so, they go on to talk of *The Prince*. Its structure is difficult and fragmentary. Precepts drawn from Livy form the chapter heads. There are whole sections that might easily be cut out to improve the book. A good editor today, receiving such a manuscript, would probably ask the author to cut it down to one-third and pull it together a bit. Yet once read, *The Discourses* stay in your mind as an impressive intellectual experience. And once read, whatever impression you have formed of Machiavelli through reading *The Prince* is rather drastically changed.

What was the intellectual tradition that lay back of *The Discourses*? In the case of *The Prince*, it was the mirror-of-princes medieval and humanist literature. Felix Gilbert has suggested in a recent article, and I think the suggestion is a sound one, that research into the literature of "the good state," both in Italian and in Greater European thought, might yield exciting results for an understanding of *The Discourses*.

However that may be, what are the basic ideas of *The Discourses*? I should say the following: first, the superiority of the democratic republic to every other political form; second, the ultimate reliance even of despotic and authoritarian regimes on mass consent; third, the primary political imperative of cohesiveness, organic unity in a state, stability and survival; fourth, the great role of leadership (what Machiavelli calls the role of the law-giver, but what we should today call leadership) in achieving this cohesiveness and survival; fifth, the imperative of military power in insuring survival and the need for putting it on a mass base (he felt that war was the health of the state); sixth, the use of a national religion for state purposes, and the choice of one not for its supernatural validity, but for its power as a myth in unifying the masses and cementing their morale (Machiavelli's count against Christianity, like that of Nietzsche after him, was that by glorifying humility and pacifism and the weaker virtues, it dulled the fighting edge of a state); seventh, the need in the conduct even of a democratic state for the will to survive, and therefore for ruthless instead of half-hearted measures when ruthless measures were necessary; eighth, the idea— later to be found in Vico and in our day in Spengler—of the cyclical rise and fall of civilizations due to the decadence and corruption of the old and the reinvigoration of the new.

This is, of course, only a sampling of the vast riches to be found in *The Discourses.* It is not a single-themed, monolithic book, such as Marx or Mill wrote. It has a catholicity and vastness of resource which will make it yield different discoveries for every reader and on every reading.

This is not the place to discuss the themes I have mentioned. I want only to say that if *The Prince* is great because of its intensity, *The Discourses* are great because of their variety; if *The Prince* is great because it is polemical, *The Discourses* are great because they have balance; and if *The Prince* is great because it gives us the grammar of power for a government, *The Discourses* are great because they give us the philosophy of organic unity not in a government but in a state, and the conditions under which alone a culture can survive.

—4—

"The authentic interpreter of Machiavelli," Lord Acton has written in his erudite preface to Burd's great edition of *The Prince,* "is the whole of later history." In the same essay he strings out a remarkable series of quotations from the great writers and statesmen of the last three or four centuries which show the impact that Machiavelli had on the European mind. The history of that impact may be called the history of Machiavellianism.

It is clear that one element in the denunciation of Machiavellianism was the use of that symbol as a weapon of the Counter-Reformation. Machiavelli was utterly secular in his thinking. And when the Church, in assuming the aggressive against the religious reformers, sought something that could be set up as a secular devil-symbol in contrast to the ethical teachings of religion, it easily found what it sought in Machiavelli's writings. At the same time also the same symbol could serve to brand with infamy the methods that were being used to set up and consolidate the new nation-states of Europe, the power of whose sovereigns was one of the great threats to church power. And so the Church statesmen who had at first accepted *The Prince,* then ignored it, finally decided to attack it. Under Leo, Clement, Paul III, it was tolerated. But under Paul IV, in 1557, a generation after the Florentine's death, Machiavelli was put on the Index. What is somewhat ironic about this is that the Church princes, like the secular princes, were among the principal followers of Machiavelli's precepts. As Lord Acton (himself a Catholic) points out, the arguments used to excuse the massacres of the religious wars were drawn from Machiavelli.

There is another important element in the history of Machiavellianism —so far, at least, as the English-speaking secular world is concerned. Machiavelli entered our consciousness largely through the Elizabethan drama. Wyndham Lewis has written a provocative, although erratic, book with the title *The Lion and the Fox.* It takes its point of departure from a fact spelled out by scholars like Edward Meyer and more recently Mario Praz—that the figure of Machiavelli dominated the imagination of the Tudor dramatists. The meeting between Italian Renaissance culture and the Tudor mind contained an element of shock arising from novelty. The English were, as is true of all cultural borrowers, at once attracted and repelled by the Italians. Moreover, Tudor drama was enormously sensitive to world currents. The result was that not only were there, as Meyer has pointed out, some 400 direct references to Machiavelli in the Elizabethan literature; but the Machiavelli figure, whether directly or indirectly, dominates it as does no other. Iago was drawn from Machiavelli, as was Barabas. Webster, Massinger, Ford, Marston, Ben Jonson, Shakespeare—they were all fascinated by the image they constructed of subtle cunning, of treachery, of the gap between outward seeming and inward being, all of which they thought of as Machiavellianism. To the Tudor imagination, which has in turn so influenced our own, Machiavelli was the symbol that stood for the decadence, the corruption, the unfathomable depths of Renaissance Italy. It was probably due to the fusion of the influence of church and stage that Machiavelli became associated in the popular mind with the Devil himself. "Old Nick" became an epithet equally applicable to both.

It may therefore seem surprising that Tudor England had scarcely read Machiavelli at all. *The Discourses* were not translated into English until 1636, *The Prince* until 1640. The Elizabethans got their knowledge of Machiavelli from a French book attacking him, Gentillet's *Anti-Machiavel.* And Gentillet gave just enough of Machiavelli to distort him, and not enough to make him either comprehensible or human. This should not surprise us. It is the essence of a symbol that its outlines should be shadowy. What has first been sifted through the intellect is unlikely to ensnare the imagination. Had the Elizabethans really read *The Discourses* and *The Prince,* they would no doubt have been more just to the author, but their drama would have suffered and one of its type figures would have had to be scrapped. By the time the translations were made, it was unfortunately—or shall we say fortunately?—too late to affect either their intelligence or their art. The symbol had become fixed.

I have spoken of various historical reasons why the Elizabethans should have responded to the Machiavelli symbol, and Wyndham Lewis adds the fascination which the diabolical holds for the Puritan genius in every age. Yet we come closer to the core of the truth when we remember that the Elizabethans had the same perverse and feverish preoccupation with the theme of death. And, I am inclined to guess, for much the same reason. It *unmasks* the human animal. But for this very reason Machiavelli became the subject of attack from still another source—the seventeenth- and eighteenth-century absolute monarchy. To be sure, we have a long roster of despots—benevolent and otherwise—who are reputed to have drunk in Machiavelli with their mothers' milk and were known as "Machiavellistae." But we must remember, so black had Machiavelli's reputation become that if you wanted to hit at a monarch, you had only to start a whispering campaign to the effect that he ruled according to Machiavelli's grammar. The supreme irony was that Frederick the Great of Prussia, while still a young man, wrote a refutation of Machiavelli. As Frederick's later career showed, Machiavelli had adumbrated the methods of the benevolent despots only too well. His offense had been only to unmask them, to lay bare to the world the mechanisms of power which were behind the authority of the ruler. Voltaire encouraged the young prince to write his treatise; but his comment on Frederick in his *Memoirs* is delicious:

> If Machiavelli had had a prince for disciple, the first thing he would have recommended him to do would have been to write a book against Machiavellism.

But if Machiavelli was a butt and a tool in the Age of Reason, he came into his own in the nineteenth century in the age of new nationalism. Men rediscovered Machiavelli the liberal, Machiavelli the democrat, Machiavelli the nationalist patriot. In Germany, during and after the Napoleonic wars, the intellectuals rediscovered Machiavelli, and turned their fine gifts of scholarship toward him, with the characteristic result of a spate of Machiavelli studies. The leader was Fichte, who made an analysis of Machiavelli part of his famous *Address to the German Nation;* and Hegel, who following Machiavelli made a cult of the state, taught that "the course of world history stands outside of virtue, blame and justice." And in Italy Cavour and the leaders of the Risorgimento found in Machiavelli their ideal symbol. What both the Italians and the Germans sought in him was what they needed for their movements of national liberation: the stress on cohesiveness, the pursuit of the main chance, the prime virtue of political survival. The Germans took from him the concept of *Staaträson*—opportunism justified by reasons of state policy; and in the field of foreign affairs, *Realpolitik.*

In country after country the rediscovery of Machiavelli seems to have had an almost magical efficacy in stirring latent national and even reformist energies. To complete the history of Machiavellianism, I need only point out that for the recent collectivist movements as well he became an evocative figure. H. G. Wells, in what is one of his really first-rate political novels, *The New Machiavelli,* dreamed of a "strengthened and perfected state" that blends Machiavelli with English Fabian humanitarianism. Both Lenin and Mussolini did their work in the shadow of the Florentine. The "old Bolshevik" Kamenev published a volume of Machiavelli selections with a sympathetic Introduction under the Soviet regime. Some years later, when he was tried and convicted in the purge trials, the Public Prosecutor used his Machiavelli editing job against him. Mussolini also wrote an introductory essay to an edition of *The Prince,* and it was included in Volume

IV of his *Collected Works,* although for a time he banned his own works from the national library. Rauschning in his *Voice of Destruction,* which recounts his conversations with Hitler, asserts that Hitler ranked Machiavelli with Wagner as among the influences shaping his thought; and that he used to keep a copy of *The Prince* by his bedside.

—5—

It has become a truism to point out that Machiavelli is the father of power politics. Whether a truism or not, it is still true. Machiavelli, as ambassador and administrator, could not afford to do any wishful thinking. If he did, the penalty was swift and merciless—failure. Which may not be a bad idea as a school for political theorists. But to say that he was the father of power politics may have curiously erroneous implications—as if we were to say that Harvey was the father of the circulation of the blood. Power politics existed before Machiavelli was ever heard of; it will exist long after his name is only a faint memory. What he did, like Harvey, was to recognize its existence and subject it to scientific study. And so his name has come to be associated with it.

To be sure, Machiavelli's role is not wholly innocent. His grammar of power brought a whole new world to consciousness. With one of Moliere's characters, the princes of Europe became aware that all their lives they had been talking prose. And the awareness led them to perfect their prose. Frederick, Richelieu, Napoleon, Bismarck, Clemenceau, Lenin, Mussolini, Hitler, Stalin, have gone to school to Machiavelli. But by bringing the world to this awareness Machiavelli did what every creative figure does. We might as well blame Shakespeare because, by creating Hamlet, he has intensified the agony of the indecisive and divided liberal.

Machiavelli has also been accused, and it is true, of being the father of the martial spirit, of propaganda techniques and of the totalitarian spirit. But here again he anticipated things latent in the very texture of society and the state. A reading of *The Discourses* should show that his thinking fathered many movements, democratic as well as dictatorial. The common meaning he has for democrats and dictators alike is that, whatever your ends, you must be clear-eyed and unsentimental in pursuit of them and you must rest your power ultimately on a cohesive principle.

May I venture a guess as to the reason why we still shudder slightly at Machiavelli's name? It is not only the tradition I have described. It is our recognition that the realities he described *are* realities; that men, whether in politics, in business or in private life, do *not* act according to their professions of virtue; that leaders in every field seek power ruthlessly and hold on to it tenaciously; that the masses who are coerced in a dictatorship have to be wooed and duped in a democracy; that deceit and ruthlessness invariably crop up in every state; and that while the art of being ruled has always been a relatively easy one, the art of ruling ourselves is monstrously difficult. Machiavelli today confronts us with the major dilemma of how to adapt our democratic techniques and concepts to the demands of a world in which as never before naked power politics dominates the foreign field and determined oligarchies struggle for power internally. It is not an easy dilemma to resolve. And in a sense, just as the seventeenth- and eighteenth-century monarchs hated and feared Machiavelli because he had exposed their authority to the world, so today we hate and fear him because he has exposed our dilemma and made it visible to ourselves and the world.

Let us be clear about one thing: ideals and ethics are important in politics as norms, but they are scarcely effective as techniques. The successful statesman is an artist, concerned with nuances of public mood, approximations of operative motives, guesswork as to the tactics of his opponents, back-breaking work in unifying his own side by compromise and concession. Religious reformers have often succeeded in bringing public morale closer to some ethical norm; they have never succeeded as statesmen. Even in the theocracies of Savonarola in Florence, Cromwell and the Puritans in England, our own New England colonies, the men of God, when they came to power, learned to play the game of power. The only difference between them and others is that, since they had a certitude of having a pipeline to God, they did not have to reckon at all with the uneasy factor of their conscience. The most destructive imperialisms of the world have been those of men who have elevated their preferences to the pinnacle of moral imperatives and who have then confidently proceeded to impose those imperatives on others.

Today, as in Machiavelli's day, our world has become a collection of principalities struggling for survival, maneuvering for position, fighting over spoils. The scale is bigger but the proportions are the same. The strong men have come forward in every state, using the rhetoric of mass interest and national glory to extend their power and entrench their class. The first law of internal policy is to hold on to power, of external policy it is to extend your imperialism. Like Machiavelli, we live in a time of the breaking of nations.

Let it be said that Machiavelli in his day blundered as we are doing in ours. He could not make up his mind whether what he wanted was a democratic Florence or a unified Italy. I think he must have felt, when he wrote *The Prince,* that democracy would somehow follow if unity was achieved. There are some today who feel the same way about the attempts to achieve world integration through establishing a Russian Century or an American Century. There are others who feel that no integration is worth the candle if democratic rights and human decencies are scrapped in the process. In Machiavelli's writing you will find both attitudes, but more often the first.

This raises sharply, of course, the interminable question of ends and means. Machiavelli would, I think, shrug his shoulders at the whole problem. He himself, he would say, was an observer of politics. And as such he would find it irrelevant to impose his own ethical patterns on the torrential flow of world history. It is for that very reason that Machiavellianism, after everything has been said about it, fails to be an adequate philosophy for a way of life. Men are not only observers, not only participants; they are also valuing individuals. Without judgments life loses its hierarchial quality of being a choice between preferences. And losing that, it loses its savor.

Machiavelli sought to distinguish the realm of what ought to be and the realm of what is. He rejected the first for the second. But there is a third realm: the realm of what can be. It is in that realm that what one might call a humanist realism can lie. The measure of man is his ability to extend this sphere of the socially possible. We can start with our democratic values, and we can start also with Machiavelli's realism about tough-minded methods. To be realistic about methods in the politics of a democracy at home does not mean that you throw away all scruples, or accept the superior force of "reason of state," or embrace the police-state crushing of constitutional liberties. To be realistic about the massing of power abroad in the economic and ideological struggle for the support of men and women throughout the world does not mean that you abandon the struggle for peace and for a constitutional imperium that can grow into a world republic. We may yet find that an effective pursuit of democratic values is possible within the scope of a strong social-welfare state and an unsentimental realism about human motives.

Note

1. I use here the translation made by Ralph Roeder in his *Man of the Renaissance* (1933).

3

Alexis de Tocqueville

1. Some Paradoxes

Alexis de Tocqueville saw America a good while before its meridian: in Emerson's scarring phrase he saw it at "the cockcrowing and the morning star." He described it, in his *Democracy in America,* with a reflective passion whose obsessiveness had less to do with the state of America itself than with his inner drive to discover the solution of the problems posed by the Western democratic revolutions, and the relevance of that solution to the problems of France. His luck—and ours—was that when he made his voyage to Jacksonian America in 1831 he came to the right place, at the right time, with the right questions, and the right preparation to see the bearing of the American experience on them. The result was not only the greatest book ever written on America, but probably the greatest on any national polity and culture.

One thinks of Polybius and Machiavelli on the Roman Republic, of Gibbon on Imperial Rome, Burckhardt on the Greeks, Emerson on the British, Michelet on the French, of Bryce, Parrington, and Beard on America—but all of them are either too narrow or fragmented in analysis or too discursive as history. Tocqueville alone knew how to

---

Originally published as the introduction to *Democracy in America*, translated by George Lawrence and edited by J. P. Mayer and Max Lerner (New York: Harper and Row, 1966), xxv–lxxxiii. Lerner published his introduction separately as a short book *Tocqueville and American Civilization* (New York: Harper Colophon Books, 1969), and this book has been reissued in a new edition, with an introduction by Robert Schmuhl (New Brunswick, N.J.: Transaction Publishers, 1994).

portray America as a case study in the nature of the democratic revolution in Europe as well as America, and democracy as a case study in the nature of political man and his institutions. What his mind was able to seize, his will and skill carved into the hard rock of his material. The profile has held, surviving the storms and buffetings of history, its meaning cutting across the varied languages into which it has been translated and the national experience through which it has been filtered. One may venture that today its influence is greater than ever, its relevance to the needs of the day deeper.

It is one of the paradoxes of intellectual history that a gentle, reflective man, who loved his secluded library and was sensitive to noises from the outside world, should have busied himself all his life with the theme of revolution; that a social and intellectual aristocrat should have become one of the early prophets, if something less than a champion, of the modern mass democracy; that a young man who spent less than ten months in the United States should have produced so fundamental a study of American civilization. Yet these paradoxes apply to Tocqueville and point to the stature of *Democracy in America.* It has gaps, wrong guesses, moralizing, and blind spots, and is often rhetorical. But it is also shrewd in observation, piercing in insight, sensitive about the dilemmas of modern political man, profound in following out the bearing of the facts it cites, all but clairvoyant about the later growth of the institutions whose earlier lineaments it draws.[1]

2. The Making of a Social Thinker

In the history of ideas, as in literature, creativeness is likely to come at the convergence of psychological need with experience. It took a young man who was at once a European intellectual and a fiercely sensitive contemporary, open to the currents of his time, to see what the America of Andrew Jackson's day was like. The young Tocqueville had an intense need to clarify his own thinking and shape his intellectual and political direction. America in turn needed someone to interpret its current problems and its historic role and destiny, to itself as well as to the world outside. When he came to America in 1831, Tocqueville was ready for the America he encountered.

He came of the Norman aristocracy, with his family roots deep in the countryside of the *departement* of Manche, only a few miles from the English Channel. His birth in Paris, on July 29, 1805, came at the height of Napoleon's world adventures and his power. While he was later (in the second volume of his study on the French Revolution) to square his intellectual accounts with the dictator in an unsparing way, the grandeur of Napoleon's scope and daring in the political realm must have left with the young men who grew up in his shadow a heightened sense of what the human mind could accomplish.

The boy grew up in a setting encased in the conservatism of status, religion, and a deep commitment to the royalist tradition. His family was strongly royalist: his mother was the granddaughter of the man who defended Louis XVI before the Revolutionary Tribunal, his grandfather and one of his aunts were guillotined, and his parents were barely saved from the scaffold. His early childhood was spent in a château at Verneuil, near Paris, amidst family memories of a vanished regime. When Napoleon fell and the Bourbon dynasty returned, the elder Tocqueville became a prefect, and showed himself a thoughtful and competent administrator, moving from one prefectural post to another. Brought increasingly into his father's confidence (there is a portrait of the father, as prefect, dictating a report to his son), he developed a lively sense of hard fact and of difficult judgments. He was later, in the *Ancien Régime,* to write scornfully of the French revolutionary *philosophes* who undercut the foundations of a society, without any experience of the concrete facts of social or political life. He attended the lycée at Metz, and found some books that shook his religious faith—a not uncommon experience at the time, but for him a matter of enduring anxiety. His reading was spotty rather than comprehensive, and while he did well in composition and rhetoric, carrying off several prizes, he was only a tolerably good student in other subjects and a failure at the classics. Thus his was not at all the kind of mind that performs well at every task in youth, but the more searching mind that picks its tasks, poses new questions for the experience it meets, and turns its experience into meaningful use.

His great leap forward came when, the family having moved to Versailles, he started the study of law at eighteen, became *juge auditeur* (magistrate) at Versailles at twenty-one, and had to face a society and world whose foundations were being shaken. He felt somewhat ill at ease in the law at the start and regarded it as narrowing. Yet he accustomed himself to the search for the relation between the concrete fact and the frame of the universe. He was lucky in having as a fellow magistrate and close friend a remarkable young man called Gustave de

Beaumont. Together they attended Guizot's lectures and plunged into the political and intellectual currents of their time.

As the son of an important man Tocqueville was at ease with the men who shaped the legislative acts and parliamentary maneuvers of his day. His friends too were the sons of the commanding elite of his day. He had the means for travel. A trip to Italy and Sicily with his brother, when he was twenty and had finished his law studies, resulted in a journal containing some striking insights into the relations between land tenure and political institutions. An early letter of his, recently discovered, on the history of England, shows shrewd perception in an area that today we call political sociology. He learned relatively early to regard legal custom, statute, and code as keys for unlocking the inner meaning of social structure and national character. On this score the influence of Montesquieu and his *L'Esprit des Lois* on his thinking must be considered a capital one.

A sharp conflict between his private loyalties and his public duty came in the "July Days" of 1830, with the overthrow of the Bourbon dynasty of Charles X, and the accession of Louis Philippe as a bourgeois monarch brought to power by a group of the *haute bourgeoisie*. Tocqueville had foreseen the 1830 revolution as part of the continuing European revolution, begun in 1789. Yet he did not like the *novi homines* who came in with Louis Philippe—their vendible values, their desire for middle-class comforts, their terrifying mediocrity of mind and spirit. He was asked (as a magistrate) to take an oath to the new regime. To the bitter resentment of many of his friends who (like his family) clung to the Bourbon cause and must have seen him as a traitor to his class, he spoke the necessary three words. It took some moral courage. "I am at war with myself," he wrote in a letter to Mary Mottley, his wife-to-be. "How simple the path would have been if duty had accorded with all the susceptibilities of honor." Tocqueville had a very small opinion of Louis Philippe, a judgment which he was to repeat twenty years later in his *Souvenirs*. But what was decisive for him was his feeling that the new regime could bring order and might be the last chance to establish a constitutional regime in France. The combination of ambivalence, inner torment, moral sensitiveness, and detached final judgment which this episode displays was one that was to remain with Tocqueville for the rest of his life.

He was restless, a child of the malaise of the era between the fall of one Napoleon and the rise of another. It was this restlessness rather than (as has sometimes been suggested) a wish to avoid further political headaches by being out of the country in the troublesome months ahead, which made him think of an American trip. Accepting the French Revolution and its consequences, he and his friend Beaumont were excited about the continuing European Revolution: we must recall that the years 1830–1831 were years of democratic revolution not only in France but in Poland, Belgium, Ireland, Italy. They both wanted to think through their basic orientation to this revolution and come to terms with it in one way or another. In addition, Tocqueville already felt the need for a "new science of politics," as he was to put it later in *Democracy*. Being fact-minded young men, rather than closet philosophers, they wanted to study the new social and political forces of their day in the setting of a particular nation, not their own, so that they could approach the subject with some detachment. America gave them the chance, and they set to work planning for the journey.

In August, 1830, one of Tocqueville's letters boldly announced the plan: "I have long had the greatest desire to visit North America: I shall go see there what a great republic is like; my only fear is lest, during that time, they establish one in France." Later letters suggest that he was also concerned about a career beyond his magistrate's post, which was not going well because of the regime's suspicions about his views. He wanted a political career and thought that if he became a specialist on America it would make him stand out from the other young men of his generation. "On returning to France," he wrote, speaking of his own return, ". . . if the moment is favorable, some sort of publication may let the public know of your existence and fix on you the attention of the parties."

This modest dream of glory, this tremulous hope of heaven, is in dramatic contrast with the fame which was to overwhelm him only five years later. There was one subterfuge which the two friends executed. Wanting official blessing for their trip from the regime, and knowing that a broad study of American democracy might be suspect, they proposed a study—harmless enough to be accepted—of the American penal system and its prison-reform measures, with a view to their application to France. They got no subsidy, but they did get government sponsorship for a project at once timely and useful. Prison reform was in the air: the new French regime was anxious to discover a base of American experience on which to build a program of its own, and the two bright young men were clearly fitted for their task and could do no harm with it.

By early February, 1831, the two young men had their leave and their appointment as government commissioners. Their boat was ready to sail from Le Havre at the end of March. They hurried their preparations. They got letters from French and American diplomats, from Beaumont's cousin Lafayette, from Tocqueville's relative, Chateaubriand, who had been among the American Indians and written an idealized novel about them, from other French counts and barons and dukes: their passport to the new democratic world was to be a strangely aristocratic one, but the patina of aristocracy was to serve them very well indeed in America. They studied English and put together a little packet of books for the boat, including an English book on the American prisons, an American history, and a volume by the French economist, J. B. Say. Tocqueville bought an array of boots and linens, a greatcoat, several hats (including a silk one), and a leather trunk. Each of them brought a gun, and Beaumont also took his sketchbooks and flute. It was a strangely sophisticated outfitting for a voyage to the rough American cities and wilderness. Pioneers, O pioneers.

They carried also a cargo of ideas. It had been only seven years since Tocqueville began his law studies, but his mind had come of age in that time. The remarkable letters and notebooks he wrote in America show amply that he was no longer a fledgling intellectual when he took the boat at Le Havre. Saint-Beuve's famous quip about the young Tocqueville, that "he began to think before having learned anything," has a light sting of truth in it. There is little question that he had a whole trunkful of ideas stored away in his mind, the result of his reading of the political classics, his work as a magistrate, his observation of men and nations. He knew France and had studied Europe and its history. Like any thinker approaching any culture to study it, Tocqueville had a collection of basic concepts—call them preconceptions, as Harold Laski did in his last essay on Tocqueville—which are at once a thinker's tools and his jailers. But, as much as anyone, Tocqueville made an effort to use his concepts as hypotheses to be tested, and not as rigid molds into which to fit the raw material he found. He did not wholly succeed, but who does? As for his youthfulness, we are less surprised to find it in the artist, the poet, the mathematician, than in the social thinker. We must remember that Tocqueville's world was still a compassable one, that he had not had to go through the protracted ordeal of a graduate school, that he had not been overburdened with what other men had thought, but had used his own mind and imagination. This imaginative creativeness was the most valuable baggage he took with him to America, when the boat—after running aground in the harbor—finally sailed after midnight, April 2, 1831.

Reading their letters from shipboard, one catches the infection of their excitement. They were heading for a new world, about which there had been many descriptive accounts in French literature but no real social and philosophical analysis. It was a world which might have lessons for the agonized society of France and Europe, if only one could read them correctly. Several weeks out, Tocqueville, on a stormy dark night, climbed out on the bowsprit of the boat and stood there with the spray flying in his face, thinking doubtless not only of the vast land that awaited him beyond the darkness but of the difference it would make in his life. "We are meditating great projects," Beaumont wrote his father. "Would it not be a fine book which would give an exact conception of the American people, would paint its character in broad strokes, would analyze its social conditions . . . ?"

After a crossing of five and a half weeks the *Havre* reached Newport, and the following day the two friends reembarked on "a tremendous steamship," the *President.* On May 11, 1831, they reached New York, docking at Cortlandt Street, and were surprised to find the next day that the news of their arrival was in the enterprising New York papers.

3. The Making of a Book

What was it like, the America of Jackson's day and Clay's and Van Buren's, of Emerson and Channing, of John Quincy Adams and Webster and Nicholas Biddle, of Justice Story and Chancellor Kent, of Josiah Quincy and Francis Lieber and the Livingstons, of James Fenimore Cooper and Mathew Carey and George Bancroft, of the wharves and the colleges, the cities and farms and wilderness? If we try to assess the justice of Tocqueville's description of this America against the historical sources, we meet the difficulty (as Marvin Meyers has pointed out) that Tocqueville is today one of the most important of those sources and that our knowledge of this America—in the sense of a grand overview—is in part derived from him.

He came at a good time for a social observer. The Jacksonian era was one of the watersheds of American history, when the driblets of small changes are gathered into a strong current of great change which conditions what is to come for some time. If America is, like every powerful society, primarily a system of social energies, then this period saw a great forward movement in American history because it saw one of its greatest bursts of social energy. There was a rapid development of a transportation system, of roads and steamships and canals, with the first railroads soon to be built. This system of transport in turn made it possible for workers and technicians to reach new production centers and for products to reach new markets, thus achieving the first great breakthrough in American economic history. The construction of a network of "internal improvements" (on which John Quincy Adams and Clay prided themselves) was reaching its height; by 1837 it had begun to decline. There was a frontier being opened rapidly, with the dissatisfied, the restless, and the ambitious streaming into it, into the Great Lakes region, down as far as New Orleans, filling out the whole area between the Appalachians and the Mississippi, opening a vast food supply, tapping the resources of half a continent for its markets. There was the early development of a factory system. There was actually a triple frontier—of geography, of industry, but also of democracy—and therefore a reassertion of the democratic impulse which was always in danger of thinning out in the seaboard cities and towns.

There was a burst of humanitarian passions, the proliferation of reform movements (prison reform, slavery reform, educational reform, sexual reform and the emancipation of women, a new attitude toward children), the surge of millenarian plans, and half-dream, half-practical projects like the communalist settlements. There were strong pressures, especially from the working class, for a public education system, open to all on equal terms, and the beginnings of a philosophy of public education. There was the all but complete triumph of universal manhood suffrage, despite the dark fears of the possessing and commanding classes in the seats of power. There was the electoral triumph of the party of the *demos,* when Jackson's followers joyfully invaded the White House to survey the symbolic field of the battle they had gained. There was the reassertion of the common man against the paradox of what Francis Grund called the "American aristocracy." There was a Jacksonian campaign against the new power of the merchant, capitalist and banking class, asserting the power of the governments—state and federal—to set the limits of corporate and banking action and to hem in the monster of the United States Bank which (by its control over currency and credit) seemed to hold at its mercy the fluctuations of price and therefore of value and purchasing power. There was the bruised feeling of the capitalists, dazed at the vehemence of the Jacksonian attack, reacting by a reformulation of the American creed to stress freedom from governmental intervention, thus laying the foundations of what was to become—a half century later—the triumph of laissez faire. There was, in the wake of all these great dislocating changes, a sense of uncertainty in manners and morals and taste, with no traditional class to act as arbiter in that whole realm, so that what Tocqueville was to call the "tyranny of the majority" was from another viewpoint a disquieting vacuum of values.

If these are some phases of the turbulent ordeal of change through which America was going, Tocqueville reached America at a meaningful period of its development. It was also the high morning of his own. Had he come earlier, before the economic breakthrough, the Jacksonian revolution, and the beginnings of a mass democracy in America, he would not have been able to see the outlines of its enduring forms. Had he come later in his own life, after the events of 1848–1851 in France had left him lonely and embittered, he would have drawn a more somber and less balanced picture of what he saw. As it was, there was a happy matching of subject, mood, and painter in that arrested moment of intellectual history when Tocqueville stepped off the *President* and America lay before him.

He was struck with surprise by what he saw, not in the hackneyed sense that he had expected painted Indians in the wilderness of New York and found instead a metropolis but in the sense that the great experiment, whose viability had been repeatedly doubted and denied, was in fact a going concern, and a vigorous, effective, and happy one.

The travels of the two young men have been traced and reconstructed by George W. Pierson: New York for two weeks, where they were received with éclat, met the governor, were shown about the city and entertained everywhere, were given a banquet by the mayor and alderman; a visit to Sing Sing, as part of their prison project; three more New York weeks in June, when they met highborn and lowborn, but especially the prestigious and powerful of the city (men like Kent, Gallatin, Philip Hone, James Gore King, Nathaniel Prime), when they went to fashionable balls and soirées, when Tocqueville asked endless questions and furiously filled his notebooks with the answers, when

Beaumont (who was the gallant of the two) walked in the moonlight with beautiful women, when both of them pushed themselves to the limits of exhaustion and excitement. Then for three weeks in July they explored upper New York State, seeing a group of politicians in Albany, including the lieutenant governor and the governor (Tocqueville discovered here that the New Yorkers had chosen a mediocre man for governor because the men of talent preferred trade, where they could make money); they held their memorable conversations with Elam Lynds, the intellectual father of the Auburn Penitentiary, and the even more memorable one with John C. Spencer on the courts, the legal profession, and the separation of church and state. Their warm reception may have been due partly to their aristocratic charm of manner, but it was also characteristic of American generosity.

Then came the most exacting ordeal the friends were to have in their American travels. It was a trip from Buffalo into Michigan Territory, to the wilderness settlements of Detroit, Pontiac, and Saginaw, and back to Detroit—the famous trip which Tocqueville recorded in his notebooks and then (on a leisurely boat trip to the Great Lakes and Canada) wrote up as "A Fortnight in the Wilds" ("Quinze Jours au Désert"). They had a rationale for making this arduous trip—the conviction that the sources of American prosperity lay in the frontier lands and their products. But a deeper motive may have been the challenge of a noneastern and nonurban America, the America that Chateaubriand had seen, and without seeing which it would be a bit shameful to return to France. Despite Tocqueville's rather frail physique, they made a trip by steamboat to Detroit, then by rented packhorses overland to Pontiac, and finally (again by horse) into the deep solitary wilderness to Saginaw. It was on this stretch that they were stalked by a silent, mysterious, but persistent Chippewa; found shelter in log huts; hired two Indian guides part of the way, whose loyalty to the project was a wavering one; lost part of their provisions and almost lost their horses; were bitten by swarms of mosquitos as they slept in the open; encountered Indian settlements, trappers, half-breeds, the heat, the insects, and even rattlesnakes.

But they came through, and they learned in the end not only their own stubborn endurance, but also some truths about the American frontier which they might not have discovered other than at first hand. In the wilderness, on July 29, came Tocqueville's twenty-sixth birthday, which happened also to be the first anniversary of the 1830 Revolution. He had gone a long way in one year, not only geographically but in seizing on his life purposes. The memories of the turbulent July Days in Paris were in strange contrast to the silence of the wilderness around him. His account of the "Quinze Jours" remains a little masterpiece, written more vividly—with less of Tocqueville's characteristic rhetorical balance and more sheer narrative *brio*—than anything he ever did.

After returning from the frontier the two friends resumed their tour of the Eastern cities. In Boston, which was cool and distant at first, the news spread of their ability, distinction, and charm, and they were overwhelmed with invitations and stayed three and a half weeks. Again Tocqueville kept notes of his interviews with scholars, preachers, and political bigwigs—most of all with Justice Story, of the Supreme Court, also with Channing, Josiah Quincy, Jared Sparks, Francis Lieber, Daniel Webster, Joseph Tuckerman, Edward Everett, and even with the ex-President, John Quincy Adams. They seemed most interested in religion, law and government, and local administration. Their great difficulty was a lack of knowledge of French administration to serve as comparison, and Tocqueville sent a hurried request home for a memorandum on it. They were besieged with material from the nabobs in Boston, who sent them their books, reports, articles: Jared Sparks even composed a long memorandum for Tocqueville. They got all sorts of information. Francis Lieber, for example, told them that there was not a single married woman in Boston who would dare carry on an intrigue, and that the young men too were pure—except for their frequenting prostitutes. There was a good deal of snobbism, cant, and Federalist-Whig conservatism in what they were told in circles like those of Justice Story, in the capital of America's commanding and creative elites. It would take Tocqueville years to disengage himself from the bias he found in Boston, and there were some Americans (notably Thomas Hart Benton) who felt he never did.

In Philadelphia they talked with Quakers, philanthropists, intellectuals, businessmen, and prison reformers, and found in it a combination of cultural polish and the democratic impulse. In Baltimore, on their first day, they went to a subscription ball where rank depended on wealth, and the next day to a horse race. They learned at once the quality of Southern "society" and the condition of the blacks. Then they came back to Philadelphia for another two weeks, the high point being a conversation with Nicholas Biddle, with whom Jackson was engaged in a life-and-death struggle over the Bank of the United States.

After this exposure to a second set of Eastern cities, Tocqueville made a second frontier voyage down the Ohio and the Mississippi, from Pittsburgh to New Orleans, and a return journey through the Deep South from New Orleans to Washington. It was a happy alternation, from the city culture to the frontier, back to the city and then to the frontier again—this time the Southern rather than the Northern. The last part of the travels was also a confronting of a culture built on slavery, which was of special moment to Beaumont when he came to write his novel *Marie,* a strange mélange of fiction and sociology, but of moment also to Tocqueville, plowing him to the depths on the great issue of freedom, and sharpening the equality-liberty ambivalence that was to be his preoccupation for the rest of his life.

The two friends had some hair-raising adventures on the Mississippi journey. It was December, in an extraordinarily cold winter. The Tennessee River froze, their boat got stuck beyond dislodgment, their carriage broke an axle, they stayed in wretched inns, and Tocqueville was very ill. They saw Nashville and Memphis, they traveled by stage, canal, and river steamer, they found themselves in Davy Crockett's district, they met the redoubtable Sam Houston on a splendid stallion and interviewed him on the river boat to New Orleans. They spent New Year's Day, 1832, in that city, then crossed Mississippi, Alabama, Georgia, and the Carolinas, and arrived in Washington, where they paid a call on President Jackson. He received them with courtesy, but for once Tocqueville had not prepared the right questions to ask: the conversation was superficial, and Tocqueville's estimate of Jackson was less than high. They were shown the honors of the capital by their many friends there, spent a day in the Senate, and left by coach for Philadelphia and New York, and then by the *Havre* again for France, on February 20, 1832.

They had been in America for almost forty-one weeks. They went home to digest what they had seen, heard, experienced, felt, and thought, and to make something of it. Once back in France, Tocqueville set to work. He took an attic flat in Paris in 1833; wanting solitude for work, he shut himself up in it, and lined up a number of books to read in order to fill in the gaps of his knowledge of America. But he grew discontented with Paris, discovered the delights of the family château at Tocqueville, and later transferred to its solitude. What he read about America was not the reports of other travelers—such as Harriet

Martineau, Frances Trollope, and Michael Chevalier—for he was unwilling to have their views influence his thought, but varied source material such as a *Life of Washington,* Jefferson's *Notes on Virginia,* volumes of legislation, commentaries on the law. He got the help of a young American in digesting some of these formidable sources. But otherwise he relied on his memories and reflections and his incomparable notebooks.

The notebooks are worth intensive study; they show how a first-rate mind went at making a first-rate book. One may ask whether Tocqueville's method was inductive or deductive, but it is like asking which of a pair of scissors does the cutting. He relied on his observations and on the many interviews which he had noted down quickly, often in dialogue form. But what he saw depended on what he had come prepared to see; the answers he got in the interviews depended on the questions he put. This had its drawbacks. His conversation with Jackson was unfruitful largely because he did not know enough about the presidency or the Bank, about American economics, party politics, and class struggles, to ask Jackson the right questions. As a result he failed to grasp the nature and potentials of the Presidential power in America. Yet some of the strengths of his book also flowed from his method. This European had come to America with an intellectual cargo such as few visitors have since equalled. He had the capacity to select the significant from his mass of observations. He was surely one of the most remarkable interviewers in the history of social thought, able to judge where a man's strength would lie, and not averse to the flattery which would unloose his tongue. The men he interviewed sensed the thoughtfulness behind Tocqueville's questions and quickly caught fire from him; he in turn, as the answers came, caught fire from them, glimpsed new vistas he had not thought of, and from them framed fresh questions. And when he had formulated a hypothesis—about the separation of church and state, for example, or about American frontier settlers, or about the relation of slavery to social energy—he tried it out on other people he talked with. Thus his conversations were a continuing linked inductive-deductive-inductive chain.

What was striking about Tocqueville was not the preconceptions which could distort the picture, but the striking capacity to move out of the domain of his own background and experience and enter that of the people he talked with. It is easy to quote passages showing that Tocqueville never wholly escaped the limits of his family and social conditioning. The more remarkable fact is that he laid himself open to the America that was there, and grasped it with an imaginative warmth, even if it cut across the grain of his prejudices.

He was not a warm person but a withdrawn and aloof one, who had a horror of mediocrity. The people in a crowd were for him faceless. Such a person could not have enjoyed the egalitarian atmosphere of a society where (as he noted) you shook everyone's hand whether you knew him or not, where the best talent pursued the dollar, leaving the mediocrities to govern. The man whose ancestors had served a succession of kings, and who himself had wept when he saw Charles X fleeing Paris, did not enjoy a subscription ball where the social pecking order was neither birth nor talent but money. He didn't like river captains whose boats ran aground and who were "insolent" when you asked them about it, nor rough inns where the beds were ranged three across, and any traveler—male or female—was expected to throw himself on them. He didn't like genial democratic bores whom he couldn't get rid of. He didn't like political cant in the press or political parties whose everyday currency was scurrility. This was not a society made to his liking, nor was it one to which he would willingly return to live in. Yet he had enough insight to seize upon the deepest sources of its strength and the mystique by which it appealed to its people, and he had enough creative sympathy to set it all down whether he liked it or not. It was a Brave New World which would some day make itself felt across the Atlantic, although in a form characteristic to Europe: there were already forces at work in Europe which were part of the same revolution which had swept over America and might now sweep over his own country. Yet he would have to understand it, analyze it, lay it bare, project its lines of energy into the future; for the survival of everything he held dear depended on the thoroughness with which his people in France, and the people in the rest of Europe, understood the lines of social force that were in motion, and on what they did about it.

What Tocqueville himself wanted was not to write a description of America but to draw a chart to guide Europeans through the rough waters of their time. "I admit," he wrote in his brilliant introductory chapter to the First Part, "that I saw in America more than America; it was the shape of democracy itself which I sought, its inclinations, character, prejudices, and passions; I wanted to understand it so as at least to know what we have to fear or hope therefrom."[2] It was in this sense that he wrote to John Stuart Mill: "America was only my framework; democracy was my subject," and he might have added, rounding out the trinity: "and France and Europe were my target."

4. Master Ideas, Structure, Style

There are four interlinked central ideas in the book: the idea of *democracy*; the idea of *revolution;* the idea of a *social style and character,* carrying a pervasive spirit which informs the total society and determines the relations of individuals to the government and of the crucial institutions to each other—of majorities to minorities, of rim to center, of the local to the central authorities. Finally the idea of *history and God and man* interacting with each other within *the* "fatal circle" of necessity and freedom.

It is a revealing fact that Tocqueville thought of calling the second volume of his book *L'Égalité en Amerique,* but—wisely or not—gave it up, for "democracy" was the term that the Americans themselves were using in Jackson's day, and Tocqueville's own use of it entrenched it both in America and elsewhere. But he uses the term in several senses: as legal equality, as a leveling egalitarian tendency in the whole of the society and in history, as constitutionalism, as the participation of the people in government through those whom they elect—that is to say, representative government. Only the context indicates the meaning he gives it in any particular passage. In the broadest terms his *democracy* sometimes means a Whitmanesque leaves-of-grass democracy, which deifies the people as the ultimate and creative source of power and of the society's energies, and sometimes the brand of "constitutional democracy" which stresses the consent of the governed while maintaining the guiding role of elites ("aristocracies") and which regards freedom and its protections as the chief aim of a system of government. One might accuse Tocqueville of commuting between the realm of equality and the realm of representative constitutionalism without ever deciding which of them marks democracy in its essence. But the fact is that the ambiguity of the term lies in the inherent nature of the dilemmas of modern man rather than in Tocqueville's own ambivalences. One thing is fairly clear: when Tocqueville talked of mass movements in history and of the role of America in the stream of history, he meant *démocratie* in the radical sense of the sway of the irresistible demos; when he talked of what France and Europe needed to learn from the American example and what to do about *démocratie,* he meant it in the sense of representative constitutional government with the stress on the creative role of the people, and at that point he was a liberal in the modern American sense; when he talked of the majority tyranny, and of what the unrestrained demos could do to the institutions which men had laboriously built, he was a conservative liberal, and the *démocratie* he wanted to salvage from the destructive forces of history and from the mass age was democracy as individual freedom.

This leads into the idea of *revolution*. With his background of European history Tocqueville saw revolutions as violent seizures of power, long prepared by repression and ferment, whose coming can be foreseen but not their timing. What was very much on Tocqueville's mind was "the revolution that is taking place in the social condition"—a continuing, almost a permanent revolution: *la revolution continue* was one of his favorite sentences. He was fascinated by the irresistible march of the demos in overthrowing first the feudal and then the aristocratic and monarchical yokes in the Europe he had studied.

When he tried to apply this concept to America, Tocqueville found himself in difficulties. He saw America and Europe together as part of the continuing revolution: but if he pressed this too hard it would strip America of the uniqueness which he knew it possessed. Tocqueville could not agree with Lafayette, who believed that the American experience could be carried over bodily to France. He recognized the quality of American uniqueness. But at least in part it came, as he saw, from the fact that Americans never had to overthrow a feudal or aristocratic regime: "The Americans have this great advantage," he writes, "that they attained democracy without the sufferings of a democratic revolution, and that they were born equal instead of becoming so." This meant, he saw and said clearly, that Americans had escaped the particular kind of alienation from man that comes with the violence and hatred of mass revolutions. But if that was true, then the American revolutionary experience could not easily be assimilated to the European. It was a happier, less violent brand, involving in essence the fulfillment of the individual through his institutions, the release of his energies for the pursuit of profit and happiness. What meaning then could such a revolution of affirmations have for a Europe caught in the struggle of estates and classes, and still encrusted in the old blood-rust of centuries?

Tocqueville was of course profoundly right in seeing America and Europe as part of the same revolutionary continuum. But the complexity of the nexus between America and Europe has baffled every student of American civilization since Tocqueville, as has the question of whether the American Revolution was a social one, or primarily legal and political. America was settled out of the unsettlement of the older European societies, in the sense that those societies were no longer adequate for the restless energies of its land-hungry peasants, its alienated intellectuals, its religious dissenters. The revolutionary impulse of America came out of the very Europe which could not use the impulse for its own liberation with the same effectiveness with which America used it. America carried over the best radical energies of Europe, but in a new setting, on a new Continent, with what was to be a mélange of peoples never before brought together, with a buoyant self-confidence (along with its defensiveness) and with a sense of mission, with a wilderness to expand into, and a clean slate on which to write the doctrines that would minister to the new experience. The nexus was there, for America could carry over the ideas and institutions it wanted from Europe without paying the blood price that had been paid in developing them in Europe. That has been its historical happiness, beyond the individual lot. It was now ready, in turn, to offer Europe in transmuted form—for Europe's own characteristic uses—the revolutionary spark it had taken from it. Tocqueville sensed this; that was why he had come. What he wanted to puzzle out was the nature and meaning of the message that America had for Europe.

He was acute enough to understand that a society is an organic whole, and that it is impossible to pick institutional shoots from the culture and transplant them on another cultural soil. The idea of the wholeness of American society was one to which Tocqueville constantly returned; and while there has been less comment on it than on other ideas of his, for our era it may prove important as any. He may have taken it over from previous social thinkers, including Montesquieu, but his own thinking had perfected it. Whenever he tried to explain any institutional segment of American life—its associations, its literature, its military system, its manners, its taste, its mobility, its morality—he had recourse to the same central principles of egalitarianism, individual self-reliance, unrestrained pursuit of self-interest, weak central government, popular participation in government, and social activity at every level. In short, what Tocqueville had written when both volumes of *Democracy in America* were completed—each very different from the other—was not another book of travels, nor even a book on America's national traits, but a book on the character of American institutions and on the American style of civilization.

True, he didn't use the term civilization in our current value-free sense but used it to mean the aspects of a cultivated society as against a savage one. In fact, he wrote before the modern sociological terms, such as "culture" and "civilization," had been given precision of meaning. But he was not greatly handicapped by their absence, because he had laid hold of the idea itself, in the words that his own time used. When he spoke of the spirit of the laws and of the customs or mores *(moeurs)* of America, he meant the wholeness of the civilization and the inner cohesion and consistency of its parts. It was because he saw this that he could not content himself with the primarily political emphasis in the first volume, but had to continue and write the second, which reached out to every aspect of the civilization. This is why it is a kind of folly to speak of Tocqueville and Bryce together, as many Americans tend to do, as if they were equals. The fact is that Bryce was an exceedingly shrewd and urbane commentator on American politics, many of whose insights into American institutions and national character have worn well. But Tocqueville almost single-handedly shaped a political sociology, a military sociology, a sociology of the intellectual life, a theory of alienation, a theory of mass culture and mass tyranny in a democracy.

The most difficult intellectual problem he had to face in his book was history itself, and the role of necessity and freedom, of God and man, in it. "This book," he writes in a famous passage in his introductory chapter, "has been written under the impulse of a quasi-religious dread." Men must come to see, he says, "that both the past and the future of their history consist in the gradual and measured advance of equality." When they make this discovery, "it gives this progress the sacred character of the will of the Sovereign Master," and therefore any "effort to halt democracy appears as a fight against God himself."

By itself this seems to mean what Engels—and Hegel before him—meant when they defined freedom as "the recognition of necessity," and it could be read as a flagrant celebration of that reason-of-history—the invoking of history as a rationalization of power drives—which has claimed as many victims as reason-of-state did in the post-Machiavellian wars of Europe. But Tocqueville knew too much about man's inhumanity to rationalize it by the naked doctrine of historical necessity. God was, for him, present not only in the stream of history itself but also in men's efforts to channel it. "The Christian nations of

our day . . . present an alarming spectacle; the movement which carries them along is already too strong to be halted, but it is not yet so
swift that we must despair of directing it; our fate is in our hands; but
soon it may pass beyond control." And the means to such guidance?
"A new political science is needed for a world itself quite new"—the
"new world" here meaning that of a possible new Europe in a revolutionary time, with lessons drawn from a country where "this great
social revolution seems almost to have reached its natural limits . . . or
rather one might say that this country sees the results of the democratic revolution taking place among us, without experiencing the
revolution itself." It was to the construction of this "new political
science" that Tocqueville devoted his book. Other political thinkers
before him had had the same sense of the need for a wholly new
formulation in a new age: Aristotle, Machiavelli, Bodin, Hobbes,
Madison, and Hamilton in the *Federalist Papers.* It is striking to see
how confidently this young man, still in his twenties, set about his
task.

One might ask wryly what role there can be for human will and
choice in such a science of politics if God is on the side of the irresistible force of revolution. Here Tocqueville fell back on the theory that
a benevolent God, presiding over the course of history, could not
allow the irresistible force to go in the wrong direction: "I cannot
believe that God has for several centuries been pushing two or three
hundred million men toward equality just to make them wind up under
a Tiberian or a Claudian despotism. Verily, that wouldn't be worth the
trouble." Here Tocqueville, who sometimes seemed to refer to God in
a detached way as a mathematician might refer to the Infinite, went
farther and invoked a principle of benevolent design in the universe.
He believed that God's design would not be done unless man's will—
as part of that design—served as the means for carrying it out. More
searchingly, however, his answer was that the irresistible historic force
is a fact, whatever notion one may have of God or Providence; but that
it is left to man's choice to decide whether that force will prove
destructive or tolerable. If the choice is made blindly, in the clash of
repression from the classes above and terrorism from the classes below,
the result will be "tyranny and degeneration"; if it is made intelligently,
by thoughtful men armed with the new science of politics, egalitarianism
will still come, but without the accompanying blood and darkness. It
was a subtle answer, and a moving credo.

Tocqueville was a conservative in a sense that American conservatives do not often take to heart. He had a deep sense of history, and of the place of revolution in it. As a political man (he scorned the abstractions of the philosophers who separated themselves from political reality) he wanted to do whatever he could to bring about an ordered revolutionary change by other political men. It has even been argued that, to be more effective tactically, he presented his views about the coming democracy not as his own preferences but as the will of Providence. We may guess that he saw himself in a mediating role between the fanatics who made a political religion of revolution, and who wanted the bright dream to be realized tomorrow or sooner, whatever the human cost, and the guardians of the old order who would pull down the pillars of the temple and die at their posts rather than surrender them to anarchy and atheism. He sought to temper the mindless haste of the first group (call them the Left) and instill in them an enlightened use of their coming power, while he sought also to convince the Right to humanize a new regime by anticipating and helping to establish it, rather than brutalize it by unthinking resistance which could only make the worse of two evils triumph.

This ran afoul of some of Tocqueville's own shrewdest insights about political man and his behavior, and had to be squared with them. Tocqueville understood very well that while accommodation to a revolutionary movement may slow it down, as indeed it did historically in the case of England, it is more likely to speed it up. In the unfinished second volume of *L'Ancien Régime et La Révolution,* he was to point out (Part III) "how the prosperity of the reign of Louis XVI hastened the outbreak of the Revolution," "how the spirit of revolt was promoted by well-intentioned efforts to improve the people's lot," and "how revolutionary changes in the administrative system preceded the political revolution." In *Democracy in America* he had already grasped that principle, pointing out that the passion for equality feeds on its own success. The all-out logic by which, at the start of his first volume, he presented egalitarian democracy as the wave of the future would have to be rethought in the five years intervening between the first pair of volumes and the second.

It was not surprising therefore that at the close of the final volume, published in 1840, Tocqueville came back to the theme which he had started, that of God and man in history. Again he affirms the irreversible trend, but his sureness about it has no buoyancy of assertiveness and is tempered with sadness. He looks at the egalitarian prospect ahead and sees only a gray uniformity of a "countless multitude of beings, shaped in each other's likeness, among whom nothing stands out or falls unduly low." It has often been noted that Tocqueville had an ambivalent attitude toward aristocratic societies. He was drawn toward their aesthetic and creative aspects, toward the cultivation of manners, that they made possible. But he also had deep convictions about a natural order—which he identified with God, or Providence— in which democracy came far closer than aristocracy to the principles of natural justice. He confesses that he would himself prefer the diversity and creativeness of the past societies, even with their inequalities. But he adds: "It is not so with that Almighty and Eternal Being, whose gaze of necessity includes the whole of created things. . . . It is natural to suppose that not the particular prosperity of the few, but the greater well-being of all, is most pleasing in the sight of the Creator and Preserver of men. What seems to me decay is thus in His eyes progress; what pains me is acceptable to Him. Equality may be less elevated, but it is more just, and in its justice lies its greatness and beauty."

This is moving, but the principle underlying it is faulty: that a democratic revolution, stressing equality, would have to wipe out diversity and creativeness, that justice is incompatible with diversity, equality with creativeness. Had Tocqueville followed this premise all the way it would have turned his picture of America into a monstrous wasteland. Actually his own book refuted it for America, although he retained a fear it would still happen in Europe. This is evidence that Tocqueville as scrupulous observer at times triumphed over Tocqueville as grand theorist. Only where the mass society has had built-in inequalities and injustices of its own to replace the inequalities of its predecessor societies, as under modern totalitarianism, has it produced a cultural wasteland. The fact is that even in the America of the 1830's, which Tocqueville visited, there was considerable diversity and great intellectual excitement. Tocqueville noted some of it, but he also missed a good portion of it. In America, the mass society, whatever its conformist defects, has had a strong, egalitarian thrust and also a strong legal tradition of the protection of individual rights. It has also as a historical fact developed a great measure of diversity and creativeness of its own, along with the conformity.

Actually Tocqueville ended on a note not very different from this. "I am full of fears and of hopes. I see great dangers which may be warded off and mighty evils which may be avoided or kept in check; and I am ever increasingly confirmed in my belief that for democratic nations to be virtuous and prosperous, it is enough if they will to be so." Thus he ends after all not as a determinist in history, but as a voluntarist and a possibilist. He goes on to attack the determinist theories, which see nations as subject to "some insuperable and unthinking power, the product of preexisting facts, of race, or soil, or climate. These are false and cowardly doctrines which can only produce feeble men and pusillanimous nations." This was an early manifesto against the determinist doctrines, which, after his time, were used by the totalitarians, and whose outcropping in the racist doctrines of his wayward and agitated young friend, Gobineau, saddened him beyond measure.

Then, in a closing passage, comes Tocqueville's solution for the whole tangled problem, in a phrasing as vivid and felicitous as any that has been used in writing about the limits of necessity and the scope of human freedom in history: "Providence has, in truth, drawn a predestined circle around each man beyond which he cannot pass; but within those vast limits man is strong and free, and so are peoples." It would not be true to say that the Americans had not quite succeeded in breaking through that predestined circle: much of Tocqueville's book was concerned with showing how the necessities of democratic societies shape a certain character in the nation and a certain style in its institutions. But while Tocqueville's references to Europe have overtones of limited options, the whole book conveys a sense of the spaciousness of the American society and the freedom of movement it made possible, for the individual, the group, the class, for the exploration not only of new frontier lands but of new forms of political and social organization.

One might argue that there are two books here, not one: a book on America and another implicit book—a subbook, as it were—on and for Europe; that in one of them the atmosphere is open and the predestined circle makes a wide sweep, while in the other there is a constricted atmosphere and a cramped circle rather than one of vast limits. A critic might even complain that the two books, while they coexist, do not fuse.

But whether they do or not, the result has been a grand one. The geography, history, social conditions, and destiny of the two continents were different, which was exactly Tocqueville's point. America had not had to carry the dark burden of Europe's frustrated fratricidal revolutions, but had made its own social revolution, in broad daylight, with the suns of the world shining on it. Europe would have to work out its own revolutionary destiny. But it could learn from the American experience—learn concretely the value as well as the problems of decentralized administration, popular participation in government, an independent judiciary, the jury system, the separation of church and state, the formation of voluntary associations to advance concrete causes, a religious respect for the rule of law and for the rights of individuals. Beyond these specific lessons for France and Europe, there was the over-all symbol of America, with its social energies, its national confidence, its thrust toward the future. Although the direct references and exhortations to France are relatively few in the first volume, while increasing in the second, France and Europe are always implicitly present in both, as they were present in Tocqueville's mind. In fact, it was this double vision of Tocqueville, seeing Europe in the perspective of America and America in the perspective of Europe, that gave the book a dimension that other books on America have not possessed.

Part I of *Democracy* appeared in Paris, as I have noted, in 1835, in two volumes. The publisher had little confidence in it, but it was an overwhelming success and made Tocqueville famous overnight. Part II, also in two volumes, did not appear until 1840. People bought it and the reviews were good, but there was no excitement about it as there had been about Part I, and Tocqueville felt the difference with some bitterness.

The two volumes are different in mood as well as scope, and to some extent in style. Among the commentators each volume has had its detractors and its devotees, like the earlier and later Nietzsche or the two Parts of *Faust*. Those interested primarily in American political institutions, or in the economic or ethnic aspects of American life, prefer the first volume. It introduces the grand themes of Tocqueville's thinking, its analyses are sustained, and it contains a number of the classic chapters—on the stream of democratic tendency in history, on the ecology of the continent in early times, on the population estimate, on the legal profession, and above all on the widely cited tyranny of the majority.

The second volume is abruptly different almost as soon as you start it. The Tocqueville who wrote it was no longer the eager young man

pouring everything from full notebooks and memory into his manuscript, developing his main themes, laying bare the anatomy of American government and ideology, making daring prophecies, communi-
cating his zest for the travel experience he had just had. He was a
success now and cut a figure in both European and American circles.
He could afford to be more magisterial: his chapters are briefer, more
clipped, with a feeling of reserve intellectual richness held in check;
but while the sheer information on America, which had filled the first
volume and delighted its readers, is almost stripped away, the philosophical consequences are made explicit in a succession of sharp,
brilliant chapters, each devoted to a particular angle of implication.
What comes to the foreground is not the excitement of discovery and
the vision of possibility, as in the first volume, but the elaboration of
the basic idea of a leveled, uniform mass society as it is applied to
every phase and segment of manners, morals, customs, taste, and the
arts. The tone becomes more detached and distant, without the urgency of Volume I; but with an edge of irony. The mood is *triste* and
somewhat worldly, as of a man who has bitten too deeply into the fruit
of knowledge—both of America and Europe—to find much of it anything but bitter to the taste.

Yet the second volume is one of the great achievements in political
sociology, with ideas as glistening as the words they are clothed in.
Tocqueville had not spent ten years on the whole American project
without thinking all its implications through as far as he could carry
them. If the first volume presents a "new political science," the second
presents a new social theory of political man, with the emphasis on his
social relations and on the way his society is held together by some
principle of cohesion. The two volumes together made an enormous
impact on the European mind, distilling the best of the European tradition and yet going beyond it to place the struggle for Europe in the
perspective of the new world heralded by America. They spoke to the
European condition out of the American experience. If it had taken
America to create a new world and a new form of political man, it
took a European to explain it—even to Americans.

Not the least of the appeal of Tocqueville's book derived from his
style. His French style was far better than the translations in which he
has been read in England, America, and Germany. One has only to
read the exchange of letters between Tocqueville and Henry Reeve,
his English translator, to see in Reeve a quality of the mid-Victorian

Florid which Tocqueville—for all his courtliness of manner—did not possess. What Tocqueville had was grace, but not without economy. For him the word was the skin of the thought, and the thought in turn took the shape of the word. In sheer expository ability he ranks with the masters of exposition in the history of ideas. He never makes the mistake of pouring too many and too varied things into his vessel at once. He deals with a single phase of a single idea at a time, turning it around and around, going at it from every angle until his meaning is amply clear and has been given richness of expression. In fact, sometimes he goes on after the reader has caught the point, and is tempted to cry, "Hold! Enough!" Yet there is little of the inflated rhetorical quality in his style, in the sense of orotund rhythms and intoxicated-with-the-sound-of-his-own-words bombast. He didn't go in for flourish. The writer whose style he most admired was Voltaire: "Nothing [he wrote of Voltaire] can exceed the clarity, finesse, gaiety, and yet the simplicity of his style." And he goes on to tell of Voltaire's answer to a lady who admired his phrases: "Madame, je n'ai jamais fait une phrase de ma vie." This use of style to play down style was Tocqueville's aim, and largely he succeeded. Every sentence of the French version has spareness and elegance; the words are chosen for the exact nuance; the rhythms are contained, although each briefer rhythmic arc builds up and converges with the others into an overarching one. These are the qualities one finds also in *Souvenirs, Ancien Régime*, and most of all in the remarkable letters of Tocqueville to his friends.

5. The Polity: Power, Law, and the Elite

An American of the mid-1960's, reading *Democracy* today, has the uncanny feeling of reading not about Jackson's America but of his own, more than a century and a quarter later, a nation not of 13 million but of almost 200 million, a nation not on the margin of the European power centers but itself the greatest power center in the world. We may thus approach Tocqueville with a double critical vision of our own, asking at once how valid his analysis was for the America of Jackson's day, and how suggestive it is still in understanding the America of ours.

I start with the broadest possible division of a civilization into three clusters of concern. One is the *power system*—political, economic, military; and the questions we ask are whether it allows for governmental effectiveness and for individual freedom. The second is the *society,* in the sense of the stratifications of class and status, and the crucial institutions like the family, the church, the school, the codes, the media of communication; and the questions we ask are how much freedom and access it allows for the development of the personality and how much content it gives to the life of the people. The third we may call the *culture,* in its broadest humanistic sense, including the whole range of social expression, whether in work or leisure, the elite arts or the popular arts; and here the question is that of diversity and creativeness. Tocqueville used some of these terms and did not use others, but they may be helpful for an appraisal that commutes between his America and ours.

In his first volume he was absorbed with the American governmental system, as was natural for a young man who had moved in political and administrative circles at home and who was watching a new polity in operation. He had a great curiosity about how the American government worked, and transmitted his findings to a European audience which had been battered by books about Europe, but responded to the brilliance of this one. It would be a mistake to see his discussion of government in America as proceeding on the level only of political mechanics. Just as Montesquieu and Voltaire studied British political institutions, Tocqueville studied American institutions for insight into the proper relation of authority and freedom. We usually think of Tocqueville as a champion of freedom, but this should not obscure his concern with power and administration: the division and separation of powers, the tendency in a democracy to centralize power, the relation of central power to local administration, the power role of the parties and of the press, the power of the lawyers and the courts, the power of the army, the dangers of despotic power. As a humanist his concern with power is from a humanist angle. He was too close to the *Federalist Papers* to see in perspective the authentic quality of Madison and Hamilton as political theorists, although his own intellectual position on government was very much like that of Madison. He did not have the fixation on power and the ruling classes that the whole line of hard-bitten European political thinkers have had from Machiavelli to Pareto and Mosca. But he was too much a European to ignore it.

Unlike many liberals of his own day and ours Tocqueville understood that power in itself (despite Acton's later maxim) need not corrupt: only a corrupt exercise of it makes it corrupt. He spoke much of the democratic principle of the sovereignty of the people, but often such a concept of popular sovereignty can be hollow, as it has proved in authoritarian societies which display the banner of popular sovereignty with great fanfare as "people's democracies," but actually fear political competition for the suffrage of the people. What counts is power exercised and popular sovereignty *in action*, and for Tocqueville the heart of that was the constant participation of the people themselves in political activity, from the local town meeting and the selection of the local supervisors to the national elections and especially their action in voluntary associations.

Tocqueville was struck with the American separation of powers, struck also with the centralization of power and the decentralization of administration. Both seemed to him far superior to the European system where powers were fused rather than separated, where there were obstructive intermediary powers between the sovereign and the people, and where administration was centralized. But with his habit of creating ideal models, he may have distorted somewhat the actual power picture in Jacksonian America. He overestimated the scope and strength of the local governmental units in America, and underestimated what could happen in developing an effective national authority. Even in Jackson's day such an authority was far stronger than Tocqueville thought, since the men with whom he talked in the Eastern centers of economic power (including Story, Biddle, and Sparks) were unlikely to assay truly the long-range meaning of the efforts of the Jacksonians to contain corporate power.

As a European liberal of a new enlightened type in his time ("je suis un liberal d'une espèce nouvelle"), which meant mainly antimercantilist and free-trade views, Tocqueville inclined toward the middle-class stance of laissez faire in economic policy. This was advocated in the comfortably optimistic doctrines of J. B. Say, whose *Catechism of Political Economy* had become a standard text in American, as in French, learned circles. Tocqueville was no economist and was rather bored by economics. He was not rigid in his thinking about economic policy. He admitted some kind of intervention in the economy, and even advocated legislature protection for industrial workers. But he was tempted to see in America an Arcadian system where men were free to do what they pleased, and where the essence of government was to be in effect *not* a government. This in fact is one of the things that recommends him to many American conservatives today, who use him as a pleader for their brand of social statics, forgetting that Tocqueville asked the aristocrats of his own day to recognize the reality of the democratic revolution. Tocqueville's view of the weak state in America was a misreading of what was already happening in the 1830's and would increase in the 1840's: the state governments were engaged in a wide arc of regulatory functions, expressing the anxieties of a rising class of farmers and workers about the untrammeled operations of manufacture and finance. Tocqueville understood that democracy leads to centralized power; but curiously he did not apply it to the economic sphere in America, which he often exempted from his broader generalizations as an exceptional case. He applied it to the direction in which continental Europe seemed to be moving in his day—that of a swollen, overcentralized state which assumed all the powers of government and administration, leaving the people apathetic, with only the enervated sense of having everything decided and done for them. At times here Tocqueville seems to glimpse the outlines of the servile state in the form of the modern "people's democracies," and more often he glimpses the liberal welfare state in something like the British or Scandinavian form. But again and again, after one of his long discourses on future trends of "democracy," it turns out that he is talking of the European trend and not of American democracy.

When he does talk broadly of state power in America, it is in terms of the weak state, which need not function forcibly because the society has no need of the state to hold it together: it is held together by *l'interêt*. "That's the secret," Tocqueville wrote in his long letter to his friend Chabrol, his first general formulation of his ideas for his American book. "Individual *interêt* which sticks through at each instant, *interêt* which, moreover, comes out in the open and calls itself a social theory. . . . Here there is no public power and, to tell the truth, there is no need of it." And a later letter to Chabrol continues the point: "What strikes every traveler in this country . . . is the spectacle of a society proceeding all alone without guide or support by the single fact of the concourse of individual wills. It is useless to torment the spirit seeking for the government; it is nowhere to be perceived, and the truth is that it does not, so to speak, exist."

This was at any rate the conventional American theory. It was fondly held by Jeffersonian-Jacksonians, even when their own state governments did not practice it and even when the Jackson administration had a showdown with the banking system; they felt that the

Bank interfered with "natural" bullion and free banking. It was also fondly cherished by Federalist-Whigs even when they demanded a set of governmental subsidies and public works under the name of "internal improvements." Each group clung to a myth it found useful at the time, which was to re-emerge with renewed strength as the grand legal and social rhetoric of the post-Civil War period. Tocqueville took it over, and in the flush of his enthusiasm over the differences between America and Europe ("What, pray, do the 1200 employees of the French Ministry of the Interior do?" he asked Chabrol with ironic puzzlement in an urgent letter), he abstracted the American situation into an almost complete power vacuum and built a model of a society that ran without governmental power. The fact was, of course, that there *was* a power: a *business* power benevolently guided by the federal power (as Hamilton foresaw), and a *federal-state* power always there in reserve (as the Jacksonians proved) to act summarily in protecting the economically less powerful against the more powerful.

With considerable prescience Tocqueville did foresee the "manufacturing aristocracy which we see rising before our eyes," and he called it "one of the hardest that have appeared on earth." This thrust, coming from a French landed aristocrat, had a special meaning as an attack on the new feudalism by one who had turned his back on the old feudalism which had sustained his ancestors. It parallels the anticapitalist tradition of American political leaders from Jefferson and John Taylor through Jackson to Franklin Roosevelt, who were rooted in the land rather than the industrial city. Tocqueville's foreboding flash of insight is also well known: "If ever again permanent inequality of conditions and aristocracy make their way into the world, it will have been by that door that they entered." This was all the more remarkable a prediction because a considerable body of European thought held that trade and commerce would level inequalities, since they would create a middle class that would challenge the power of the aristocracy. While agreeing that Tocqueville foresaw the big concentrations of corporate industrial power, one may question strongly whether the "inequality of conditions" they brought with them will prove "permanent." Certainly they have not proved immune in America to government control.

A reader today, looking back at America since Tocqueville's time, can trace how the operation of centralized business power led to great governmental counteraction, and how big labor took its place alongside big business and big government. Tocqueville was aware of the "condition of labor" in industrial countries, as he showed in his moving description of the deadening effect of the division of labor upon the mentality of the workers. He saw in the American worker the expression of a new kind of serfdom in the new business feudalism ("in the midst of universal movement he is struck immobile"), with a deadly constriction of social vision (with the division of labor, "the workman becomes weakened, more limited and more dependent"), and with an inner dehumanization ("what is one to expect from a man who has spent twenty years of his life making heads for pins?").

Much of this came not so much from Tocqueville's observations in America as from his English experience, as is clear when we compare these comments with his discussion of Manchester and Birmingham in his English diaries. Much was accomplished even in Jackson's day by this "immobile" worker, militantly organized in pushing not only universal suffrage but universal education which would provide social mobility for his children. Much more was accomplished later, at the height of industrial capitalism, when the trade unions made the American working class as effective as any in the democratic world in achieving both collective bargaining and social legislation. Tocqueville agreed that the worker in a democratic society could advance by his own efforts, but he distinguished between the industrial society and the larger democratic one, and (as Jack Lively suggests) he seems to assume that industrial society would remain a small segment of democratic society. We are in Tocqueville's debt for his flashing insights into the sociology of industry, on the side of both business and labor. But the reader must set these insights within a new frame of collective bargaining, a new welfare corporation and trade union, and a new welfare state, all of them inside what is, in effect, a new functioning economic constitution and a changed over-all cultural ethos.

As the great analyst and prophet of the mass society, Tocqueville could not have failed to glimpse the Leviathan state that has accompanied it in every case. He saw it clearly when he thought of the paternalistic state that would come in Europe to govern an inert people. Did he see as clearly what has proved to be, in the American case, a Leviathan sprawling over a huge power network, subsidizing, protecting, controlling, coercing, cajoling, but always (as if in answer to Tocqueville's bemused "it does not, so to speak, exist") unmistakably *there*? I should say that he foresaw it—both the fact and pervasiveness of it—but he hoped that the spirit of American institutions, especially the American sense of law and passion for freedom, would keep the Leviathan from strangling the society.

As with all his thinking, he had an explanation at hand. In a discussion of county administration in New England, he speaks, in contrast to the European "disorderly passions," of the American "love of order and legality." "No one thought," he points out, "to attack the very basis of social power or to contest its right; the object was only to divide up the right to exercise it. By this means it was hoped that authority would be made great, but officials small, so that the state could still be well regulated and remain free." And he adds: "There is nothing centralized or hierarchic in the constitution of American administrative power; and that is the reason why one is not at all conscious of it." Here the striking fact about America for Tocqueville was that it did not have the European "mania for centralization." The same separation of powers that he saw in administration on the county level existed also on the state and national levels. Hence his conviction that America could "still be well regulated and remain free."

One may doubt how adequate Tocqueville's explanation is, even while recognizing his insight. A generation later Walter Bagehot used the American separation of powers to argue that the American system was too rigid for effective functioning. The development of a flexible Presidential power has made his argument archaic. There is still a formal separation of powers in America on the national level. But the modern student knows that there are today not separated powers but separated agencies of government, each tending to work with fused powers. He also knows that in the case of the President, or the Secretary of State or Defense, or the Attorney-General, or the Chairman of the Rules Committee, the officer as well as the office is powerful. If America is at once regulated and free today, as it still is despite the Leviathan state, it is not because of any one principle, whether the separation of powers, or the system of dual federalism, or the party system, or the judicial check, or any other single institutional mechanism. It is because of the functioning of all of them with a will to both flexibility and effectiveness that counts for more than mechanisms.

All through the book Tocqueville keeps coming back to the question of whether the American government is a success. Tocqueville had strong doubts about whether the American Union would last, but they had to do with the slavery issue, not with the essential strength of

the American scheme. He saw in the American power system something of a grand design, whose outlines were shaped by the state-
federal equilibrium, the separation of powers, the lack of a strong
executive power, the decentralized administrative system, the strong
judicial power. But above all the grand design was held together by
the American political psychology, which came from the individual's
active identification with the process of government, particularly
through the habits of dispatch of government business formed in local
government and the habits of judgment and decision formed in the
jury system. Tocqueville identified this political psychology with his
well-known insistence that the American system was not "revolutionary." He meant the term in the European sense, of violent changes
produced by resentments against feudal institutions and tyranny from
within, which were inflamed by the new doctrines of intellectuals, and
translated into action by rioters in city and village and by political and
military adventurers.

In assessing this doctrine of Tocqueville's, a good deal depends
upon how the concept of revolution is grasped. America had indeed
had a revolution, and a violent one, but it had not been the European
model: it had been its own kind, carried through by an elite of lawyers,
planters, merchants, writers, farmers. It was even in its own fashion a
social revolution—creating the "first new nation," as Lipset has put
it—but not in the European fashion. For it was an anticolonial revolution, using the symbol of British oppressive colonial power cohesively
to blunt the force of interstate and class frictions and achieve some
measure of unity, and affirming the possibility of a society on a new
base. After independence was won, America continued its revolution-
by-consent, which so bemused Tocqueville by its difference from those
he feared in Europe that he allowed himself at times to deny its revolutionary character. It was in a sense a built-in revolutionary process,
which was held in control by the political grand design and the psychological style I have noted. It was able to absorb changes in technology and industry, the surge of immigration, the crowding of the cities
with a polyglot population, successive wars, wild cyclical business
fluctuations—and survive.

The American political grand design was further strengthened, as
Tocqueville saw, by a mystique for which it is difficult to find a term.
It has acted as a principle of social cohesion without which any system
of government, however good in principle, could not work. It was a

kind of *civil religion*. Call it an attachment to institutions and a respect for them flowing out of self-respect and self-restraint. Call it an accepted disciplinary understanding between the people and their rulers, a habit of consensus which Americans developed and fortified, which they broke radically only in the Civil War, and which has had its ups and downs since but has not again been wholly broken.

Certainly it must be distinguished from the *political religions* of Europe which mark the difference between the European revolutionary spirit and the American. The political style of the European revolutions was to be found in the urban convulsions and the jacqueries which at once fascinated and repelled Tocqueville, and which have since led out of the French Revolution to the political religions of Lenin, Mussolini, and Hitler. It is true that the Civil War was a brutal fratricidal conflict, but while it generated hatreds it was not primarily ideological in origin or overtones. The political style of the American revolution was to be found in the civil religion which held in restraint a power-mass far greater than any in Europe, and which—while not escaping the interior tyrannies of a mass society and the crude wartime and postwar repressions of civil liberties—kept them within the bounds of a tolerably humanist democracy.

I turn to some of the specific political institutions on which Tocqueville had busily asked questions and taken notes. He saw the President's power as severely limited both by the federal system (he viewed the states as little other than a group of republics) and by the superior power of Congress, in which the President had no hand, and which could overrule his veto. Tocqueville thought "the weak and indirect influence" of the President "on the conduct of affairs" something of a blessing, since it reduced the "instability" which he regarded as "one of the principal defects of the elective system": the President could get rid of every "removable functionary employed in the Federal service" and could thus, Tocqueville felt, make a "national crisis" of every Presidential election. On Andrew Jackson himself Tocqueville was more grudging and condescending than the historians have been: he thought Jackson's conduct of his office "one risk now facing the federal authority."

One must take account of Tocqueville's bias arising out of the French situation: He may have seen Jackson as courting the people too much. He despised any trace of the demagogue, who fawns on the popular passions or uses them to ride to power. Later, in his *Souvenirs*, he drew an unflattering portrait of Napoleon III on this score. True, he saw that Jackson was no military adventurer but a Democrat committed by his party doctrine to a states'-rights view. But he thought that Jackson's power was personal and would enfeeble the office itself. More is involved here however than a faulty estimate of Jackson: Tocqueville cast what was at best a dim and flickering light on the Presidential office itself which has become in some ways the most powerful of any in nontotalitarian systems and has had a far-reaching influence on other constitutions. Because of his fear of the Presidential power Tocqueville failed to glimpse the mutual invigorating relationship that has proved possible in American history between the President and the demos—the political dialogue upon which leadership in the affirmative democratic state has been based. Tocqueville, who saw so much else, missed the true meaning of this dialogue and its bearing upon the possible strength and survival power of a democracy. He did point out that the powerless President and the weak state, along with the high degree of decentralization, were made possible by the happy accident that America had an ocean between itself and Europe, and no foreign enemies, and no fear of invasion. There was thus an escape-valve in Tocqueville's thinking which could allow for the later expanded Presidential power. In France itself, when a constitution came to be written for the Third Republic in 1875, it called for a weak president. This was not only because of the reaction against Napoleon III, but also because the conservative framers of the constitution included friends and admirers of Tocqueville.

For all his enthusiasm about the American social system as a whole, Tocqueville had something less than a high opinion about how a democracy operates its government. Just as he tolerated the Presidency on the theory that it doesn't have much power anyway, he thought that democracies conduct their foreign policies badly as compared with "aristocracies," since they cannot "persevere in a design"—that is to say, carry through some sustained strategy of foreign policy. He cited American behavior during the French Revolution, when the popular passion for the French revolutionaries almost involved America in the European "deluge of blood," and was prevented only by the "austere arguments" of George Washington. In principle Tocqueville was right about democracies and foreign policy, yet under strong presidential leadership in an era of global dangers this weakness has at least been recognized, if not wholly dealt with.

Nor did Tocqueville have much respect for lawmakers and lawmaking in a democracy. He considered aristocracies "infinitely more skillful in the science of legislation"; he considered democratic laws "defective or unseasonable" and the legislators themselves (along with other officeholders) as "often inept and sometimes contemptible." What made the difference was not the instruments but the ends—the fact that in America the lawmakers, however inexpert, identified themselves with the people, and their own interest coincided with the national interest. The people in their turn were drawn into the legislative process, especially by the town meetings, which Tocqueville saw as the "free schools" of the voluntary associations. The whole became a web of involvement whose absence formed the fatal weakness of aristocratic and dynastic systems. "Let it not be said," Tocqueville wrote in one of his noblest passages, looking ruefully from America (with all its legislative faults) to his own Europe, "that it is too late to attempt that experiment; nations do not grow old as men do. Each fresh generation is new material for the lawgiver to mould." And the nature of the experiment? It was to "make men care for the fate of their country through the laws," and so to frame the laws that they get "linked to the everyday passions and habits."

Has the quality of American legislators improved much since Tocqueville wrote? The answer is doubtful. Congress is still largely composed of rather ordinary men with a sprinkling of extraordinary ones, all of them under extraordinary pressures; the state legislatures rarely contain distinguished minds. There are still a number of great figures in both houses, as there were in the day of Calhoun, Clay, and John Quincy Adams. The bleak period of American legislative history, that of business domination between the end of the Civil War and the turn of the century, has largely been overcome and now energies are flowing into Congress. But what has chiefly happened is that the weight of the elites has shifted, and an expertise has developed outside Congress and outside the legal profession, from which Congress has traditionally been recruited. Much of the legislative burden has had to be shared by them.

Tocqueville was understandably impressed by the public finances of the American government of his day. But today the annual governmental budget of over a hundred billion dollars, and the defense budget of roughly half that sum, can be framed only by technicians; yet they must be understood by the legislators, and scrutinized and changed by them. While shaped outside Congress, they condition the entire legislative program. The direction and essence of the budget, like the changes in nuclear strategy, cannot be grasped by most of the voters. The legislators must increasingly be generalists, ready to make use of the expertise of their own committees and of technicians advising them, and capable of using their judgment on the basis of the material submitted to them by those highly trained in tax, weapons, social welfare, or foreign aid systems. If the laws that emerge from this process are to be "linked to everyday thoughts, passions, and habits," it is a task in the end for popular education and for the President as political educator, both in his role as party leader and as head of state. This educational function may in fact prove to be the President's most important one.

It is not surprising that Tocqueville missed something of the nature and point of the American party system. Even the authors of the *Federalist* had seen parties merely as "factions": Tocqueville a half century later saw them as a necessary evil, as vehicles of "agitation," and he groaned at the incessant elections—with their resulting changeovers and their spate of new laws—as the source of the "endless mutability" in American government. He generalized brilliantly on a typology of political parties, and suggested polar party types—Parliamentary and mass parties, ideological and personal parties, hierarchical and egalitarian parties—that have proved suggestive to recent students of the party system. He was especially good on the major division between parties in every political system: between the party that wishes to limit and the party that wishes to extend the sway of the people. He saw and resolved the paradox that the limiting party wanted to centralize governmental power and the extending party wanted to distribute (or federalize) it to the rim. It is striking that the paradox, in our day, has doubled back on itself and come all even again: that the people-limiting party (the Republicans today) seeks to limit governmental power, and the people-extending party (the Democrats) has swung around— except for sectional reasons in the South—to extending the governmental power as well as the popular.

As for his generalization that the "great" parties come first, in the crises and convulsions of forming the state, and are succeeded by "small" parties, he was perhaps betrayed into a Golden Age nostalgia which still persists among us. He saw the "great" parties at the dawn of the Republic, when Madison had seen only "factions"; he thought the parties of the America he had visited were mean and petty; yet they proved to be the seedbed of the modern party system, and we look back to the time of Clay, Webster, Calhoun, Jackson, and (immediately afterward) Van Buren as the time of the party giants and of the memorable party battles. In our own time the parties have become massive organizations, loosely held together for the power-and-policy stakes in the states and the nation, with the liberal-conservative wedge dividing each of the major parties internally, thus yielding four parties rather than two—at least between Presidential elections. Tocqueville saw the triumphant party as rushing a batch of new and unconsidered legislation through the Congress. This reads strangely after an era of what James M. Burns has called the "deadlock of democracy"—between "Presidential" and "Congressional" parties. Even the unparalleled hard-won legislative achievement of Lyndon Johnson's Administration is proof, by the very fact that it stands out from the rest, of the kind of leadership talents and the kind of party majorities that are necessary for a triumphant legislative record. Even in that instance, where so much was achieved in so brief a time, it would be hard to call it "unconsidered" legislation.

Nor was Tocqueville much happier about American office-holders than he was about the party-system. He noted sardonically that frequently "men only undertake to direct the fortunes of the state when they doubt their capacity to manage their private affairs." It was a shrewdly expressed half-truth—that in a democracy where the prestige lies with economic action, those who can, do, those who can't, govern. But it was only a half-truth. In a number of the big-fortune families the pursuit of money has yielded decreasing psychic satisfactions, and the sons of the rich—a Roosevelt, a Harriman, a Rockefeller, a Kennedy—have increasingly preferred public office to the further amassing of private wealth. To Tocqueville, an administrative insider who had followed his father from prefecture to prefecture and felt that an administrator must have training and knowledge, the American administrators seemed fly-by-night transients, in and out of office with every political wind, untrained to their jobs, committing little to writing, keeping few archival records, heedless about precedents, casual, atomistic, in a society that "seems to live from day to day like an army on active service." He concluded that a democracy could not make an art of administration—a curious conclusion in the case of a country which has carried the administrative arts as far as any country has, and has used the lessons carried over from the management of business units to the management of government. The archival and dossier societies do not necessarily produce the best administrators. When a society moves too fast for archives (as Tocqueville's America did, although perhaps not ours) it may jolt the administrators into innovating practices and principles.

It was when he came to study the American legal system that Tocqueville was most at home. He looked at American society, as he was to look at English society and later at French society under the *ancien régime*, as a historical analyst with legal training. He could read a legal text and ask: what is a society like which has produced a legal system of this sort? He could talk to the lawyers he constantly met in America and see how they and their work shed light on the essential character of American society. He could attend a trial, watch the judge and the jury, and draw far-reaching consequences from them about the American national character.

There were some things that he missed about American constitutional law. He did not grasp the full power and prestige of the U.S. Supreme Court, nor did he have much inkling of what class and party forces lay behind the struggle over the judicial power between Marshall and the Jeffersonian-Jacksonian group. He carried over from Justice Story a sense of the importance of cases involving the sanctity of contract, but he gave mainly the conservative view of men like Story and Webster, and he did not see the elements of personal enrichment and corporate power behind those cases. Except for a passing remark on the class nature of the bail system ("The surface of American society is covered with a layer of democratic paint, but from time to time one can see the old aristocratic colours breaking through"), which lights up the whole relation of law to the class structure, his interest in the economic impact of the law was mainly directed toward the system of land inheritance, where he went somewhat astray and at first misread the American practice.

Tocqueville somewhere got hold of the idea, doubtless from Kent's *Commentaries*, that the Americans had abolished primogeniture and entail as a result of their revolution, and that this had forced a division of the big landed estates by the great leveling force of democracy. Characteristically, he managed this idea until he was in danger of being swept away by it, making a good part of the American national character a kind of footnote to the changed law of inheritance. Tocqueville held a number of later conversations which put the law of inheritance back in perspective: great estates could be left intact or could be divided by a man's will; usually they were divided, and if a man died intestate they had to be. But there was another reason for the vanishing of the estates—the shortage of labor available for them, since so many had their own small farms or struck out west to make their fortune, in a society where land-hunger was linked with the hunger for quick speculative gains. Tocqueville wrote his analysis anyway, in brilliantly sweeping terms, on the social consequences of the "changes in the law of descent." Yet, even if he overplayed the particular point, he was profoundly right in seeing a deep relationship between the laws of land tenure and inheritance and the social structure (and therefore political character) of a civilization.

Another of his master ideas about American law was that of the psychological consequences of the jury system, which he considered on the same level of importance as universal suffrage. The fact that laymen sat not only on criminal but civil cases gave them self-reliance and a personal stake in the administration of justice; it also gave them (Tocqueville felt) a respect for the judge who guided them through the technicalities of the civil law, and therefore a sense of judgment and balance in the whole of public life. The fact that most Americans today flee jury duty, and also that the jury as an institution is under attack, does not demolish Tocqueville's line of reasoning but makes us ask what else has changed psychologically in a society where the jury no longer has the impact that Tocqueville noted.

As for the American common law itself, Tocqueville wrote exactly at the time when the triumph of the common law "reception" was assured. He made much of the case-mindedness and fact-mindedness of the common law, which were to interweave so happily with the pragmatic outlook of Americans, giving law a hard grounding in the empiricism of everyday life and giving that empiricism in turn the sanction of the law. He would have been delighted with Holmes's famous summary: "the life of the law has not been logic: it has been experience." Tocqueville was impressed by the role of the legal elite in American life, but he also feared that a common law governed by precedent would turn the whole society (as in England) too insistently toward the past. Yet the doctrine of *stare decisis* has proved to be a frame for continuing change as well as for conservatism, and the history of American constitutional law from *Marbury v. Madison* to *Brown v. Board of Education* is evidence of how precedent not only presents the courts with something to stick to but also—as social urgencies dictate—something to break away from.

There remains to speak of the pattern of the elites ("aristocracies") that Tocqueville noted surviving, or emerging, amidst the egalitarianism of American democracy. We have seen how much stress Tocqueville placed on the erosion of the landowning aristocracy: without the landed family traditions to which they might attach themselves, he felt that the great families, with their virtues as well as their vices, could not survive. As for an elite of office-holders, whether executives, legislators, or "magistrates," Tocqueville had little esteem for politics as a career in America. He foresaw that in a democracy—where statesmen "are poor with their fortunes to make"—there was the constant pressure of the money spirit upon public affairs. He noted ironically the industry of "place-hunting," and foresaw the local corruption which later so impressed James Bryce in the big American cities. In a remarkable passage he noted the envy of ordinary men toward other ordinary men who had risen to power and success, and he saw how it would lead to that belittling of politics which has until recently worked against the emergence of any commanding American political elite. He was equally shrewd about the clergy as an elite, noting that the successful separation of church and state kept them in their own domain, outside of the secular and political. Today the clergy of all faiths are involved, both as organized pressure groups and as citizens, in reform movements as well as on the side of established power; but Tocqueville was still justified in writing them off as an '"aristocracy."

The elites that Tocqueville took seriously were the lawyers, the businessmen, and the military officers. The important role of the American lawyers was a genuine discovery for him, and he dwelt on it in a classic chapter. He felt that they were bound to play a revolutionary role in the European democratic struggles ("lawyers will be very active agents of revolution"), yet in America he saw them as a powerful conservative bulwark against mass rule, both because their craft made them conservative and because it made them "secretly scorn the government of the people." There have been lawyers from Patrick Henry to Louis D. Brandeis who identified themselves with democratic egalitarian movements; more recently the younger lawyers have devoted their talent to the constitutional struggles for civil rights and voting reapportionment. Yet given the breed of corporate lawyers and their "law factories," Tocqueville was not far from right about the close links between the lawyers and the existing power structure.

His insights into the "industrial aristocracy" have also stood up pretty well. He understood the double beat of envy and attraction which the Americans of his day felt toward rich men. His picture of the rich American, who shows his wealth and taste only privately in his home, and who on the street becomes an egalitarian democrat, would not have jibed with the "conspicuous consumption" that Veblen noted and satirized in the garish decades at the turn of the century; but it jibes better with the more subdued behavior of the moneyed elite today. Similarly the free-wheeling, free-swinging militancy of the corporate barons in the half-century between the 1880's and the New Deal, when they fought welfare laws and collective bargaining with every weapon, when they built up their structures of monopoly power and had the courts largely on their side, contrasts with their present acceptance of the premises of a welfare state. It is worth noting that while the business and legal elites combined forces during that whole militant period, and had large segments of the political elite with them, they were unable to establish the kind of tyranny which Tocqueville feared in his discussion of the industrial aristocracy, and which has disfigured the recent history of Europe.

One reason America has been thus free may lie in the refusal of the military elite to lend its support to such movements. In a long discussion of the role of the military in a democracy, Tocqueville felt that a cabal of young officers in a democratic army will always restlessly seek war and revolution because a nation at peace consolidates the high officers in their seniority. These young men would be eager to advance in rank and eager to capture power in a society with which they have few psychological links. If Tocqueville was right about them, they might in time have found corporate adventurers with whom they could join forces and fortunes. Yet the striking fact about American military history is not that there have been many efforts at a military coup but that, despite some imaginative plots in recent fictional thrillers, there have been none. It has not been cabals among fire-eating young officers that have brought about America's wars, but instead land-hunger, sectional conflict, and economic and ideological interests.

This does not diminish the impact of the salvo of brilliant insights in Tocqueville's chapters on war and peace. He is profoundly right in saying that a democracy like the American is slow to get into a war, slow in gathering its energies at the start, but massive and resourceful when it does gather them, giving its people a fighting faith worth more than many divisions of soldiers. He saw also that a war is always a threat to internal freedom in a democracy, since it concentrates governmental powers and awakens extreme and intolerant military emotions. Viewed as a general essay, rather than as a specific commentary on American institutions, the five chapters on war and peace are among the most important in the book. Tocqueville knew the military case from the men he knew in his own circles of the nobility; he knew something of the attitudes of discipline and subordination required— and achieved—in European armies, and of how different these were from the discipline in the American armed forces. He knew something about the French Revolution, and knew the effect that the *levée* of a mass army—a nation-in-arms—had exercised upon modern warfare, making population and resources count rather than the old feudal military virtues, and bringing into the military a new mobility and restlessness. When he spoke of the lower rank of officers in a democracy he may have had in mind a young officer called Napoleon Bonaparte, with his smoldering careerist ambitions. He calls Napoleon *cet homme extraordinaire*, but notes that he derived his strategy, of aiming at a nation's heart by striking decisively at its capitol city, from the "state of society in his time." Throughout his discussion Tocqueville's strength lies in seeing the complex relation between the inner structure of a military establishment and the inner structure of the society. In a sense these chapters form a brief introduction to the sociology and social psychology of military power.

One of Tocqueville's striking paradoxes is that an aristocratic (caste) army expresses its society far better than the democratic army expresses its own: there is a harmony between the two former, a split between the two latter. At first view this seems right, and the military instability of post-revolutionary regimes in the emerging nations of today would seem to underscore it. Yet historically it has not applied either to America or Great Britain, and it seems far truer of developing than of developed democracies. The clue may lie in the extent to which the civilian tradition has authority and civilian life offers chances for power and career transcending those of the Army. In the American instance Tocqueville did not reckon enough with the capacity of the

larger democratic society to exert its contagion on the army, although
he does foresee the possibility that it might prove so, in a paragraph
starting, "It is in the nation, not in the army itself, that we must look
for the remedy for the Army's vices," where he warily hedges his
bolder original formulation.

Those who know the American armed forces today know that the
officers as well as the soldiers are civilians in uniform. One reason for
the military stability of American democracy is the tenacious hold that
the society and its civilian values have upon the junior officers as well
as the senior. In fact, the reason for conscription (as Tocqueville saw)
has been the difficulty of getting men to give up the high rewards and
careers of civilian life. The young officers in the Command schools,
where general officers are trained, find the military coups of the Latin-
American, Arab, and Asian countries alien to their thinking and experience. The precarious MacArthur-Truman incident showed that a democracy must still reckon with the political ambitions of charismatic
generals who are chagrined at seeing their grand strategy rejected. But
it also showed that the idea of civilian control of the military is a
master idea in the armed forces. The civilian control of defense decisions has never been put to a more sustained test than in the struggles
in the 1960's between the Secretary of Defense and the service units.
But thus far the control has held. General Eisenhower's farewell warning against a "military-industrial complex" which might threaten
American liberties is still worth heeding. The reasons for it have to do
with the new military technology and its relation to billion-dollar defense installations, and therefore to service status and power and the
profits of great corporations, rather than with the restless ambitions of
minor career officers. But there is another aspect to these links of the
military with giant technology. They have technicized the defense
services and brought their dominant leaders into positions of profiting
from consulting posts after their retirement, thus adding another element
of economic security to the security which their military careers have
given them. This ties more closely into the civil society a group of
men who might otherwise have remained outside it and played with
the notion of military dictatorship. Even the space-exploring heroes,
who have had terrestrial business and political offers showered upon
them, have been absorbed by the civilian society. What remains to be
seen is how the military-industrial elite complex reacts to the inevitable
cutbacks in the defense industries when the time comes for drastic

arms reduction, and how strongly it is backed by local groups, Congressmen, scientists, and trade-unions whose interests are interlocked against the cutbacks. That is when American freedom will be put to its most exacting test.

6. Freedom in a Mass Society

There is at once a spaciousness and subtlety in Tocqueville's view of freedom which ranks him with Milton, Mill, and Acton. As an inheritor of the French Revolution, but as a highly critical one, he took the first term of its trinitarian slogan with entire seriousness, where others were willing to see *Liberté* submerged by its sister terms *Egalité* and *Fraternité*. "I think that at all times I should have loved freedom," he writes in the second volume of his *Democracy*, "but, in the times in which we live, I am disposed to worship it." Perhaps the French were less concerned with freedom than with independence: the independence of the middle and lower classes from the power of the monarchy and aristocracy. But once independence and therefore a measure of equality were achieved in France, the scramble for power inside the new regime left little room for maintaining freedom. Tocqueville must have had this distinction in mind when he wrote that "the Revolution in the United States was caused by a mature and thoughtful taste for freedom, and not by some vague undefined instinct for independence." He was deeply impressed by the public spirit of the Americans, and their feeling for the authority of the law, which he did not find in Europe. American freedom, he pointed out, did not mean an absence of social obligation or an anarchic vacuum of social order, but a responsible assertion of individual autonomy within a social frame of equal rights and distributed powers.

This was not an easy concept for Tocqueville to hammer out in his day, any more than it is for us today. The path he had to traverse was difficult, sometimes even treacherous. He had some fixed conceptual points. I have noted his distinction between freedom and independence, and between anarchic and responsible freedom. He also had the problem of making these square with equality and individualism, both of which he saw as potential dangers to freedom, although historically, the pressure for all three of them had developed in recoil from a despotic order. Tocqueville sometimes used *equality* to mean only the abolition of hereditary class distinctions and privileges—not much more than an equality before the law. Sometimes he enlarged it to mean an equality of material conditions which enabled an individual to feel equal to others. But his characteristic use of the term was in the sense of the more extreme trend in democracy—the leveling and corrosive trend, which he feared, rather than the equal participation of all in a common concern, which was for him the healthy phase of a democracy. He used *l'individualisme* (see the succession of chapters on that concept in his second volume) in the French sense of his time rather than in the present American sense. He meant by it, more than anything else, the loneliness of the individual and the atomization of the society, while we use the term to stress the self-reliant assertion of individual differences in talent and character. Today we see individualism as opposed to the leveling emphasis of egalitarianism; Tocqueville saw it as one of the consequences of egalitarianism. "In ages of equality," he wrote, "every man finds his beliefs within himself, and . . . all his feelings are turned in on himself."

Writing as a Frenchman about an American society that had presumably made freedom into a passion, Tocqueville nevertheless developed a theory of freedom which no American thinker has surpassed. On the issue of freedom and the state, there have been American anarchist thinkers, including Thoreau; there have been radical egalitarians; there has been the liberal tradition of freedom, starting with the Founding Fathers and stretching to the diverse liberal views of Justices Holmes, Learned Hand, Frankfurter and Black. The American tendency has been to see a freedom system as the kind that succeeds best in achieving a competition of ideas. Tocqueville's memorable sentence on freedom—"he who seeks in liberty anything more than liberty itself is destined for servitude"—must stand as abiding witness to his refusal to see freedom instrumentally. He saw it, as it were, existentially: it was a thing in itself, a subject, not a means or object. It was the condition which fulfills a man by the very fact of being the essence of his existence as himself, and not a creature or puppet of others.

As an heir of the European revolutionary tradition, Tocqueville was committed against arbitrary government by any aristocracy; but he was equally committed against oppressions by the new revolutionary majorities. In the American experience he saw a free people in the flush of their freedom, but he was concerned also about the increasing oppression of the nonconformist creative spirit by an oversimplifying majority given to stereotyped thinking. This was not a contradiction in his thought nor a failure of commitment to freedom, but an effort to define the nature of that commitment. In fact, some critics have felt that his commitment to freedom was too absolute and "pure," and have scored him for his failure to recognize what the French Revolution was about: that coercion of some people is necessary to secure freedom for others, perhaps for the majority. Tocqueville very early saw that this could lead to a liberalism tainted by totalitarian passions. He sought to protect freedom not only from the aristocracy of birth and privilege, and from the new industrial and military aristocracies, but also from the coercions of the new mass society; he sought to protect it from tyranny in any form, whether from tyrannical minorities or tyrannical majorities.

His chapters "The Omnipotence of the Majority in the United States and Its Effects" and "What Tempers the Tyranny of the Majority in the United States" are the best known of the book. Tocqueville expected his American contemporaries to be angered by them, but they and the succeeding generations have embraced Tocqueville's thesis on majority tyranny—which should give us pause when he tells us how sensitive to praise and blame the Americans are as a nation. Both in wartime and in postwar periods Americans have known of the danger that national hysterias present to liberty of thought and expression. Periodically a great fear seems to sweep over America, not only during and after exhausting wars but in other crises of the national spirit. In this mood, sometimes of fear, sometimes of frustration, a wave of intolerance becomes impatient of minorities out of harmony with it and seeks to bring them into line. It is this pressure toward a general conformity of opinion which Tocqueville had in mind, and his prescience in foreseeing it has made him into something of a major prophet for American intellectuals, and has made even some of the Marxist-oriented among them forget the basic moderation of his thought, as they did for a time with Justice Holmes.

When he spoke of the tyranny of the majority, Tocqueville meant both an arrogance of power and a conformity of opinion. He was scornful of the idea that the people can do no wrong, and that the voice of the people is the voice of God. The notion that there is "no need to fear giving total power to the majority" is, he said, "the language of a slave." On this score, in good eighteenth-century natural-rights fashion, he appealed "from the sovereignty of the people to the sovereignty of the human race." But basically he was not talking of majority power as embodied in unjust laws, but of the even harsher majority power as embodied in mass opinion. What he feared in a democracy was the tyranny of narrow minds and mean spirits which would crush diversity and compel conformity. Even more than the external pressures on the minority he feared the internal censor operating in the mind of the majority which would inhibit individuality and stifle dissent from within. It was the first of these two strains in Tocqueville—that of majority pressures on the minority—which fascinated John Stuart Mill, evoking two remarkable essays on him. It influenced American liberals during the struggles of the McCarthy period in the early 1950's, giving a fillip to the study of political repression and to the political sociology of the "Radical Right." It gave the prevailing tone to the studies of American mass culture in the 1950's and 1960's. In a sense almost the whole of Tocqueville's second volume, written five years later, and stressing the mediocrity of opinion, belief, literature, the arts and the mores in a democracy, may be seen as an extended footnote to the seminal chapters in the first volume dealing with the moral tyranny of the majority and its constricted inner psychic universe.

Tocqueville's portrait of the role of the dissenter and intellectual in American life is a bleak one. He cites the "fury of the public" in Baltimore against a hapless fellow who dared oppose the War of 1812, the alienation (as we should now call it) of writers who oppose the prevailing opinion, the drastic punishment imposed on any who offend the sensibilities of the "power which dominates"—that is to say, the majority itself. In aristocracies, he points out, a writer may find shelter from the people with some patron or with the throne itself; he can find ways of eluding the censorship, and he can even slip antireligious books past an Inquisition. But America, which in theory allows him to write whatever he pleases, is in fact a naked society which holds no hiding place for him from the "irresistible power" of a people which, by ostracism and neglect, can impose a silence upon nonconformists more effective than any *auto-da-fé.*

It is a biting portrait of a mass society in action. Anyone who has studied the history of conformity in America will recognize its considerable measure of truth. Mill, in his second (1840) essay in the *Edinburgh Review*, noted that what Tocqueville ascribed to the despotism of the democratic principle was as true in England as in America, and that it was due less to the idea of majority rule than to the rise of industrial society and the triumph of the middle class. Tocqueville was not swayed from his analysis, although he did acknowledge that there were institutions which tempered the majority despotism: the absence of a strong central government, the jury trial (there would be many today who would wish he had been more critical of the jury system), the strength of the legal profession, the voluntary organizations that often joined in some reform cause or championed an unpopular one. But the important fact, as Tocqueville noted about the Americans, was that "freedom is not the chief and continued object of their desires; it is equality for which they feel an eternal love . . . . Nothing will satisfy them without equality, and they would rather die than lose it."

If one were to cite against him the long history of American reform movements and of the intellectual passion behind them, it would only play into his thesis: it is the movements embodying the passion for equality that succeed, and when they have succeeded they become themselves vested interests and vested ideas. More to the point would be the continual intervention of the American conscience, even at such low moments of the American story as the Mexican war, the slavery compromises, the imperialist adventures of the turn of the century, the "Red scares," and the McCarthy adventurism in the era of Communist espionage and spy trials. It is John P. Roche's contention that the deterioration story of American civil liberties has been overplayed, and that there is a more vigorous "quest for the dream" in American life today than ever, the "dream" being not only egalitarian but libertarian. But his is a minority viewpoint, although a close reading of history might bear him out. The drive among the American creative elite to be nonconformist, by underscoring the conformity of the American mass society, has itself threatened to become a new kind of intellectual group conformity. Perhaps this new trend bears out the Tocqueville thesis as strikingly as any in the past. Tocqueville was talking of "some mighty pressure of the mind of all upon the intelligence of each," and his insight could apply not only to American society as a whole but also to the particular groups within it. This gives point to Henry S. Commager's remark, that in our absorption with the tyranny of the majority we tend to forget about the tyranny of minorities. The pressure toward conformity within the "Radical Right," which itself laments the intolerance of the "conspiracy" of academic liberals, is so great that a moderate conservative is hard put to resist the urgencies of the extremists. The same may be said of the pressures within the militant Negro civil rights movement, or of the liberal and Leftist intellectuals who would lose their in-group status if they cut against the grain of their fellows.

The disease that Tocqueville saw in America was the disease of a mass culture and the mediocrity it demands. But the conformity he saw applies not only to the pressures from the mass but to the pressures from the elites as well. James Fenimore Cooper, himself a Jacksonian, also uttered a cry of desolation in his novels at the falling-away of savor and distinction in the America that Tocqueville studied. It was not only a "tyranny" or "despotism" that both men—and many since them—have feared, but a deterioration of life style and a vacuum of values. Nor did religion help much, because the rigidity of its codes was calculated to "check the passion of innovation." For Tocqueville these pressures made for a certain flatness in the American national character. There is a tendency among the American social theorists today to attribute much of this flatness to recent changes in the society, whether toward the suburban housewife or toward her organization husband or their other-directed children. Tocqueville's book suggests that long before the suburbs, bureaucracies, automation, and status anxieties of today, what he called the "courtier spirit" of the American had already become a burden upon the culture. He faced the possibilities of this future with some nostalgia for the past: "The sight of such universal uniformity saddens and chills me," he wrote in the powerful concluding chapter of his second volume, "and I am tempted to regret that state of society which has ceased to be." It was less the tyranny than the bleakness of a mass culture that Tocqueville carried in his fears like a smoldering city. Yet when the reader goes on to finish the whole passage he finds that Tocqueville saw compensating qualities in a society of egalitarianism: "not the particular prosperity of the few, but the greater well-being of all. . . . Equality may be less elevated, but it is more just, and in its justice lies its greatness and beauty."

Such a portrait of unrelieved bleakness left little room for depicting the pluralism of American life. Tocqueville devoted a chapter to the "three races," but the ethnic pluralism of America developed much more rapidly after the great migrations of the turn of the century. While he gives us a magnificent descriptive overview of the face of America, in his early chapter on its "exterior form," there is little suggestion of the regional pluralism which was to form part of the diversity of the American character. Nor, despite his stress on religion in America, is there a vivid sense of the religious pluralism, nor of that fusion of religion, ethnic origin, region, speech, and even occupational diversity that were to form so many pockets to relieve the standardized flatness of the larger society. Curiously Tocqueville, who himself noted that democratic peoples have a way of personalizing the formless movements of mankind, did exactly that with the movements of opinion in American democracy. The American "majority" is usually a cluster of minorities whose diverse motivations happen to result in a similar stance. In his use of the term "the tyranny of the majority" Tocqueville turned what is pluralistic into something monolithic. True, the impact on the dissenting minority is the same, however diverse the groups are that compose the "majority," and Tocqueville was perceptive in seizing upon this impact. But as a political sociologist he overdid the simplicity of his "model" of American society, making it less complex in order to make it more compassable. Except for the "associations," he seemed to see little that could mediate between the monotony of the sprawling inorganic society and the loneliness of the atomized families and individuals.

He did not have a "class" approach to politics and society, as Madison tended to have. When he had to use a class division (as in his discussion of taxes and public finance) he used the three-class system of the wealthy, middle, and working classes. In his later writings, on the French Revolution, he dealt with the rhythm of the classes in a historical era, each coming up with a sense of its identity and power, and thrusting the others down. He wrote a sketch along these lines, on the state of French society before 1789, for Mill's *Westminster Review*. But in his book on America his attention was not on the division but on the tendency toward the abolition of the classes. He was impressed, as I have noted, with the way in which the laws of inheritance had largely done away with the old landed class, and he felt that the new businessmen—while they might someday form a dangerous aristocracy—were not yet a class in the accepted sense: their mobility was too great, men came into their ranks and left them too swiftly, and the pursuit of profit was rampant throughout the society instead of being restricted to them. There was moreover no proletariat in the European sense, no deep *ressentiment* (as Nietzsche was to call it) of the underlying population against the wealth and privileges of the upper orders: "Everyone having some possession to defend, recognizes the right to property in principle." Thus Tocqueville was perhaps the first great theorist of the modern era to recognize the classless society built into the American principle of equality—not a "permanent equality of property," for which "no other country" had a "stronger scorn," but the principle of an equal chance at life chances.

This principle of the abolition of classes cropped up later, as we know, in the Marxist canon, although in a different context. Marx said: the rich will get richer, the poor poorer, until the poor will overthrow the rich. Tocqueville said: the rich will get richer, but the poor will also get richer, until the divisions between them lose their old meaning. Marx said: the dialectic of history will abolish classes, and then man will at last be free. Tocqueville said: the logic of a democratic society is a classless logic, and its history moves toward the abolition of classes, but it will not bring freedom automatically; men will be free or unfree, depending upon what they do collectively in preventing either a despotism of laws or a despotism of opinion. Of the two, it was Tocqueville who was the realist, and it was Marx who—for all his talk about "scientific" socialism—was following an abstraction.

Marx and Tocqueville never met; in the early 1840's, however, Marx and Proudhon met frequently, and Proudhon knew the Tocqueville volumes and may have told Marx about Tocqueville's idea of a classless society. Tocqueville was no revolutionary and did not mingle with the new group of Anarchists and Socialists on the fringes of French political-intellectual life. Along with a reference to Proudhon there is only one other reference to them in his *Souvenirs,* when he recounts meeting George Sand, who told the liberal aristocrats in Tocqueville's group of the ferment of the new radical energies under the crust of the old society, and warned them, "If it comes to a fight, believe me, you will all perish."

Whatever might happen to the democratic revolution in Europe, Tocqueville saw its American future more confidently. He had hopes about the future erosion of the white-Negro caste system, and saw some sort of impending showdown over slavery. In his mind it took the form of an internal conflict "between the Blacks and the Whites of the South of the Union," a danger "more or less distant, but inevitable," and "a nightmare constantly haunting American imagination." Thus while Tocqueville did not foresee the sectional form that the Civil War took, he had a foreboding of the nightmare years of the

Reconstruction period afterward in the South. Nor did he have many illusions about what would follow abolition. "The Negroes might remain slaves for a long time without complaining; but as soon as they join the ranks of free men, they will be indignant at being deprived of almost all the rights of citizens; and being unable to become the equals of the Whites, they will not be slow to show themselves their enemies."

The apocalyptic vision of Tocqueville—"the most horrible of civil wars [Tocqueville meant inside the South] and perhaps the extermination of one or the other of the two races"—has happily not taken place. But America is caught in a protracted civil rights struggle in South and North alike, which Tocqueville foresaw, missing only its timing. The difference between the current civil rights revolution and the struggles of the past lies at least partly in the crisis of conscience which the whites have undergone, and which challenges the implied assumption in Tocqueville that the whites could not accept the Negroes as equals. But it lies even more in the new willingness of the Negroes to "show themselves their enemies" if they are not accepted as their equals. The reason why Tocqueville could uncannily call the turn on the current civil rights revolution lies in his insight into the dynamics of all passionate movements. It is the principle that every such movement "grows by what it gains" or (as Tocqueville sometimes put it) "grows by what it feeds on." This insight is so basic to Tocqueville's thinking, and so repeatedly applicable in every era, that one may think of it as the "Tocqueville effect."

What it amounts to, as Tocqueville notes in the *Ancien Régime,* is that once the passion of revolutionary claims and demands has seized hold of a movement, concessions and reforms must be seen not as ways of stopping or even of moderating it, but as steps toward its final fulfillment. This was true of the American Revolution, from the time when the intellectuals took up the cause of the people, and the King and nobles made the first concession to them. It was true of the French Revolution. Tocqueville noted in the *Ancien Régime* that the movement to sweep away the aristocracy "which started as a political revolution proceeded as a religious revolution." This tendency of intense social movements to become political religions gives them at once their effectiveness and their potential destructiveness, unless their own leaders can learn to channel and discipline them. Tocqueville is not necessarily happy with the operation of this "Tocqueville effect," for with all his passion he was not a revolutionary. But he faced unflinchingly the nature of social reality and the character of social movements as he saw them. One suspects that Tocqueville today would have little doubt about the ultimate and irresistible success of the movement for equal Negro civil rights, not only in law but in social actuality, in South and North alike. It has engaged the energies and imagination of men, and has developed a mystique against which it would be hard to find a counter-mystique. But one must also suspect that Tocqueville would make the same agonized appeal to its leaders that he makes to Americans and Europeans alike about the democratic revolution as a whole: an appeal to ride the whirlwind, to command the storm, and to tame the egalitarian energies of both to the purposes of humanist values.

7. Culture, Personality, and the Good Life

We have thus far been concerned with Tocqueville's thinking on revolution and history, on democracy, on power and freedom. In a broad sense these deal with political man on the American continent. But his book also goes beyond the political to the American cultural style. Here he is concerned mainly with the egalitarian principle and how it has worked itself out in America in the industrial society, in the philosophy, history, and literature of the new civilization, in its work and leisure, its family relations, its public image and its sense of privacy, its moral codes and religion, its life purposes, its personal alienation and social cohesion. There are few aspects of the current studies of the American civilization pattern that he did not touch upon, directly or glancingly.

In this phase of his work Tocqueville is absorbed not so much with the "spirit of the laws," in Montesquieu's sense, as with the spirit of the mores. We sometimes forget that Tocqueville was not only a political and social theorist and a historian, but (in the French sense) a *moraliste*—that is to say, a writer who focuses on values, *moeurs,* psychological and spiritual factors in a society. Tocqueville in this volume was interested in the relation between the life of the mind, the impulses of the heart, the drives of the personality, the everyday quality of living, and the style of the culture. If there is one theme which pervades the whole it is that the egalitarian principle takes a heavy toll from the human personality, sacrificing depth to busyness, and courtesy to vulgarity, putting easy social relations ahead of meaningful human

ones, restlessness ahead of rootedness, independence ahead of authority, private decision ahead of public taste, materialist well-being ahead
of the intangibles of the mind, the belief in progress ahead of a sense
of complexity in society and history, and the "indefinite perfectibility
of man" ahead of the mystery of the supernatural.

One of the crucial questions Tocqueville asked about any society
was: where is the seat of authority over opinions and *moeurs?* Unlike the
aristocracies of Europe, where such authority rested with the nobility
and the intellectual elite, it rested with the American democracy in the
people themselves. In politics, in morality, in literature and the arts, to
some extent in religion, the authority principle had to be fashioned as
the nation and people grew. Tocqueville didn't like it: he preferred a
social system in which there was a clearer definition of the locus of
authority, and where the mores (*moeurs*) of the culture could be more
clearly shaped by men of taste, if not always by intellectuals. But this
was how it was in a democracy, and he accepted it as such. This, he
said in effect, is what happens to the culture and the personality under
the pervasive impact of egalitarianism. Every man becomes his own
center of intellectual and moral authority. He is constantly in motion,
so that there is no chance for him to come under the sway of traditions. The revolutions that shake his time reduce the accepted opinions
to "a sort of mental dust." He is no more content to have a traditional
class shape the ideas he must accept than he is to have them shape the
rulers or taxes or vocation he must accept, without his consent. And so
he becomes a unit of autonomous judgment, sufficient unto himself.

But is he in fact sufficient unto himself? Tocqueville was shrewd
enough to see that this vaunted intellectual and moral autonomy of the
individual in a mass democracy might be self-defeating because it
could not be sustained. In one of his sharpest insights he saw both the
pride and the pathos of the individual autonomy: "The citizen of a
democracy comparing himself with the others feels proud of his equality with each. But when he compares himself with all his fellows, and
measures himself against this vast entity, he is overwhelmed by the
sense of his insignificance and weakness." Hence his helplessness
before the "intellectual dominion of the greatest number," hence the
majoritarian flatness (as Tocqueville saw it) of a democratic culture.
"In times of equality . . . no matter what political laws men devise for
themselves," Tocqueville wrote, "it is safe to foresee that trust in
common opinion will become a sort of religion, with the majority as
its prophet."

Thus Tocqueville saw the American as a deeply split personality: "feeling the need for guidance and longing to stay free"; "finding life at once agitated and monotonous"; feeling pride in his nation and in his own equality with others, yet ravaged by a sense of his own loneliness and insignificance—and, out of that sense, seeking to assuage his loneliness by huddling with others and to cure his insignificance by joining the majority composed of other men who in turn wished to join the majority which included him. Tocqueville saw through a good deal of the surface bluster and optimism of American life. He saw that the mania for gregariousness was a less striking fact than the driving privatism that led each man—after the hurry and worry of the day—back to his home and family circle, atomizing American life into "a multitude of little societies." In today's jargon we call the American "alienated," "isolated," "atomized." Tocqueville was content to note that American egalitarianism made "men forget their own ancestors," that while "aristocracy links everybody, from peasant to king, in one long chain, democracy breaks the chain and frees each link." Tocqueville even saw that a good deal of the single-minded money chasing of the American-on-the-make was one way of breaking through the facelessness of American society and of leaving a personal mark on life. Thus long before the psychoanalysts came to set up camp in the American mind, Tocqueville knew that Americans were not pursuing money and power in themselves but only as a way by which a man could achieve identity.

Who can fail to note how contemporary this is for us? There is not much in the latest dissection of the insecurity, anxiety, and loss of identity of the American of today that will not be found in the portrait of the estranged American in Tocqueville's second volume. Lord Acton was wrong in saying that the "despondency" which many have found in Tocqueville came from his doubts about the future of freedom in America: they came rather from his despair about the future of the American personality as it surrendered itself, in its fear of isolation, to the mass; and from his doubts about the quality of American culture which would arise from this surrender.

No democratic society can survive, Tocqueville was convinced, without a philosophy and a religion. The American philosophy derives from the "equality of conditions": it is the method of self-decision—every man thinking and deciding for himself, with a kind of amateur skepticism that leads him to get most of his notions "from the very

nature of man" and thus to build a stock of "general ideas about
political affairs." If Tocqueville meant that Americans have few inhi-
bitions about becoming amateur economists or scientists or political
and constitutional thinkers, he was right. If he meant that the American philosophic method is inherently one of "general ideas" as abstractions he has not been borne out by history: the New England
reformers and Transcendentalists of his day were later followed by a
pragmatic school which expressed much better the underlying premises
of a working American democracy than did the neo-Platonists of Boston
and Concord. In this sense he attributed too much influence on American philosophy to the equality of conditions, and too little to the march
of the machine, which had already produced an empirical tradition in
England and was to do so in America. More likely he had in mind the
tendency to think in corrosive "natural rights" terms, which gave a
revolutionary thrust to political thought. But he was shrewd in seeing
that the dissolving influence of "general ideas" in France, from the
philosophes onward, was checked in America by the deeper hold of
religious belief in a religion-founded and religion-saturated society.

There may seem to be today a strangely traditional note in
Tocqueville's many chapters on religion. But it would be rash to judge
this out of perspective, especially in the present era when the corro-
sion of religious faith has not been replaced by other strains of belief
and commitment. Believing in the role of religion in maintaining social
order and continuity, Tocqueville was more willing to accept dogma
in this area than in any other. In almost every passage where he discusses the difference in political fiber between the anarchic democratic trends in Europe and the orderly democracy of America he
attributes a major share of the difference to the religious quality of
American institutions. He called religion "the first of American political
institutions." He saw that the Puritans who settled New England had
brought with them not only a religious doctrine but one with radical
democratic implications, and that the same innovating spirit which
made them carve out their own religious beliefs had made them carve
out also their own political practices. He even saw what Max Weber
and R. H. Tawney were to see later: that there was an inner relation
between the religious spirit and the strength of the capitalist impulse in
America, and that the single-minded pursuit of wealth and personal
property was linked with the single-minded quest of God. Despite
Tocqueville's own reservations about American Protestantism, which

may be found in the sharp references in his letters, he saw how religion organized much of American life.

He was convinced not only that it played a strong role in America, but also that it was necessary for the functioning of any democracy. As a post-Enlightenment man, with the sophistication of one who has had his doubts and come through them, he argues not so much for the theological validity of religion (although that too crops up in a number of moving passages) as for its secular existential utility. "Despotism may be able to do without faith, but freedom cannot. . . . How could society escape destruction if when political ties are relaxed, moral ties are not tightened?" Thus Tocqueville saw the role of religion as the cohesive stuff of a democratic society which has lost the old cement of authority and must find a new cement of some sort if it is not to dissolve into atomistic dust.

For Tocqueville was well aware, as he shows in his chapters on individualism, how socially disintegrating the passion for individual autonomy can be. Time after time he confronts the paradox of a society which is fragmentized by self-interest and self-seeking but which seems nevertheless to have found a principle of inner order: his answer to the paradox is the binding force of the religious principle. Speaking of absolute governments he says that it is religion, not fear or authority, that has given them their hold on people: "Patriotism and religion are the only things in the world which will make the whole body of citizens go persistently forward toward the same goal." In the American democracy, as I have suggested, he found the fusion of these two—of religion and politics—in a kind of civil religion.

One may guess that what Tocqueville missed most in the Europe of his own day was the *corpus mysticum* of the Age of Faith, preceding the great economic and political revolutions, when Europe was an organic whole with a mystique holding it together whose image was taken from Christian doctrine. He was too much the child of his time to ask for a return to the universalism of the Middle Ages, or to expect his contemporaries to rediscover a divine sanction for the civil society. But he did find in the American democracy the mixture of political and religious sanction which he considered the minimum for holding a society together: the "civic spirit" which the Americans showed in their participation in politics, the enthusiasm which sometimes became an "irritable patriotism" but was far better than apathy, the strong fiber of the laws (the more readily accepted because the people had a hand in making them) the sanctity of the marriage tie, the "severity of *mores,*" the fixity of moral principles because "the sway of religion extends not only over the *mores* but even over the reason of the people," the "perfect picture of order and peace which the American finds in the bosom of the family" and which exercises a restraining force upon even the turmoil of political debate and experiment.

It is an idyllic picture, contrasting strongly with the America of today and—to the extent that it was faithful to Jacksonian America—giving ammunition to those who feel that American moral standards have degenerated. Tocqueville found in America that sense of a fixed point of reference which Walter Lippmann has pleaded for in his *Public Philosophy,* which Lippmann calls a "mandate of Heaven" built into the habitual thinking and the political institutions of the society. More than anything else the civil-religious cement, holding the political society together, might account for the failure in American history (except for the Civil War) of those waves of political fanaticism which ravaged Europe and brought a number of its nations under an evil spell.

On the role of religion in America, Tocqueville stressed the element of hope in it—a religion of hope and of awe, not of political power or of worldliness. Exactly because material well-being was so important to Americans, he felt they needed to balance it by an other-worldly sense. When materialism went too far it evoked, as a counterforce, the camp-meeting religion of the frontier, "filled with an enthusiastic, almost fierce, spirituality such as cannot be found in Europe." He notes dryly that "forms of religious madness are very common" in America, and we who have witnessed the continuance of Fundamentalist passions in our own time find ourselves at home in his description. As for the politics of religion, he applauded the separation of church and state as preventing the corruption of each. He noted the exemplary behavior of the Catholic clergy in America, saw the strong proselytizing pull of Catholicism as "single and uniform," and predicted (at a time when there were scarcely more than a million Catholics in America) a steeply growing strength for it.

He wrote before the widespread decay of faith, not only in America but in the Western world. This has given way in turn to a renascence in church membership and activity which may mark less an authentic rebirth of religion than a desire for a more secure standing in the community. But even the latter would confirm Tocqueville's insight into religion as an institution in America. While he could not have foreseen the proliferation of dissenting sects, the growth of a religious pluralism, the renewal of the religious impulse among the scorned and rejected in the Negro churches, he did see that religion in America was a matter of code making and moral role playing, less a way of believing than of belonging, a bridge between God and an orderly community. He understood that, whatever the frictions between the confessions (it is interesting that he said nothing about the Jews or anti-Semitism), there would be no religious wars in America as there were in Europe. What has happened since his time—the ordered parceling out of roles to the Protestant, Catholic, and Jewish communities, and the drawing together of all three faiths into three branches of an enveloping official American faith—is wholly in line with the picture he drew of religion in America. Less so is the newest trend of a secularist liberalism which is still restricted to a minority but has received the support of recent constitutional decisions.

As with religion, so with American education: its function was a public one; its chief aim was the making of citizens, not the fitting of men for private life. Tocqueville made his discussion of the "instructed" Americans, although brief, part of his chapter on "the main causes tending to maintain a democratic republic in the United States": he saw education, as he saw religion, as a form of social cohesion. What Tocqueville called *les lumières*—the enlightenment or instruction of Americans—was never as elegant as in Europe nor yet as squalid. Americans were neither as erudite nor as illiterate: they struck an impressive mean. Comparing them with the learning and the libraries of antiquity, said Tocqueville in a stirring passage, "I am tempted to burn my books, in order to apply none but new ideas to such a new social state." He was especially taken with the pioneer "plunging into the wildernesses of the New World with his Bible, axe, and newspapers."

This is at least a glimpse of what was to become the American cult of education, counted upon to solve every public and private problem. Far more even than in Tocqueville's day education has become part of the social reality and the social myths which serve as a cement of American society. The American ideal has moved beyond civic or political education, exactly into the realm of private life where Tocqueville did not find it in his day. It is a way of bettering yourself, of rising in the economic and social hierarchy, and a way also by which your children find a better means of living and way of life than yours. It is now becoming also a way of resolving the new "problem" of giving content to the leisure created by automation—a problem that would have seemed strange at a time when work was part of the prevailing ethos.

One of the most searching sections of his book is Tocqueville's analysis of the impact of the democratic principle on the American family pattern. He saw that, while the formal authority of the father had been weakened in America by the principle of equality, and the sons quickly grew away from him and asserted their independence, the family had closer natural ties of affection and respect than in the "aristocratic societies" of Europe. It is in the chapters on the American woman that he grows almost lyrical about the consequences of the climate of freedom. The portrait of a lady, Tocqueville style, depicts her in sharp contrast to the European woman: she is educated and prepared for her life in an informal society; she is scarcely an innocent, she is knowledgeable on many matters kept from a French *jeune fille;* "her morals are pure rather than her mind chaste"; yet she is also self-reliant and self-controlled. Tocqueville has some doubts about this kind of training, lest it "make women cold and chaste rather than tender and loving companions of men." Yet he feels that the American matron after marriage, formidable as she may seem, and sometimes (especially on the frontier) sad and resigned as well as strong, is a force for stability in the society.

"Now that I come near the end of this book . . . if any one asks me," he writes, "what I think the chief cause of the extraordinary prosperity and growing power of this nation, I should answer that it is due to the superiority of their women." This was more than gallantry; it was a tribute to the workings of the principle of freedom of marriage choice, as expressing the larger principle of freedom in the society. It gave to women for the first time in Western history the chance to develop a self-reliant grace without losing their femininity, and without becoming those George Sands and Madame de Staëls of whom Tocqueville had something of a dread.

It is curious to note how uninterested Tocqueville was in childhood and the growing-up years: in fact, he even believed that "in America there is in truth no adolescence." He thought that their commercial civilization would leave Americans too busy to value love: "One hardly finds any Americans," he wrote, "who care to let themselves indulge in such leisurely and solitary moods of contemplation as generally precede and produce the great agitations of the heart." Thus there is no warning in Tocqueville of the reign of the romantic ideal of love in America today, nor the place it has occupied in American fiction and the American imagination. He overstressed the built-in strictness of the American moral standards, attributing to the inherent nature of a democratic society what was due mainly to the overlay of Puritanism. His picture of American morality was taken mainly from the after-dinner conversations with his Boston friends, rather than from the sort of view of American sexual behavior that one gets in reading the radical sexual reformers of Jacksonian America. Thus there is little in Tocqueville to suggest either the breakdown or patterned evasion of the moral codes, or the heavy toll of mental conflict and anguish in the American personality as we know it.

But what is striking, is not that he failed to foresee some things but again that he saw so much. He saw that the father-son relation must be different in a new democracy, on a continent to be opened up, from what it is in a tradition-soaked society, and that relations between brothers are also easier ("democracy loosens social ties, but it tightens natural ones"). He saw that free marriage choice puts the burden of working out marriage differences upon the two freely choosing partners. He saw the inner emotional structure of the family which parallels the political structure of the society. Above all, he understood the nature of the American woman, and saw that a rivalry with the American male (such as took place in the feminist revolutions which had started in his day) would not resolve the problem of her identity as a woman: it could be resolved only by balancing her intellectual vigor and independence with a basic femininity. "As a result American women, who are often manly in their intelligence and in their energy, usually preserve great delicacy of appearance, and always have the manners of women, though they sometimes show the minds and hearts of men." This description of the American woman of the 1830's has, after all the movements for liberation, become more applicable today than ever in the intervening time.

On other aspects of the American personality Tocqueville was more somber than on the family. He saw American life as restless, lonely, fragmented into "small private circles." He recoiled from the constant furor of activity. While he defended American manners against the British travelers who had mocked them (he noted that the travelers had rather absurd middle-class manners of their own), he found "little dignity of manner in America" when compared with the aristocratic refinements for which he still had a lingering nostalgic sadness. He found Americans as incapable of genuine recreation and play as they were of sustained attention to ideas: "this astonishing American gravity," even greater than that of the English, made them insensitive to either. He saw deeply into the role of work in the Protestant economic ethos, and found men so committed to work that it continued long after they had become rich, which suggests Veblen's later observation, in his *Theory of the Leisure Class,* that conspicuous leisure had to be vicarious.

The flatness of the landscape of American values left Tocqueville depressed: "I confess that I believe democratic society to have much less to fear," he wrote, "from boldness than from paltriness of aim." He found a people so permeated by a widespread middling ambition that there was no room left for the lofty ambitions; he found a sense of the career open to all, and therefore no notable instances of the vaulting careers that overleap the succession of obstacles in the usual obstacle race. He noted that the sense of honor, while it has a role in democratic as in aristocratic societies, is very different in the former because of the dead level of the economic virtues. The ethos he saw in America was an economic ethos. Even courage was prized differently—not a martial valor, but "the courage which . . . makes a man almost insensible to the loss of a fortune laboriously acquired, and prompts him instantly to fresh exertions to gain another." Because Americans all aim at the same prizes, the diversities of personality are leveled out. What is left as the object of desire is "not any particular man, but man in himself"—a generalized, impersonal, standardized and therefore dehumanized ideal.

Were Tocqueville alive to study the history of the eager reception of his book in America, despite the unflattering picture it gives, he might explain it by saying that every American reader shifts the burden of criticism from his own shoulders to the rest of the nation. But by following the logic of his analysis, which reduced everything in American life to a dead level, Tocqueville somewhere left out a quality of generous openness to the world of experience and ideas, including the harshest ideas. This has proved especially true of the intellectual elites. Tocqueville saw shrewdly enough that the Americans of his day had done little in theoretical science and much in technology; what happened in the succeeding century bore him out. But its slowness may not have been due wholly to the lack of a contemplative climate or the inherent character of a democracy. The fact was, as Tocqueville himself noted, that Europe had been carrying the burden of theoretical science for centuries; it would take time for American university so- phistication to take over that burden, and for Americans to be prodded beyond their exclusively pragmatic concerns. In the last twenty-five years, when the refugees from Nazism fused the European tradition with the American, the United States took the lead in scientific theory as well.

While he noted the colonialism of American literature up to his time, Tocqueville was confident that it would assert its independent spirit and "have a character peculiarly its own." This prescience of a nativist American literature and intellectual life was confirmed when, only a year after Tocqueville went back to France, Emerson made his first visit to Europe to come to terms with it, and came home to meditate on the need for an "American scholar"; while Whitman's *Leaves of Grass* appeared fifteen years after the publication of Tocqueville's second volume. Tocqueville guessed that the drama, which he saw as the democratic art *par excellence,* would develop in America despite the overlay of Puritanism in the American mind. But he might have added that the same attraction which the stage offers to a middle-class society—not "pleasures of the mind" but "lively emo- tions of the heart"—would make the novel and short story a more central genre for Americans; he could have taken the hint from the emergence of the novel in the middle-class society of eighteenth-cen- tury England. As for poetry, he felt that Americans were impatient of the legends and old traditions which spurred the poetic imagination in Europe: "all these resources fail him; but man remains, and the poet needs no more"; he moves in a democracy from the gods and Nature to "certain dark corners of the human heart." The life of the individual American might be "petty, insipid, crowded with paltry interests . . . anti-poetic." But Tocqueville saw an *élan,* in America's conscious- ness of itself, which is vastly poetic—and thus foresaw Whitman.

Even more striking was his insight into the richness of American speech and the American language, as Mencken was to celebrate it, stemming from the lack of those sharp divisions between a literary and a popular language which plagued aristocratic Europe. And there are more than hints of the core problem of a democratic aesthetic—the cheapening of the product with the enlargement of the market, the passing off of the fake for the genuine, the easy harping on realism, and above all else the intrusion of the spirit of the marketplace into the studio and workroom. The rise of the mass-opinion industries and of the big media—the movies, radio, TV, and the slick magazines—came long after Tocqueville's day. But he foresaw the concern of their being when he spoke of the "ever-growing crowd of readers always wanting something new," the flattery of the mass, the "idea-mongers," the introduction of "an industrial spirit into literature": "democratic literature is always crawling with writers who look upon letters simply as a trade." As for the audience in a mass society: it "often treats its author much as kings usually behave toward their courtiers: it enriches and despises them." All of this is overstated, but exactly because Tocqueville is so savage about a democratic aesthetic he has left his imprint on American intellectuals who look down at their own popular culture. No one has ever put more sharply and succinctly than Tocqueville the reach of the commercial spirit into the world of the arts, with the big prizes it brings, the gawking admiration for the successful, and the underlying contempt and self-contempt.

The weakness of the historian in a democracy was, for Tocqueville, of a different kind—not the trading spirit but determinism. He saw democracies as playing down the role of great men in history, as assigning large causes to small effects, and as linking these causes in a chain of determinism. "If this doctrine of fatality," he wrote with a tinge of despair, ". . . passes from (historians) to readers . . . and gets possession of the public mind, it will soon paralyze the activity of modern society, and bring Christians down to the level of Turks." There was an element of truth in Tocqueville's indictment: in Tocqueville's own era George Bancroft wrote with a simplistic determinism about the role of Providence in American history; it was in a later generation that the determinism of Henry Adams, Frederick J. Turner, J. Allen Smith, Charles Beard, and Vernon Parrington gave substance to Tocqueville's prophecy. Yet the interesting fact is that determinism in history proved to be European far more than American, and that the historians and other social scientists in America, after serving their apprenticeship to a single-key determinism in the early part of the twentieth century, have moved beyond it sooner and more radically than the Europeans. What is even more damning about Tocqueville's judgment is that while the French and the Germans, despite their aristocratic traditions, developed a great school of social history, the Americans have excelled in history as dramatic narrative, as witness Parkman, Prescott, and Motley, and have also created a great school of biographers. Instead of playing down the role of great men, American writers have focused on the individual career and the individual will in the face of obstacles, and have played up the personal as against the impersonal.

Tocqueville had, of course, some elements of determinism in his own historical approach: the "predestined circle" was there, beyond which man could not pass; but within the "vast limits" of that circle Tocqueville insisted on seeing him as a free man. He accepted from European progressive thought the idea of an irresistible stream of tendency in history, but he rejected the idea of a "general will," whether placid or malignant, and counted on the creative individual will for effectiveness. The greatest enemy of the human spirit he found in what he called "individualism," by which he meant the separation and loneliness of men in a mass society, without a principle of social authority to serve as a cement between them. He was not certain, he said in the last of his Appendices, whether anarchy or despotism offered the greater danger, but he was certain that both came from *"the general apathy,* the fruit of individualism." His descriptions of a not impossible future society, in which the few will govern with a paternalistic efficiency, sustained by the "general apathy," have an Orwellian nightmare quality of the placid society of sheep and the Big Brother shepherd. Where Tocqueville missed out was (despite some insight in his second volume on the French Revolution) in failing to see the coming of a dictatorship elite, like the Communist or Nazi, armed with the gospel of dynamism. He was, however, profound in depicting the passive underlying population which embraces its masters because it has lost its will to freedom and seeks to escape from the burdens of decision. It is a kind of "post-historic man," vegetating in material comforts but no longer able to act upon history.

The reverberations of this theme in our minds today are bound to be disquieting. The hedonic society that Tocqueville professed to praise, but did not really like, has grown in its cult of material well-being and atomized fulfillment. The ethos which, born out of religion and the civil consensus and out of the "double movement of emigration," helped hold America together has begun to disintegrate. The dynamism of the industrial drive may slacken as the advance of automation makes post-industrial men the carriers of leisure rather than of industry. What is it that will save the American from the society of "general apathy" about which Tocqueville had such forebodings?

Perhaps the answer is mythic: perhaps it lies not in any institution but in the buoyancy and *élan* of the total American experience, in the slowly increasing historical consciousness of Americans, in the faith that the experience has meaning for generations to come, and that each generation of sons will have greater hopes and successes than the fathers. Tocqueville speaks once or twice of the self-corrective faculty that Americans have shown: "The great privilege enjoyed by the Americans is not only to be more enlightened than other nations, but to have the chance to make mistakes that can be retrieved." But this capacity for recovery and for continuous experimenting, with social as well as technological forms, goes beyond the particular tinkering. It is, says Tocqueville, the sense of identity of the American nation "marching through wildernesses, drying up marshes, diverting rivers, peopling the wilds and subduing nature." And he adds, "That is like a hidden sinew giving strength to the whole frame." We have called it recently by various names—"*élan*," "national purpose," the "American style." But Tocqueville's "hidden sinew" is still as good as any.

8. Last Years: Politics, History, and Belief

After the second volume of *Democracy,* with its indifferent success, Tocqueville was in his early thirties, in the prime of his life, with a political career still ahead, and with another great book to write in rounding out his view of history and social theory. He had followed up his travels in America by a journey to England in 1833, and his study of English institutions helped put in perspective what he had seen in America and what he thought about Europe and hoped for it. In his political career he was intent on applying in practice the theoretical guidelines he had developed for the healthy functioning of a democracy—in France, and through France in Europe.

Following an initial failure due to his refusal to accept government support and his insistence on his political independence, he was elected in 1839 to the Chamber of Deputies from the constituency of Valognes, in the department of La Manche. He represented this constituency until the end of the Second Republic. Coming in as an independent, he tried to steer a course between the government and the opposition, but had a hard time of it. He also played a role in the provincial *Conseil* in La Manche, looking into railroads and harbors, into poor relief and the problem of foundling children. But in the main he put his energies into the various phases of his parliamentary career. He worked hard on prison reform, on French colonial problems (from which come his remarkable writings on Algeria), on foreign policy. But he was not a party leader, being unwilling to run with any Parliamentary gang or pay the price of party maneuvers and corruptions for wielding power; and he was on the whole a poor speaker. Thus he remained almost isolated between the two great parties, with only his intellectual power and his moral earnestness. "You drive me to despair when you speak of a great part for me," he wrote to Beaumont in 1842. "The great parts in politics need great passions to fill them. No man can battle with éclat against apathy, indifference, and an entire nation's discouragement. In vain I pile up a great fire in my imagination; I feel all about me a chill that penetrates every part of me; do what I will it extinguishes the word in me." While he gave formal and unenthusiastic support to the first two governments under which he sat, he quickly shifted to the opposition with the Guizot Ministry. An admirer of England, he persisted in criticizing the politics of the English alliance with Guizot. Yet while he could not work with a Guizot government under Louis Philippe, neither could he give his wholehearted support to Thiers and the opposition. He felt condescending about Thiers, with whom he usually voted. He had some sense of identification with Guizot, whom he usually opposed. He was a man of ambivalences, torn between ideas that attracted him and measures that he opposed. He felt, moreover, the hollowness of the whole Parliamentary system, in which 200,000 had the vote out of a population of close to 35 million.

While he had expected the February Revolution of 1848 and even predicted it in his speech of January, 1848, Tocqueville was none the less dismayed when it came. But he was re-elected to the Assembly, and was chosen as one of the members of the Constitutional Committee. In the tug of war between a constitutional and a Jacobin revolution, Tocqueville supported the former. He opposed the unsuccessful June uprising of the workers, who sought to use the Revolution to extend their power. His aim, he wrote later, was "to make the evident will of the French people triumph over the passions and desires of the workers of Paris; by so doing, to conquer demagogy by democracy." The principles he had evolved in the quiet of his study, writing on America, were being put to the test in the fires of French revolutionary action. When Louis Napoleon was elected President in December, Tocqueville had forebodings. But in June 1849 he agreed to serve as Foreign Minister under him, in the second cabinet of Odilon Barrot. He remained Minister until the end of October, a period of just under five months.

These were easily the most memorable months of Tocqueville's life, more so even than the American months, yet he noted that with all the excitement came a deep serenity. "The sense of the importance of the things I was then doing lifted me at once to their level, and kept me there." His troubled role in political action was yielding at last some rewards. Yet clearly the Cabinet was doomed. "We wanted to call the republic to life; [the President] wanted to bury it. We were only his ministers, and he wanted accomplices." A little more than two years later, in December 1851, came the *coup détat* which turned Louis Napoleon's regime into a dictatorship. Tocqueville, in an uncompromising letter to the London *Times,* spelled out the meaning of the epochal event which ushered in modern plebiscitary rule, and with it a varied succession of Right-wing dictatorships and Left-wing "people's democracies."

For several years after his dismissal as Foreign Minister, including a winter at Sorrento to repair his health, Tocqueville wrote his *Souvenirs,* which may be seen as a reflective literary corollary of his political career. It was an unsparing account of his political role during the 1848 Revolution and a penetrating analysis of its social dynamics— certainly one of the classics in the history of political memoirs. But Tocqueville had another quarry in view. It was more than a decade since he had published the second volume of *Democracy.* He had been caught up now in the political fortunes of his own, had failed, and wanted now to trace back some of the main themes of his experience to their roots in the French Revolution. "I must find somewhere," he wrote his friend Kergolay, "a solid lasting basis of fact for my ideas. I can find this only as I write history." He had written an article on the French Revolution for Mill in 1836. Now he returned to the grand theme, one worthy to stand alongside his American one in scope and daring. He worked for eight years on it, quarrying in archives in Paris and the provinces, teaching himself German so that he could study Germanic medieval social forms which shed light on the Revolution.

The result was *L'Ancien Régime et La Révolution*, one of the great historical works of the modern age and at the same time (like *Democracy*) a masterpiece of political sociology. For Tocqueville history was not narrative but an analytical sequence, not a storyline but an idea-line. Its impact was great, and along with the notes for another volume, which Tocqueville did not live to complete or publish, it rounds out Tocqueville's work and his life.

He died in the midst of his labors. Always sickly, his last years were plagued by a developing tuberculosis. They were also lonely years. Tocqueville had a haunting sense of political failure which even his resounding European and world reputation as a thinker could not assuage. He turned increasingly to religion, and became more absorbed with Catholicism: in these matters he found a friend and confidante in a remarkable lady, Madame Swetchine. His letters to her and other friends reflect an agonized inner debate in which he sought the sources of his own malaise and sought also the answers to the deepest of life's riddles. He died April 16, 1859, not quite fifty-four, still a young man by the standards of today. He never relented his intellectual honesty, to the very end. "The problem of human existence," he wrote Madame Swetchine, "preoccupies me ceaselessly, and ceaselessly appalls me." The man who, next to Karl Marx, must be seen as the greatest historian and political sociologist of the last century had to confess that he could "neither plumb this mystery nor cease to peer into it." [3]

Notes

1. Throughout this essay I am heavily indebted to my friend and coeditor, J. P. Mayer. Everyone who works on Tocqueville starts from his pioneer book, *Alexis de Tocqueville: A Biographical Study in Political Science* (1939; Harper Torchbook, 1960) and from his monumental definitive edition of Tocqueville's writings (Gallimard, 1950–   ), of which twelve volumes have already appeared in French and perhaps another twelve are to come. He has been a generous but also exacting critic of my ideas on Tocqueville for fifteen years; I have found his scholarship scrupulous and his over-all view of Tocqueville admirably balanced. Without burdening him with the faults of this essay, I am grateful for the discussions of it we have had at every phase.
2. This and other excerpts from Tocqueville's book are quoted from the new George Lawrence translation of the *Democracy in America,* edited by J. P. Mayer and Max Lerner (Harper & Row, 1966).

3. For their helpful and vigorous criticism of this introductory essay I am deeply indebted to Raymond Aron, Daniel Bell, James MacGregor Burns, Henry Steele Commager, Seymour Drescher, Gertrude Himmelfarb, Jack Lively, John Lukacs, R. R. Palmer, George W. Pierson, David Riesman, and J. S. Schapiro. I want to express my indebtedness to my assistants, Roslyn Mass and Alice Delvecchio Cowan, for the invaluable help they gave me in preparing this essay.

4

John Stuart Mill

There are two kinds of successes in intellectual history—that of the thinker whose originality revives each time we read him, and that of the thinker whose influence spreads imperceptibly over the generations, so that his originality has become part of the intellectual air we breathe. John Stuart Mill belongs with the second kind of thinker. No figure in the history of Western liberal thought can match his impact and achievement, yet none has been more taken-for-granted as a good grey liberal, a slightly stuffy eminent Victorian, a man who had the right sentiments on the right occasions, a writer who seems to have written in classical quotations because we have warmed ourselves for generations on his glowing sentences and their luminousness has made them cosily familiar.

The fact is that Mill is a towering intellectual who is as fresh as tomorrow morning's newspaper and as relevant as the latest publicized crisis of our time. But it will take an effort of the imagination to think ourselves back into the issues and conditions of his time, out of which his thought grew. More than most great political and social theorists he was in the center of every melee of his age, as reformer and social radical, as anti-colonial fighter, as libertarian, as shaper and critic of democratic institutions, as a working social theorist. His was a many-faceted mind, any one of whose facets would have made the reputation of a lesser man.

Originally published as the introduction to *Essential Works of John Stuart Mill,* edited by Max Lerner (New York: Bantam Books, 1961), vii–xxx. Lerner also contributed individual prefaces to the five works he selected.

Not the least interesting of his facets is the story of Mill's education—
one of the strangest, most dramatic stories in the history of educational
literature, at once exhilarating and tragic. The best source for it is in
Mill's own *Autobiography*.

John Sterling, who had the rare distinction of being a friend both to
Mill and to his bitter opponent, Thomas Carlyle, said of Mill that he
was a "made or manufactured man." This expressed the consensus of
the intellectual group in England which watched with fascination the
experiment that James Mill carried on in the laboratory of his own
home—the experiment of turning his son, John Mill, into a trained and
disciplined genius. James Mill had aspired for the ministry, but he
failed to get a post, and turned to the blandishments of philosophy and
the rigors of radical social reform. Perhaps he carried into these pursuits something of the unsparing commitment which he might have
invested in a religious vocation. As a tutor to a young Scottish noble-
woman, and later as a divinity student, he had extended his reading
and become a most learned young man. He became a magazine writer
and newspaper editor in London, married a pretty girl whose mother
(the proprietor of a house for lunatics) was able to give her a not
negligible dowry, and settled down to raise a family and make a name
for himself. His growing family had to be supported by the rather
irregular income of a free-lance writer. But London was the center of
an imperial cluster and—next to Paris—the focus of a bourgeoning
intellectual life. James Mill placed himself deliberately at the center of
it. He could discourse on psychology, philosophy, or politics, on the
classical and modern authors, on revolution and reaction, on God and
man, and he was able to transmit the flame of his intellectual excitement
to others. He was a writer who didn't quite make the first-grade, but
he had an almost matchless magnetic talent to attract young intellectuals from every rank and party, and to shed an incandescent glow in
whatever areas his mind touched. The fact that he was utterly bored
with his wife meant an increasing withdrawal into the life of the mind
and the give and take of intellectual discussion. His *History of British
India* made something of a reputation for him and got him a post with
a regular income in the East India Company. He could devote the rest
of his life to the not ignoble goal of absorbing all relevant knowledge,
building it into a rational body of thought, and using that body of
thought as an engine for reforming society and bringing "the greatest
happiness to the greatest number." This phrase was used by his friend,

Jeremy Bentham, whose chaotic flow of thought James Mill system-
atized.

His first-born child, John Stuart Mill, was scheduled both as test
and instrument of the doctrine of the James Mill-Jeremy Bentham
group. At the age of three, he had started his reading of the Greek
classics; his father, sitting across the narrow table and working on his
own writing, would stop occasionally to explain a Greek word or
phrase, since no Greek-English dictionary was yet available. At eight,
after having read a list of Greek works that would make the reputation
of a classics instructor today, he started Latin. At the same time, he
became the teacher of his younger sister, transmitting to her his father's
instructions, hearing her recite the reading, and correcting and com-
mending her as his father had corrected and commended him. It was a
heavy burden to place on a child's shoulders, but Mill carried it—
although I suspect this was one of the things for which he never for-
gave his father.

Beyond Greek and Latin lay mathematics, on which James Mill had
started his son, but which John had to carry on for himself when he
moved into its higher reaches, beyond his father's memory and competence. Along with the art of studying under his father, and that of
acting as a teacher to his sister, John had to learn the art of teaching
himself—charting out an unfamiliar subject, getting at its rudiments,
exploring its nuances. As he had gone beyond his father in mathematics, so he went beyond him in logic as well. But his great delight lay in
history. He picked up with ease most of the great classics of historical
writing—Greek, Roman, and European. He even ventured into poetry
and a bit of fiction, but these were trimmings, and their marginality
came back to plague both pupil and teacher later.

Francis Place, one of the great leaders of the working class of his
day, a self-educated master tailor who was involved in every reform
movement of his time, visited the Mill family during one of the summers which they spent with Jeremy Bentham at Ford Abbey. John
Mill was eleven, and the impression this half little-prodigy and half
little-monster made on Place was startling. "John is truly a prodigy, a
most wonderful fellow," Place wrote his wife, "and when his Logic,
his Languages, his Mathematics, his Philosophy shall be combined
with a general knowledge of mankind and the affairs of the world, he
will be a truly astonishing man; but he will probably be morose and
selfish." It is clear from Place's reports to his wife that the young boy

irritated the older man by challenging and contradicting him and by always having the right question, the right answer, and—what was worst of all—the right logic and reasoning. It was at this period that James Mill, the father, was working hardest, getting up at four in the morning, capturing only a few hours sleep, and working away at a series of articles for an English encyclopedia. The eleven year old helped his father with the galleys of the *History of British India,* adding to his regular chores this rather delightful apprenticeship to a working writer.

Young Mill may have been something of a monster at the time, and something of a prig, but when he came to write his *Autobiography* he looked back at himself and gave the sober verdict that he had been neither—only a boy whose natural gifts had responded so well to his father's educational methods that "I started, I may fairly say, with an advantage of a quarter-century over my contemporaries." He was probably accurate about the head start he was given, but over-modest about what he started with. The boy clearly had the stuff of genius in him. Yet while the potential was there as seed, the soil and nourishment which it needed for flourishing were furnished by that relation of tension between student and teacher which we call an "education."

In our own day, when we are straining to rethink and rebuild our educational system, and recanvass the ingredients of a viable educational theory for the so-called "gifted children," the carriers of promise in America, John Stuart Mill's education has a special relevance. One can draw from it several clues to an educational theory for an intellectual elite. One is to start the child young, while his learning impulses are still utterly spontaneous, while he is open to every influence and can absorb languages and literatures. Secondly, demand the utmost. John Mill said that his father "demanded of me not only the utmost that I could do, but much that I could by no possibility have done." Francis Place's comment on James Mill as teacher was that "his method is by far the best I have ever witnessed, and is infinitely precise; but he is excessively severe. No fault, however trivial, escapes his notice; none goes without any reprehension or punishment of some sort." There were times when the younger children were denied their dinner because they had not said their lessons well, and John suffered the same penalty because he had allowed their mistakes to pass. His later judgment in his *Autobiography,* as he looked back at these chastisements, was that "a pupil from whom nothing is ever demanded which he cannot do, never does all he can."

A more important principle is that of the milieu in which the teaching and learning are carried on. James Mill's household was indeed, to borrow Barzun's phrase, a "house of intellect." Ideas and events were constantly being discussed in it, theories analyzed, logic scrutinized, fallacies pointed out. There was a constant stream of writers, journalists, politicians, working-class leaders, reformers, both in James Mill's house and in Jeremy Bentham's, where the family spent a number of summers. When the life of the mind is taken for granted, when it is given part of the natural universe, there can be no need to cozen or seduce the child into commitment to it. The commitment comes as part of the growing up.

There are few, if any, families in American mass society which are like Mill's and Bentham's in this respect. But the school or college has the chance to create an intellectual community which can provide this sort of atmosphere—although unfortunately at a much later period, when other influences and images may already have become established. The experience of John Mill may suggest that the first duty of a college is the creation of an authentic intellectual community, within each classroom and on each campus, in which the things that are taken for granted are the things that count.

Then there is the question of the dialogue of the generations. American educational theory has been saddled, since John Dewey's day, with the notion that children learn best from their "peer groups," since the experience of one's peers is most easily transmitted. The fact about Mill was that he had no real peer group. He was from the start, except for his chores as a teacher of the younger children, in converse with older people. Aside from his father, he learned most from John Austin, a brilliant if somewhat neurotic legal theorist who founded the Analytical School of jurisprudence, and who seemed drawn to young Mill and taught him much of his own sharpness of analysis and discipline of mind. Charles Austin, his younger brother, was also an influence on Mill—a half-generation removed, and for that reason perhaps the more attractive as a kind of older brother. And Thomas Carlyle was for a time a shaping and disturbing force in Mill's development; but that came later when the young man had already astonished the intellectual world of England with his accomplishments. There has been considerable research recently to indicate that in a high percentage of the known historical instances of genius, the child in his mental growth responded far more to an older generation than to his own.

With this history of education, John Mill's success in the intellectual circles of his day was almost inevitable. He wrote letters to the editor which blossomed into regular newspaper contributions. He formed a fighting nucleus of young writers and thinkers, and the name he picked for their doctrine—"utilitarianism"—has been accepted as the designation of a whole era of English thought, starting with Jeremy Bentham. He formed a debating society and did brilliantly in it. He started a literary magazine for the new philosophical radicals, with the high hopes that it would serve as a counter-force to the organs of the Establishment. And all of this before he was twenty-one.

But he had to pay a heavy price for it, a price in anguish of mind and barrenness of spirit. The dialogue of the generations had evoked young Mill's intellectual promise, but had left him emotionally immature, with his aesthetic side almost wholly undeveloped, and without having developed the capacity of feeling for which secretly his spirit longed. The result was the breakdown that Mill describes in his *Autobiography*—probably the most important part of it, and certainly the most poignant and human. It was not a "nervous breakdown," in the sense in which that term is now used. Mill went on functioning in all his intellectual activities, and his friends scarcely noted the crisis through which he was passing—which is probably the final commentary on the sources of the crisis and the lack of intimacy in his friendships. As Mill expressed it, "If I had loved anyone sufficiently to make confiding my griefs a necessity, I should not have been in the condition I was."

But the sickness was none the less real, even if it was an ambulatory one. Mill diagnosed it well as an incapacity for feeling, and indeed for love itself. His "habit of analysis" had worn away his feeling, with a dissolving force that threatened to dissolve his whole being. He played with thoughts of suicide. What dismayed him was the knowledge that even if his dream of a perfected and rebuilt social system were to be achieved on the next day, it would be of no account to him. He was suffering from over-rationalism, a disease which his father had as surely communicated to him as the disease of tuberculosis, during those early days when they had sat across the narrow board table while the father wrote away at the *History of British India* and the son wrestled with Greek syntax. This was, Mill wrote later, "a perpetual worm at the root both of the passions and of the virtues." As for his father, Mill never gave him an inkling of what he was going through: "I saw no use in giving him the pain of thinking that his plans had failed, when the failure was probably irremediable."

Mill's crisis had its first resolution when he read a passage in Marmontel's *Memoirs,* where the author's father dies, and the boy has a rush of feeling and pictures himself as being everything to his family that his father had been. "A vivid conception of the scene and his feelings came over me, and I was moved to tears." A. W. Levi, writing in the *Psychoanalytic Review,* surmises that Mill's crisis was the result of a repressed death-wish toward his father, that he had harbored a hostility against him during the course of his training, that the unwillingness to recognize the death-wish led to an attrition of his whole feeling-capacity, and that the passage in Marmontel, by resolving his conflict, released his capacity for feeling as well as his fears. This is as good a clue as any. Mill was unable to love because his father had never loved him but had used him as a test of his educational ideas and an engine of his reformist zeal. In his search for the sources of feeling, Mill was characteristically methodical and turned to the reading of the English romantic poets. Byron proved unrewarding, but Wordsworth suited Mill's mood and his love for the natural scene, and in the reading of Wordsworth he found a second resolution of his mental crisis.

But I suspect that the real resolution came several years later, when at twenty-three, with a fluttering readiness for emotional experience, Mill was introduced to Mrs. Harriet Taylor, and thereby met his life's destiny and the greatest shaping force of his mind. Mill fails to connect his mental crisis with the completeness of his response to Mrs. Taylor, but the connection seems clear enough. She was young, married to a worthy man who had few intellectual interests, felt arid and starved for an outlet to her restless talent and some meaning to her life. Mill helped her to find new interests, and saw in her the fusion of beauty and grace, intellect and character, the answer to his longings. She in turn saw his greatness, and the possibility of developing a body of thought and writing unparalleled in intellectual history. She was a bluestocking, but more; more also than an Aspasia to his Pericles. There is little doubt now, after the publication of the letters that passed between them until her death, that she was a woman of commanding intellect who furnished exactly the motive force and the critical sense that Mill needed for his books. For the next twenty years they were constantly together, in her husband's household, and on trips through France and Italy. When, for any reason they were away from each other, they kept up a constant exchange of letters. Mill was married to her in all but name and fact. Spiritually and intellectually they were husband and wife, although Harriet felt bound to her own legal marriage, perhaps unwilling to hurt John Taylor too much, perhaps welcoming the frame he gave her for her real life with Mill. Those who have studied the letters and diaries most closely have concluded that Mill did not have any sexual intimacy with Mrs. Taylor during those twenty years. They both felt that there were "lower" and "higher" feelings and experiences, that sex definitely belonged with the lower, and that a creative relationship between a man and woman transmuted the baser impulses into something loftier. In short, Mill was a proper Victorian in his attitudes toward sex, and Harriet Taylor was in all probability a frigid woman. One might add, as Crane Brinton adds about her, that her frigidity was a matter of principle rather than of neurosis.

When Taylor died, the two platonic lovers who had defied public sentiment in order to be together while the husband was alive, now found themselves with freedom to marry but without much will to do so. They waited for several years, wore out each other's nerves and became thoroughly entangled in family feuds, and finally married. Mill testifies that their life during the seven years of marriage was Paradise. It was not Paradise for his mother or sisters or brother, with all of whom Mill broke relations because of fancied slights toward Mrs. Taylor. There is a ruthless quality in the way he treated his family—a ruthless quality not wholly unrelated to the strength he had shown in maintaining his unconventional relationship with Mrs. Taylor for twenty years.

His public testimony to her greatness is well known. The reader will find it in the pages of his *Autobiography* and in the dedication page to the essay *On Liberty,* Mill's greatest book, on which there is pretty good evidence that it was a joint product. It will also be found on the tombstone that Mill set up for his wife when she died, of tuberculosis which she had probably caught from him. "Were there but a few hearts and intellects like hers," Mill said on the tombstone, "this earth would already become the hope for heaven." And in the dedication of *On Liberty* he wrote, "were I but capable of interpreting to the world one half of the great thoughts and noble feelings which are buried in her grave, I should be the medium of a greater benefit to it than is ever likely to arise from anything that I can write, unprompted and unassisted by her all but unrivaled wisdom." Mill genuinely believed that his was the inferior mind of the two. Certainly hers was a mind he needed, whether for intellectual or emotional reasons. She lent his thought a quality of radicalism which it had not had without her, a willingness to associate itself with the new and daring experiments of the time, an identification with revolutionary movements, and with the new classes making a bid for power in Europe. Mill's basic mental stance was one of balance; his mind was many-sided. It was Mrs. Taylor who was responsible for the chapter "On the Probable Future of the Laboring Classes" which he added to the later editions of the *Principles of Political Economy,* and in which he expressed his sympathy for Socialism and his prophecy of its triumph.

Harriet was buried at Avignon, and Mill took a small house nearby so as to be constantly near her, living out the remaining years of his life in the shadow of her memory and influence, and adopting her daughter, Helen Taylor, as his own. Helen quickly assumed the role that her mother had filled, of assistant and collaborator in Mill's work, and he transferred to her much of the devotion and dependence he had felt for Harriet. It is hard not to conclude that Mill's nature, for all the independence of his thinking, was one which was incomplete without some complement. At the start it had been his father, later Mrs. Taylor, still later Helen Taylor. In the case of his father, Mill's estimate of him was at once affectionate and judicious, as given in the *Autobiography,* although he never overcame an underlying hostility. In the case of the two women, however, he could not do without superlatives which are today embarrassing to the reader. In a sense he required a teacher all his life, even while he was himself the guide and teacher of half of Europe. With all his own thin-lipped strength of will, he required strength in another person, especially in a woman, on which he could lean, with an emotional urge which compelled him to realize from the relationship nothing less than a community of two loving people—that is to say, the beloved community.

Without quite knowing it, Mill was in search of the Beloved Community all his life. He gave it a number of names—"utilitarianism," "the greatest happiness of the greatest number," "liberty," "diversity"— but always he was driving his mind toward clarifying the conditions under which as many people as possible could find their fulfillment within a good society. He was (let the truth be told) what Justice Holmes used to call half-derisively an "onward and upward thinker." Which is to say that he was at once the product and in part the shaper of the eighteenth and nineteenth century conviction that men can mold their destiny by molding and remolding their society. The French *philosophes* were part of this movement, and the French and English Utopian socialists, and the "Philosophical Radicals" of the first half of the nineteenth century in England, with whom Mill belonged and whose ideas he brought to their clearest and most orderly form. Mill was in this sense a child of his age, and he suffered from the disease of his age—the gnawing doubt about whether the institutions that Western civilization had built would live or deserved to live, the sense of complicity in guilt for the great inequalities of distribution in a prosperous society, the question of what to do with the new wealth and new power which Europe had piled up, the bewilderment about how to reconcile the belief in education and democracy with the obvious fact that the former was linked with a minority and the latter based on a majority, and quite generally the anxiety about the new and somewhat barbarous classes who were knocking at the gate of history. (Remember how in the 1820's and 30's and 40's the flaring, fitful fires of libertarian revolutions swept across the face of Europe, from the Carbonari in Italy to the July days in Paris and the Chartists in England.)

I stress these doubts, guilts, bewilderments and anxieties because Mill's era has usually been described as one of optimism, and Mill as a High Priest not only of reason but of the complacencies. This misses the meaning both of Mill and his age. True, it was the century of the Great Hope, when the dream was of the perfectibility of man, when the foundations of the old religion were sapped and new religions of science and of humanity were being invoked. In Paris and London alike there were young men eager to reform the world, to resolve the problems of poverty, to organize thought into a single system. The middle class had come into its golden hour and was seeking some principle to cement its power—a principle whether of material progress or Reason or Liberty, which would enable it to rationalize its position by morality. And Mill was part of this current of history, the child of this era. But he was an anxious child of his time, and one whose dominant passion was not complacency but dissent, not dogma but the use of the critical intelligence for the benefit of man's condition.

One of the best ways to get at the quality of his vision is to note the enemies he fought. He waged a continuing smoldering war against all forms of authority that demanded unquestioning faith, and were not bolstered by man's independent mind. This meant a war with all supernatural religions and established Churches, with Natural Law, with Protestant morality, with intuitionism in philosophy, with mysticism of every kind in thought, with the arrogance of the male in subjecting woman to an inferior position, with the privileged power of the few and with the tyranny of the many in crushing dissent. His enemies were superstition, unreason, privilege, conformity. They were good enemies for a young man to have as he felt out his strength.

He went at them with a lusty vigor. Mill never became the kind of political thinker, like Hobbes or Machiavelli, who had a feeling for power and its ways and its location. Harold Laski, contrasting him with the masculine strength of Hobbes, was later to call him a "hermaphrodite" thinker. But he did have a feeling for intellectual power, and he knew how to fight the battles for the sovereignty of the little Republic of Ideas of which he became part. London in his day was compact, compassable, and somewhat insular. It was governed by a handful of literary magazines, newspapers, intellectual leaders. Mill set out to win over the newspaper editors to his cause, rounded up a new group of magazine contributors for his *London and Westminster Review*, assigned them books and subjects, read and criticized their copy; he invaded the two great Universities and sought out the most promising student leaders; he set up a correspondence with the Saint-Simonians, Comtists, and others of the intellectual avant-garde in Paris. Very quickly he became a force in the intellectual—and therefore the political—world.

But he was an independent force. The best instance of his independence is his break from Jeremy Bentham. The *London and Westminster Review* was the organ of the young Philosophical Radicals, such as Roebuck, the Grotes, Molesworth, who in turn were tied to Bentham's hedonic calculus and his "Table of the Springs of Action." It was a pretty sectarian affair, and Carlyle wrote Emerson that it was "Hidebound Radicalism; a to me well-nigh insupportable thing! Open it not: a breath as of the Sahara and the Infinite Sterile comes from every page of it." Yet in the end Carlyle wrote for it, as did others who were anathema to the Radicals. Mill insisted on turning it into an organ of liberalism in politics and the broadest cultural interests. There was a

saving quality in Mill which kept him from ever becoming a political
sectarian, or a slavish disciple of any thinker. He broke from his
father, from Bentham, from Carlyle, from the Saint-Simonians, from
Comte, although each had eagerly hoped to use his talents. With
Bentham, as with his father, Mill's objection was to the excessive
rationalism which squeezed out everything else. The pure milk of
Benthamism no longer held any nourishment for him. He saw Bentham
as a man who, himself almost without experience, sought to generalize
from his own poverty of experience and impose a rule of motivation
and ethics upon mankind. "He never knew prosperity and adversity,
passion nor satiety. . . . His own lot was cast in a generation of the
leanest and barrenest men whom England has yet produced."

No, Mill was not content to be a sectarian politician nor a free lance
journalist nor a narrow rationalist reformer. He saw his own function
as going down to the roots of thinking, and charting the domain of
knowledge. In 1830, at twenty-four, he started his first important book,
System of Logic, and he kept at it (with interruptions) for thirteen years.
He saw it as a seminal work. "Good seed is never wasted," he told a
French friend, "it takes root, and springs up somewhere. It will assist
the general reconstruction of the ideas of the civilized world for which
ours is but a period of preparation." He was fighting the forces of
reaction, but he knew that their deepest fortifications were in the minds
of men, in the things they took for granted and which they therefore
held as a matter of faith or intuition. In his *Logic,* which is now read only
by the specialists but was a sensation in its day, Mill attacked this cita-
del of unreason entrenched in the syllogism. He showed that deductive
reasoning by the syllogism presented no new truth that was not already contained in the major premise. His principal target, Dr. Whewell,
argued that there were universal, necessary truths, as in the laws of
geometry, which went beyond experience. Mill answered that the principles of geometry were useful assumptions, that there were no necessary truths, and that every general proposition—and therefore every
major premise in logic—is taken from experience. You arrive at your
major premise by induction, you apply your minor premise and get
your conclusion, and you then submit the conclusion to verification by
inductive experience again. This was the method of science, and Mill
classified the sciences by their reduction of experience to scientific
method, starting with mathematics and going down to the social and

moral studies. Even the latter, he hoped, would some day become exact sciences—a hope which still persists today.

What is worth noting here is that Mill was a philosopher of experience. The whole school of American pragmatists, from Peirce through Dewey, rests on him. When William James wrote his pathbreaking lectures on *Pragmatism,* he dedicated the book to Mill, "whom my fancy likes to think of as our leader, were he alive to-day." Bertrand Russell, in tracing his own philosophical development, writes "I did not come across any books, except Buckle...which seemed to me to possess intellectual integrity . . . until I read Mill's *Logic.*" In fact, if one were to seek a parallel to Mill in our own more recent time, it would have to be a blend of William James, John Dewey, John Maynard Keynes, and Bertrand Russell, with a dash of Walter Lippmann thrown in. He had the open-mindedness and far-roaming interests that James later had, the grounding in science and experience of Dewey, the interest in logic and economics that Keynes had, the luminousness of style and the moral clarity and gravity that Lippmann developed, and the anti-clerical rebelliousness and the feel for unpopular causes of Russell. But note that it has taken a whole platoon of thinkers to replace him.

He never limited his interests, and refused to be hedged in behind the trim boundaries of particular disciplines, but roamed through logic, metaphysics, ethics, psychology, economics, religion, politics, education. He was in the best sense a generalist, not a particularist. He was a great name in the history of each of the disciplines I have mentioned, exactly because he refused to restrict himself to any one of them, and was thus able to break down the boundaries between them, and shed fresh light on each by focusing on it searchlights from the others. In a sense he was the Aristotle of the Victorian Age, as Aristotle was the Mill of the Alexandrian: in fact, Mill refers (in *On Liberty,* II) to the "judicious utilitarianism" of Aristotle, thereby conscripting the Stagirite into his own little phalanx.

I don't mean to slight Mill's weaknesses. Although a good logician, and although he longed to be a master of metaphysics (hence his *Examination of Sir William Hamilton's Philosophy,* a long and today pretty dull piece), he lacked the metaphysical genius of Berkeley and Locke and Hume, as in politics he lacked the sense of the organic state and society one finds in Edmund Burke. He failed to go as deep as Bentham did into the meaning of meaning, and the distortions produced by language itself. While he took up Tocqueville's insights into the inner dangers of mass culture, it was he who followed the lead of the French thinker, rather than the other way around. He recognized the role of the irrational, yet did almost nothing to chart it, as Nietzsche and William James, Freud and Jung were to do. And while he knew the limits of science as a method and saw its barrenness as an exclusive way of life, he did not fight stubbornly against its sway, as he did against dangers about which he was clearer.

What he failed to see was that, once he had knocked out religion and natural law, intuition and mysticism and faith, as the underpinnings of men's conduct, he had nothing left except science and materialism. In his recoil from them, he was compelled to appeal from the "lower" to the "higher" sensitivities and tastes, but here again he had to fall back either upon subjectivism (a man's tastes are his tastes) or upon the authority of some intellectual and aesthetic elite in whose keeping would be the "religion of humanity." (Hence his disastrous, if short-lived, flirtation with August Comte's pedantocracy.) With the fluid movement of classes, and the *embourgeoisement* of Western society, the arbiters of taste, culture, and morals had vanished. The middle-class which was to be guided to a proper appreciation of these values had become the arbiter of its own values.

I have run ahead of my story, since Mill was not yet aware—when he published his first book, the *Logic*—of the depths and whirlpools he was getting into. He was enjoying his newfound power. It was good to have some sport with Dr. Whewell's history of the sciences and his deductive logic, especially when—in Book V of his *Logic,* "On Fallacies"—he could illustrate the various species of fallacious reasoning by examples from Whewell and his other targets. He was later to have the same kind of fun with Sir William Hamilton. The task of being a working social thinker was not all lugubriousness: there was a joyousness in it, and Mill let it shine through his grave historical excursions and his rolling periods.

Nor was economics for him the dismal science it had been for his predecessors. The success of his *Logic* emboldened Mill to put out as a volume a group of articles he had earlier written in his spare hours as a functionary in India House, just as he had written his *Logic* there, since he spent only three or four hours of the day on his official work. These appeared as *Essays on Some Unsettled Questions of Political Economy* in 1844, the year after the *Logic.* This led Mill to attempt the bigger task of setting down, in the wake of Adam Smith, Ricardo, McCulloch, and Nassau Senior, his own *Principles of Political Economy*. There is a legend, unfortunately picked up by some recent popularizations of the history of economic thought, that Mill wrote the book in six weeks. But he did it fast enough: over a period of eighteen months he spent only ten months at it, and then took nine months to rewrite his first draft. It was as if he had been waiting all his life for the chance to survey the whole realm of economics. The sentences came tumbling out of his well-stocked memory, mainly in recall of the conversations of the Ricardo group when he was still a stripling, and the discussions at the Debating Society, and all the books he had read then. They came tumbling out much too easily. For a decade or more Mill had not kept up with the new insights into economics. He came at the tail-end of the classical system of economics, giving the work of the earlier and more original thinkers a clarity and gloss they had never possessed from the start; he put it all into the seemingly rigorous frame of his theory of logic and scientific method; he dealt with production, distribution, and exchange, with value theory and profits, with wages and rent, with the theory of international trade. He thereby gave an appearance of finality to a system of thought which he himself recognized as belonging to a specific historical period, rather than as part of the eternal laws of society—gave it the appearance of finality exactly at the point when it was most sharply challenged by the rise of new classes within the system of capitalist production, and their claims for a new deal. Thorstein Veblen, in his essays on "The Preconceptions of Economic Science," was later to lump Mill's economics with that of the rest of the classical school, as taking the same things for granted. And both in England and America, there were men who either wilfully or ignorantly misread Mill, and tried to use him to bolster both the status quo of economic power and the method of laissez-faire.

They were unjust on both scores. Mill shook rather than bolstered the structure of economic power and its buttressing theory. He distinguished between the realm of production on one hand, where the problem was the relation between man and the forces of Nature, and where therefore one could speak of fixed laws, and on the other hand the realm of distribution, where the problem was the relation of man to man and there were no fixed laws. "The things are there," he wrote. "Mankind, individually or collectively, can do with them as they please...The distribution of wealth therefore depends on the laws and customs of society." This left the door open for at least one brand of Socialism—the kind that sought distributive justice. In a famous passage Mill expressed his aesthetic as well as moral dislike of "the trampling, crushing, elbowing, and treading on each others' heels, which form the existing type of social life." But Mill was against revolution to change this. He thought that the struggle for riches kept the energies of most men better employed than if they rusted or stagnated. "While minds are coarse they require coarse stimuli, and let them have them." His hope was that in time the better minds would "succeed in educating the others into better things."

But Mrs. Mill, who had helped Mill all through the book, was scarcely satisfied with this brand of mildness. After the revolutions of 1848, which were a watershed for so many thinkers in England as throughout Europe, she pressed Mill to make revisions in the later editions of the *Principles*. Mill had ended with a group of chapters which he called "Of the Influence of Government," which were delicately balanced between laissez-faire and governmental intervention. Under Mrs. Mill's pressure he changed much, sharpened much, added a chapter (which she largely wrote) on the future of the laboring classes, and in general managed to push the book over from its original liberalism into a tract on the margin of Socialism. In fact, there was even a passage in Book II, Ch. I, "Of Property," which was inserted in 1852 and was much quoted by the Left-wing group of Mill's disciples, starting "If therefore the choice were to be made between Communism with all its chances, and the present (1852) state of society with all its sufferings and injustices . . ." and ending ". . . all the difficulties, great or small, of Communism would be but as dust in the balance." It should be added, of course, that Mill used the terms "Communism" and "Socialism" interchangeably, that he knew next to nothing about Marx who was then working away in the British Museum, and that he had in mind chiefly the Utopian Socialisms of Fourier and the Saint-Simonians. Yet even with this caveat, it remains true that any effort to classify Mill as a traditional individualist liberal is very wide of the mark. True, much of this was due to the curious hypnotic effect of his wife upon his mind. Carlyle explained this effect in terms of "those great dark eyes, that were flashing unutterable things while he was discoursin' the utterable concernin' all sorts of high topics."

In 1854 Mill thought that he would die of tuberculosis. "The most disagreeable thing about dying is the intolerable ennui of it. There ought to be no slow deaths." When he recovered he re-planned his life and his writing career. His mood was similar to John Keats' "When I have fears that I may cease to be . . ." He wanted to make certain that the "full-ripened sheaves" of his thought would be gathered before he died. For five years, until after his wife's death in 1858, he published no books, but wrote steadily with her help, after drawing up a table early in 1854 of the subjects he wished to treat. They were to be essays—"on Love, Education of tastes . . . Foundation of Morals . . . Utility of Religion . . . Liberty," and a number of others. It will be seen that each of the essays grew into a book. The "Education of Tastes . . . and Foundation of Morals" became *Utilitarianism.* The "Utility of Religion," along with *Theism* and the essay he had just finished on Nature, were ultimately published as the *Three Essays on Religion.* "Liberty" became *On Liberty.* Work on the *Autobiography* was started immediately. The years between 1854 and 1861 were the incredible years in Mill's life. His six greatest and most readable books— the foundation and summary of his thought—were written in that period. It would be hard to point to any comparable period in the life of any of the great social thinkers of the modern age that could match it for sheer fertility and for the quality of the writing. Despite the changes that took place in his thinking in the course of his lifetime, the fact that these crucial books were all compressed within a brief seven years gives them a unity and an interrelationship, like panels on a central theme.

Utilitarianism was meant as an attempt to find a basis for the principles of moral behavior. By a rough formula, Mill's aim was *humanitarianism* (the Benthamite "greatest happiness of the greatest number"), his means was to be *reason,* his guide was *utility,* by which he meant well-being, or what we should today call *welfare.* It is an earnest and somewhat plodding book, welcome for its brevity and lucidity, admirable for its courage at the time in breaking morals away from the sanctions of religion. There was also something admirable about it in another sense. Mill sought nothing less than the regeneration of man. But instead of building it on the wishfulness of altruism, he insisted on appealing to every man's self-interest. This was to be, in a phrase William James was later to make current, a "tough-minded" approach to morality and the conduct of life. What Mill was driving at was that the justification of life was not to be found in the hereafter, nor in codes imposed from above by an aristocracy of power and privilege—

by the Establishments of the day, but that the test of a good life, was whether it was good for the man who lived it. And the test of the rightness or morality of any action is its consequences for mankind—whether it increases the sum of human happiness.

One can admire the boldness of this without concluding that Mill was able to bring it off. There were too many unsolved difficulties. There was the qualitative problem, and Mill answered the argument from hoggishness—that his system was that of "a hog from Epicurus' sty"—by saying that there are higher and lower forms of happiness, that it is a matter of training, that "men lose their high aspirations as they lose their intellectual tastes, because they have not time or opportunity for indulging them," and that with education and with equality of opportunity for all, the quality of welfare can be raised for all.

One must note here that Mill evades the question of objective standards for the quality of happiness, or utility. What is best, he says in effect, is what the best men practice. Fine, but who decides who are the best men? His answer has a Gertrude Stein quality in it: they are best because they are best because they are best. The thinkers with an organic concept of society have the merit of assuming candidly that the established arbiters of morals and taste, in the Establishments of a society, are the best. Mill has discarded that, but is unwilling to follow skepticism or relativism all the way, and he bases the principle of utility and happiness within man himself: a man knows when he is happy, and what it consists of.

A second difficulty lies with sanctions: what will keep men in the path of their right conduct? If the penalties of society are largely removed, what takes their place? Mill answers that "this firm foundation is that of the social feelings of mankind; the desire to be in unity with our fellow-creatures, which is already a powerful principle in human nature, and happily one of those which tend to become stronger." But alas, the experience with the totalitarians has shown us that this "desire to be in unity with our fellow-creatures" can lead to a mystique of submission, and in mass democracies it leads to a mystique of conformity.

A third difficulty lies with Mill's basic optimism. He sees quite rightly that the unhappiness of many people is due to their being denied, by the injustices of society, the same life-chances that the more fortunate have. This was linked with his doctrine of liberty as requiring a base or frame of social action—a theme strongly marked in

On Liberty and also in his essay *On Social Freedom.* But he goes further, and while disposing of the pathetic in the human condition, seeks to dispose of the tragic as well. "All the grand sources of human suffering," he writes in Chapter II, "are in a great degree, many of them almost entirely, conquerable by human care and effort; and though their removal is grievously slow—though a long succession of generations will perish in the breach before the conquest is completed . . . yet every mind sufficiently intelligent and generous . . . will draw a noble enjoyment from the contest itself." Thus, in the noblest terms, Mill manages to squeeze the universe almost dry of the element of the tragic, which is not man-made and cannot be man-unmade but is part of the human predicament.

I do not say it is an easy universe, this universe of Mill's. It involves ardors and rigors. But it is a curiously limited universe. The "pursuit of happiness," in the phrase that Jefferson took over into the Declaration, becomes self-conscious in it and almost obsessive; and the calculus is still there, although Mill has moved from Bentham's rather crude pleasures and pains to more refined standards of happiness.

Most of the pleasures turn out to be not very different from the virtues of a middle-class society which the preachers of Mill's day preached—without the theological trappings. True, Mill was furious at the lack of sensitivity of many members of the British middle-class, and Harriet and he were drawn into a kind of *égoïsme à deux* in defying their stuffiness. Yet when he set down his verities of the life of reason, they were strangely those of the best of middle-class England. The tragic and the irrational are squeezed out. The psychology is shockingly weak. There is no hint of any inner nature of man, because Mill rejects "innate ideas." The strain which Freud cultivated as pessimist—the death-urge in man, and the extent to which society is itself organized repression of the erotic drives—of that too there is no hint. Sex itself is treated discreetly, but we know from the letters between Mill and Mrs. Taylor that she was a frigid woman sexually, and that she and Mill agreed that sexuality was something of the lower order of values, something more than faintly disgusting. In *A History of Western Morals,* Crane Brinton speaks of Mill as "that ascetic hedonist, so incapable of anything you or I could accept as *hedone,* or pleasure." And as for society, Mill cannot go much farther than to define its happiness as the sum of the individual happiness of its members. Thus, despite Mill's references to "the desire to be in unity with our fellow-creatures," his society is an atomized one. It was a mistake that the conservative thinkers like Burke and Carlyle did not make.

The key question about morality was not a question about the intellectual and cultural elites, but about the big majority of men and women. In an age of mass culture, of passive spectator sports, of violence and dehumanization, how were Mill's elites to teach them values, instruct them in the authentic character of happiness? The successive trial answers have been given by the British welfare-state, from Keir Hardie through Sidney Webb to Aneuran Bevan: to shape welfare through social construction, so that the beneficiaries will have an artificial identification of interests with the better groups, and thus learn to appreciate life. The Communists have a short-cut, in the indoctrination of the many by the Party elite with Party-line truth. Much as he wished to spread happiness among the many, Mill was too committed a believer in liberty to suffer any attempt at indoctrination.

It was his recoil from any betrayal of the method of Reason which also set the frame for his views on religion. In his approach to this problem, which no great thinker of the nineteenth century could leave alone, Mill was not wholly disinterested. He knew the extent to which the established supernatural religions fortified the established social institutions. He wrote his three essays to undercut the hold which religion had on men's attitude toward society. His first essay, *Nature,* is a devastating refutation of the idea of religion as based on natural law. To say that the universe is part of God's design, and that God reveals himself through Nature, is (says Mill) to ignore the cruelty and injustice of Nature. "In sober truth," he writes in a great and terrifying passage, "nearly all the things which men are hanged or imprisoned for doing to one another are nature's everyday performances. . . ." And then comes a recital too long to quote and too powerful to summarize. But in throwing out the laws of Nature, Mill also throws out the whole cluster of the human instincts. His position is that of the extreme institutionalists: that everything about man is socially learned and socially conditioned, and just as there are no innate ideas there are no innate instincts.

In *Utility of Religion* Mill argues that religion is not a necessary base for morality, being capable of neither proof nor disproof. If he were cynical he might have taken the view of Edward Gibbon, that in the Roman Empire all religions were equally true and false and all religions were equally useful. Machiavelli held this view of religion, like Plato before him. But Mill's drive is different: he wants to extract the "essence" of religion from its supernatural trappings. The essence turns out to be, not so surprisingly, the religion of humanity—or, as it now tends to be called, humanist religion. As a young man Mill had been drawn far more than he knew to the Comtian religion of humanity. But Comte, who was one-third genius, one-third charlatan, and one-third madman, could not long hold Mill's respect. What his religion finally turned out to be, with all its rituals and trappings but without any sense of mystery and wonder, was (as someone put it) "Christianity without Christianity." Mill discards all the trappings, but he too ends without either wonder or worship—with something that is not much more than morality itself, but that casts a mystique of a sort around the body of moral principles.

Mill's true religion, one must conclude, was neither morality nor the religion of humanity, but quite simply the idea of freedom. What must be noted here is the relation of his thinking about freedom to the general body of his thought. Here was something he could write about with passion, because it embodied his whole being and striving, and more than any other idea it was linked with his sense of identity. Liberty was for him (to paraphrase a sentence of Holmes's) not a duty, but only a necessity. Without it the growth of a person was unthinkable, since Mill defined liberty as essentially the frame of freedom needed for fulfillment of potentials. But it followed from this that without liberty a good society was also impossible, since without liberty there could be none of the benefits of the diffusion of the relatively true ideas, nor the deposit which even the relatively false ones have left on history, nor the balancing and competition of true and false, nor the diversity of personalities (each based on the freedom to select his truth, and to grow with it) which makes a rich culture.

Nothing as eloquent, weighty, luminous as this has ever been written in so sustained a way on freedom—not even, I venture to say, Milton's tract, the *Areopagitica,* while Acton's essays are fragmentary, and Holmes's decisions atomistic. For once Mill can dispense with much of his abracadabra about utility, since he is dealing with a value so fundamental to society and to meaningful life that he makes out of it almost a first principle. He handles the problem of negative and positive freedoms well. He is vulnerable, however, when discussing the limits of freedom and he is in danger of forgetting that there is more to the universe than individuals revolving in interstellar space.

But his real problem comes with the question of the tyranny of the majority. He had learned much from Tocqueville on this, especially from the second set of volumes of *Democracy in America.* If you give the majority the freedom to push others around, you have tyranny. But he would not adopt an iron attitude toward the majority, nor allow it to adopt an iron one toward minorities. As a result the book becomes a lonely, agonizing debate between the claims of a freely growing man to be free of state and majority and all, and the claims of the many to impose their will in order to have effective government, or perhaps only in order to give themselves the illusion of security. "It may be necessary, wrote Rousseau, "to compel a man to be free." Mill would be in violent disagreement. And so he stands, a lonely figure on the shores of the world, weighing the conflicting claims of the two principles, without knowing quite how to integrate them.

Let us leave him thus. He outlived his wife by fifteen years, working mostly in France, near her grave, sometimes in London. He came to be almost revered as a "saint of rationalism." He had, as a young man, been arrested for distributing birth control pamphlets. As an older man he still had his hand in almost every cause, whether it was women's suffrage, or the Northern side in the American Civil War, or proportional representation, or farmers' cooperatives. It was as a moralist, however, that he had his greatest impact. Intellectuals living under a tyranny as far away as Czarist Russia read his works, and caught from them a vision of a not impossible reconstruction of society and regeneration of man, and their minds were stirred by the controlled passion in his words.

Primarily he was a working thinker, intent on finding the best sources and conditions for his thought, reading books and conversing with their writers for the light they might shed on whatever problem he was tussling with. I do not say that he was a dehumanized thinking machine. No one who reads his *Autobiography* or his Letters could fail to see that, for all his apparatus of rationalism, he was a committed and incurable romantic. He saw everything in more than lifesize proportions, whether it was Mrs. Taylor or the idea of liberty or the blind malevolence of a Nature over which there could be no presiding Deity. But he had the same romantic dedication to his craft as a working thinker, a dedication which kept him going through all the years of illness and struggle, with an obstinacy of will which recognized no obstacle, and a passionate fire (on such issues as women's rights or anti-colonialism) which left his opponents incredulous at its intensity.

Here was no man, then, of gruel-water intellect and thin emotions, no sawdust-stuffed Victorian moralist, no prim and unctuous spokesman for a carefully ordered world. Here was rather a man of strong passions, large vision, tenacious will, powerful intellect, who used and fused all his qualities in the service of a vision of a better world for all his fellow men. This is what he meant by the principle of "utilitarianism," which can be redefined simply as social happiness and the good life for all.

I am by no means certain that Mill ranks with the really first-rate minds of world history—with Newton and Hume, with Burke, with Tocqueville, with Marx and Freud. The sum total of his books give him however a rank in intellectual history almost equal to those I have named. It is possible to be a genius, and to use one's genius to the full, and yet not be among the great creative minds. It is hard to associate Mill with any very original theories, yet it is hard *not* to associate him with a powerful and comprehensive system of thought. His strength lay in extracting the implications of what was known, drawing the inferences, examining the proofs, and fitting everything together into a system of relation. His strength lay also not so much as an intellectual innovator, as in the world of values which he helped to shape and clarify. He was at once a moralist and a militant. He brought to its highest point of perfection the system of liberal thought which gave expression and meaning to the mid-nineteenth century in Europe. But while his passion grew out of the events of his day, he gave his thoughts and values the imprint of the universal. That is why today they have a relevance as fresh as when they were newly minted.

"He has nae roots in his mind," said Carlyle once of his dearest enemy. To which Justice Holmes answered, when Harold Laski reported the anecdote to him, "I doubt if Carlyle gave the world as great a shove as Mill." There are many who will query whether the direction in which he shoved was the right one, but a shove it was.

5

Thorstein Veblen

—1—

America, which has produced the most finished and tenacious brand of business civilization, has also produced the most finished and tenacious criticism of it. That is the core meaning of Thorstein Veblen's work. It was a body of work bounded on both sides by the image of economic power. Veblen began his formative thinking in the 1880's, when trusts were emerging and the new "dynastic corporation" was planting itself squarely in the path of the traditional political ideals. His first published economic essay appeared in 1892, two years after the Sherman Anti-Trust Act. His last writing was done in the 1920's during the boom period of what was being called the "New Capitalism," when the monopolies came into their present power. Among all the thinkers who sought to analyze the nature and consequences of this new business imperium of the West, vaster than any comparable imperium that history had produced, Veblen is easily the towering figure. His critique of our civilization is as unsparing as the Marxian, and at the same time more subtle because it is an analysis in depth, with a psychology, an anthropology, and a theory of civilizations.

Veblen has worn well. Very little in him dates. Very little bears the stamp of the manipulator and propagandist which must be refurbished with the new moods of every generation, or of the tender-minded which seems mawkish as soon as the print is dry. The years since

---

Originally published as the introduction to *The Portable Veblen,* edited by Max Lerner (New York: The Viking Press, 1948), 1–49.

Veblen's death in 1929—years of economic and cultural disintegration and dynastic war—have borne out the main lines of his thought. They have strengthened the conviction that Veblen is the most creative mind American social thought has produced.

—2—

What tricks of inheritance, what social conditionings, what turns of personal history combined to produce a mind as corrosive and a style as distinctive as Veblen's? His life is a curious one in the American saga. American biography has dealt mainly with success-stories and recent American fiction with deterioration-stories. Veblen's story was neither. It was one of outward failure and inner tenacity, of a continuing creative fire admist a social wasteland, of a life of scholarship whose victories did not bring fulfillment and whose triumphs ended in the most desolating loneliness.

Veblen was born in 1857, of Norwegian parents on the Wisconsin frontier. His mother was a talented woman who often served as an amateur doctor for the frontier community. His father was a master carpenter and builder who turned into a skilled farmer, and whom Veblen later described as the finest mind he ever knew. One of twelve children, Thorstein grew up on a farm in Minnesota, a "Norskie" boy in a culturally insulated region where English was an alien language to be acquired. There was a continuing feud between the land-hungry, largely populist newcomers and the "Yankee" storekeepers and lawyers who owned and ran the small towns. There are echoes of this feud in Veblen's now classic discussion of "the country town"[1] with his contemptuous dissection of the mentality of the Main Street merchants and lawyers and bankers who embody in miniature the tactic and the ethic of Big Business. One may also find in Veblen's work a sweep of inner geography to match the outer sweep of the plains on which he grew up, along with something of the tongue-in-cheek hyperbole and wry deflationism which marked the American frontier.

Veblen's father, Thomas Veblen, believed in the life of the mind. At table there was always sustained talk about what was happening in the world. Thomas Veblen was the only farmer in his community who sent his children to college, girls as well as boys. In his boyhood Thorstein knew German and Latin as well as Norwegian, and could print an anathema in Greek on the fence of an offending neighbor.

Packed off in a buggy at seventeen by his father, Veblen was sent to Carleton College, a little Minnesota institution with a theological atmosphere, where he got three years of preparatory schooling (he knew little English) and three of college. His interests ran toward philology, natural history (as biology was called), philosophy, and economics. It is easy to see, after the fact, how these interests could converge upon the broad-gauged study of cultures-as-wholes of which Veblen was one of the pioneers. Before the fact, however, it took a pattern-breaking mind to make them converge.

The record gives few clues as to how Veblen developed it. His best teacher at Carleton, John Bates Clark, became a first-rate economic theorist—but he was a strict traditionalist. The only strong intellectual influence that broke into the tight Norwegian community was that of Björnson, the playwright, who had become a Darwinian and free-thinker, and was making a lecture-tour of the Middle West. At Johns Hopkins, where Veblen did graduate work for a spell, he listened to lectures by Charles Peirce, perhaps the most original mind in the history of American philosophy, who insisted that "the whole function of thought is to produce habits of action," and who may thus have helped start Veblen on his war against the passive psychology of the economists. At Yale, where Veblen took a Ph.D. in philosophy under the staid guidance of President Porter, he studied economics under William Graham Sumner, who was a passionate (and at that time daring) champion of Herbert Spencer and evolution but whose economics was a defense of the existing class order.

Meanwhile what Veblen wanted most was a job and even a slight niche in life. It was a long time before he got either. He left Johns Hopkins because he could not get a scholarship. At Yale he lived the life of a penniless student, working for his board, skimping on clothes, always in debt. His classmates found him irreverent, and his type of wit irritating. The only market for obscure young men with Ph.D.'s seeking teaching posts was in the denominational colleges. But which of them would take a strange-looking Norwegian—even if he did have a degree in philosophy—whose chief enthusiasm was Ibsen, who joked about the doctrine of atonement, and who was more than half suspected of being an agnostic? Veblen got no job, and spent seven wretched years (1884–1891) eating his heart out. Added to his idleness was the fact that an attack of malarial fever at Yale had broken his health. Yet these waste years were not wasted in his development.

He read endlessly, if with a seeming aimlessness; tended his garden at Stacyville, Iowa; discussed botany and Bellamy with his wife; commented on national events with a detached raillery during the "gilded age" when sensitive men were beginning to ask whether the moral and political promise of America was played out. Ideas were piling up in his mind, clamant, unused.

In 1891, as J. Laurence Laughlin often told the story, a strange-looking anaemic figure, in coonskin cap and corduroys, showed up at his office at Cornell and announced, "I am Thorstein Veblen." It was Veblen's effort, since he had reached an impasse in his job-hunting, to get a fresh start by going back to graduate study. Laughlin got him a fellowship at Cornell, and the next year—when Laughlin headed up the economics department at the new Rockefeller-founded University of Chicago—he took Veblen along as a teaching-fellow at $520 a year. It was four years, moving at a turtle's pace up the sub-hierarchy that President Harper had built, before he became even an instructor, with the chores of managing editor of the *Journal of Political Economy* added. But it was the start he had longed for. He had books around him, a magazine to review them for, courses to give, colleagues like Jacques Loeb and Lloyd Morgan, Dewey and Boas and Caldwell to talk to. He had the great mushrooming World's Fair city of Chicago, with its continental energy and tinsel strivings and social tensions, as the focus of his skeptical observation. He was like a stretch of soil that had lain rich but neglected for years and was finally in cultivation.

The decade of the nineties saw Veblen's first harvest. The articles he wrote during that decade for the learned journals contain most of his important ideas—emulation, workmanship, the industrial and pecuniary employments, the beginnings of ownership, the economic theory of women's dress, the attack on the formalism and the laying bare of the "preconceptions" of received economics, the plea for an evolutionary economic science. Obviously Veblen was ready for his first book. When *The Theory of the Leisure Class* was published in 1899, "it fluttered the dovecotes of the East," as the great sociologist of the day, Lester Ward, put it in a letter to Veblen. "All the reviews I have seen of it so far are shocked and angry. Clearly their household gods have been assailed by this iconoclast." One must add, however, that not quite all the reviews were shocked. William Dean Howells, who ruled the literary world and was the friend of young talent, devoted two leading articles to the book and gave it an irresistible send-off. He had himself been something of a Socialist, and five years earlier he had written his own heterodox doctrine in a satiric novel on the money-spirit in America, *A Traveler from Altruria.* Howells' review touched off the acclaim and abuse which made Veblen overnight a national literary and intellectual figure.

The curious fact about the reviews was that attackers and acclaimers alike—and this included Howells too—took it wholly as a satirical study of aristocratic ways. Veblen insisted he had not meant to write a book of jokes, that he had been in dead earnest. He told a graduate student that if you tried to do serious creative work in social theory, people would either neglect you or giggle at you. Veblen had been writing not of the social aristocracy but of the business power-group of the middle class which aped the ways of an aristocracy. He attacked less the titled wasters than the captains of industry and the lesser men cast in their image. When he used terms like "barbarian" and "preda-tory," they were synonyms for "business" and "capitalist." When he talked of gentlemen and ladies, of lackeys and lackeys' lackeys; when he spoke of the head of the household who dressed his wife and daughters with a conspicuous display of waste consumption, kept his sons at archaic studies, hired servants as vicarious signs of his leisure, kept a large number of people uselessly engaged in devout obser-vances, took part in sports whose principal elements were guile, fraud, and predation, surrounded himself with subservient animals, and orga-nized his whole world to show off his prowess: of all this Veblen might have said to his American era—*de te fabula.* For he was analyz-ing an America in the sleaziest decades of its civilization—an America of crassness and money-lust, of boodle and greed, of men of power whose garish pecuniary values were made the subject of emulation by the whole people. Of course he did not give a factual survey of his culture. As an artist he picked his symbols and organized his analysis around them. Joseph Dorfman has shown in a remarkable textual analysis how closely parallel Veblen's symbols and themes are to Herbert Spencer's *Principles of Sociology*—except that Veblen took Spencer's attack on socialist society and stood it on its head, making it an attack on capitalist society. His book was a masterpiece of literary outlandishness and attack by indirection. But enough of his meaning came through so that for the Philistines he became a marked man.

He did not follow up his literary triumph with quick and easy repetitions of the formula. He worked five years on *The Theory of*

Business Enterprise (1904), which contains his formulation of the crucial economic institutions, notably of the machine process and its cultural incidence, the business depression, and the ramifying of business power in law and politics. He took ten more years to do his most difficult—and, in his own eyes, his most important—book, *The Instinct of Workmanship* (1914). It contains the affirmative side of his thought—how man's deepest drive is to create and not waste or destroy, what the main phases have been through which Western history has passed in the development of technology from the New Stone Age to the modern machine industry, and what has happened in each phase to man and his unyielding instincts. Graceless, cumbersome, and opaque as much of the writing is, the book is a deep and venturesome one. Veblen was wooing no one. He refused to be patronized or dismissed, turned into a cult or giggled at. The important thing was to build a social analysis that would encompass modern culture, and make men reckon with it.

By this time (he was fifty-seven when the book appeared) he had been forgotten in the world outside the universities, but in the academic world itself he had become a legend. On more than one campus the younger instructors and the more mature students walked about with a fire in their brain that his words had kindled.

What went into the making of the legend? There was his erudition, his stock of languages, his lore in Icelandic sagas, his ransacking of every literature, his knowledge of archaeology and racial history—of kitchen middens and skull measurements; there was the precision with which he knew the homely and workday details of cultures as well as the big abstractions, the ease with which he moved about in history from neolithic times to the report of the latest Congressional Committee on American industry. He was, as has been said, "the last man who knew everything"—and if he did not know quite everything he could distract your attention from the gap by a wry witticism. There were his strange books, any one of which could have made a lesser man's career, and each of which had the knack of standing the accepted doctrines on their head. There was his polysyllabic language, and his slow acid style that corroded the sanctities. There were his courses, with his mumbled lectures which only the better students understood, his reluctance to give or correct exams, and the even-handed indifference with which he dealt out the same passing-grade to each student. There was the way he looked: shaggy brown eyebrows, wrinkled skin, a white ashen face with unforgettable eyes, rough clothes that hung too loosely on a shrunken body, a shell of silence into which he seemed to have retreated for good and from which only the most persistent strategy could draw him. Finally there was his domestic economy, more original and radical even than his political economy.

It was on this rock that Veblen's academic career seemed repeatedly to break. His first marriage, in 1888, proved after a few years a stormy one. Veblen was scarcely a philanderer, but he was a striking figure and not a few women found him an interesting one. He on his side scorned the furtiveness that academic life required in such matters, and his wife was not averse to making scenes. After one of these he had to leave Chicago, and with some difficulty got a teaching post at Leland Stanford. Here he was happy for a time. Robert L. Duffus, one of the Stanford students who lived with him and helped him with the chores, has given us in *The Innocents at Cedro* (1944) a graceful portrait of Veblen in his mountain cabin, with his irregular hours of work, his primitive furniture that he had himself built, his highly civilized conversation when he could be induced to talk, his mixture of the tender and the deflationary. But again there was an episode ("What is one to do," Veblen shruggingly asked his friends, "if the woman moves in on you?") and Veblen moved on to the University of Missouri where his friend Herbert J. Davenport finally succeeded in getting him a place. He taught there for seven years (1911–1918), and for a time—until his second marriage in 1914—he lived in Davenport's cellar, where he wrote some of his greatest work.

One's first impulse is to wish that the university authorities had concerned themselves less with Veblen's private difficulties and more with his public talents. But, on reflection, that was perhaps exactly what they did. The Philistines knew that a giant was among them, but he was the wrong kind of giant, whose strength they feared, and they were glad to see him go packing before he pulled the temple down around their heads. What outraged them in Veblen, one may surmise, was less his unstable *ménage* than his dangerous thoughts. They got back at him in many ways. He was "not sound," they said; "not scholarly"; and—most damning indictment of all—he was "not an economist": a sociologist perhaps, but not an economist. They made his path hard from the beginning, his salary small, his promotions slow; the range of teaching posts available for him shrank, despite his fame; and he never got a grant of funds for any research project he ever submitted. These facts, as we look back at them, may dismay those who believe that a great civilization cannot live without great critical thinkers, and that while the road of social criticism must always be lonely it need not be made bitter as Dante's exile. Veblen felt keenly the *cordon sanitaire* that had been thrown around him.

He felt it, and understood it. But his understanding it did not make his mood any less bitter. He made no direct answer. But one must take as an indirect answer (to jump ahead a bit) a book he finished at Missouri in 1916 but did not publish until 1918. It was a book on the American university, *The Higher Learning in America.* When asked, while the book was being written, what the subtitle would be, Veblen answered with more than half seriousness "A Study in Total Depravity." It eventually became "A Memorandum on the Conduct of Universities by Business Men." No other book like it has ever been written on American education. Veblen's dissection of the governing boards of colleges, the faculty, the faculty wives, the system of promotion, the kind of man who gets along in the university hierarchy, the endowments, the mummery of the big plants, the competition for students, is pitiless. But all of it is mild when compared with his climactic description of the university president as a Captain of Education modeled on the Captain of Industry. The book differs from other Veblen books in being two-dimensional: its scope is limited; there is no enrichment of the main theme by excursions into psychology and anthropology; the economic interpretation is direct rather than indirect. Nevertheless the book contains some of Veblen's best writing, with an elaborately detached and precise vocabulary whose emotional overtones are at once icy and sultry. Veblen's friends thought it was too explosive, and he seems to have played with the thought of publishing it only after his death; but when he left Missouri in 1918 to come to New York as an editor there was no longer need for silence. The academic moguls had their revenge in a review by Brander Matthews who complained that Veblen knew no grammar and queried how he had earned his Ph.D. Veblen wrote a scorching retort in the form of a proposed preface to a second printing, but never had a chance to use it because the book did not sell and no second printing was required until after Veblen was dead.

The First World War quickened the pace of Veblen's writing and thinking. He had worked for fifteen years on his second and third books. In the remaining eight years of his writing (1915–1923) he published six books. What he had written before the war had a cosmic and timeless quality; what he wrote from then on contained the reverberations of the volcanic events of the day. The first two books of this period, *Imperial Germany* (1915) and *The Nature of Peace* (1917) are still transitional in the sense that they are still excavations rather than constructions. Combining the erudition of his earlier period with the heightened contemporary emphasis of his later one, they hold the best elements of his work in balance.

Imperial Germany and the Industrial Revolution is easily one of Veblen's masterpieces, and stands with *The Theory of the Leisure Class* and *The Instinct of Workmanship* to form his great trilogy. It has imaginative boldness, intellectual sweep, sureness of style. For the historian, the political theorist, the student of cultures and their contacts, it is his most exciting book. He uses two of his key-ideas—the state of the industrial arts and the cultural incidence of the machine process—to explain the difference in strength of the German and British economies, their divergent political systems, their different place in world politics. He saw the German talk about *Kultur* for the delusional rubbish it was, and made a cold analysis of the hybrid racial composition of the German people that undercut (he wrote in 1914) all the racist nonsense the Nazis were to talk for three more decades. Instead he explains the superior German economic strength by the fact that the Germans borrowed the British technology but did not take over with it the institutional encumbrances that had slowed up British industrial efficiency. Hence what he calls, with an edge of paradox, the "merits of borrowing and the penalty of taking the lead." But since the Germans did not take over British democracy along with the technology, they imposed their new technology directly on their old dynastic state, and out of the fusion came a new dynastic imperialism aimed at world conquest. It had to make its bid within a limited number of years, because people under the discipline of the machine process would not long tolerate a system of privilege and authority based on social status and military caste.

Anyone reading *Imperial Germany* today, and remembering that Veblen published it in 1915, will be startled at how clearly he foresaw the mixture of racism, industrial efficiency, military caste, and imperialist adventure that were to form Nazism, and how close to the totalitarian state the German dynastic state described by Veblen comes. That a professor in a little Missouri town should have seen all this so long ago is a tribute less to his specific political foresight than to his insights into what makes a culture. On America's entrance into the war George Creel's propaganda office tried to use the book because of its anti-German thesis, but the Post Office (perhaps because the book was harsh on the British and had some sharp things to say about the superiority of the German business imagination to the American) barred it from the mails as pro-German. It was not the first time that Veblen had baffled unwary readers who thought in terms of trivia rather than central ideas.

An Inquiry into the Nature of Peace and the Terms of Its Perpetuation appeared in 1917 just before America entered the war. It left no doubt, so far as Germany and Britain were concerned, that Veblen feared the dynastic imperialism of the Germans (and the Japanese) more than the amiable inefficiency of the British. But Veblen could not forget his main doctrines. His analysis of patriotism was deadly— and he applied it to the fears and manipulations of the possessors of economic power in every state. He saw at the heart of the state's nature the constant readiness to use the apparatus of force and war in putting down threats against the system of ownership. The book supplies the bridge between Veblen's economic thinking and his political thinking. In *The Leisure Class* he had scorned a too bare economic interpretation, but had shown the common people tied to the ruling class by all the intangible bonds of emulation and identification. So too in *The Nature of Peace* he sees nationalist feeling as having emotional roots and meaning of its own, but he shows also how it is used by the economic rulers. Patriotic loyalty takes its place in Veblen's scheme alongside pecuniary emulation, and dynastic ambition alongside business enterprise. Between the two pairs the traffic is heavy. There can be no lasting peace, Veblen concludes, until the price system—the system of ownership and property which requires nationalist loyalties for its purposes—has been removed.

So little did Macmillan think of the book's chances that the author had to pay that firm $700 to get it published. Yet it got a reception none of his books had had since *The Leisure Class*. Francis Hackett saw the book's importance and the author's courage, and the other reviewers debated its merits. People wanted to find a solid ground for peace, and Veblen's probing, uncompromising mind met that need. Again he became a national intellectual figure.

On America's entrance into the war, Veblen offered his services to

Washington. He wanted to be made use of in the planning for peace, and wrote several memoranda on a "League of Pacific Peoples," and on a plan for international control of foreign investments and of the economic penetration of backward areas. But the Wilsonians—including Secretary Baker, Justice Brandeis, and the peace research group under Colonel House and Walter Lippmann—were not interested in the ideas of the radical professor. He was finally given a minor post in Washington, and for several months did statistical surveys and memoranda for the Food Administration. Here too he had constructive proposals: to end the prosecution of the leaders of the I.W.W. migratory workers in the Prairie States and get the wheat crop in; to do away with the merchants in the country towns and get supplies to farmers by a centralized governmental mail-order system; to levy a steep progressive tax on employers of domestic servants. The memoranda remained memoranda. Veblen was by-passed and boxed up. He was evidently the wrong man in the wrong job. For his own part he concluded that the men of Washington already regarded the war as won, and were chiefly concerned about protecting the vested interests.

In 1918 he came to New York as an editor of *The Dial,* which had a subsidy and some ideas about post-war reconstruction. But he remained as much an outsider among the philosophic liberals of New York as he had been in the atmosphere of a Midwestern country town. He did not have the stamina to cope with New York living, and his former students—Wesley Mitchell, Leon Ardzrooni, Isador Lubin—took turns in watching over him. Nor could he write the surfacy and straight-forward journalistic style that editors and readers demanded, and he was furious when anyone tampered with his copy. Yet surely there had never been any editorials in the history of American journalism quite like those he wrote in his year on *The Dial.* They were on the two big themes of any post-war era—the struggle for the peace and the anti-radical hysteria. He called the first an effort to "make the world safe for the vested interests," and the second he termed variously "acute *paranoia persecutoria*" and "*dementia praecox.*" He scoffed at the fears the "Guardians" had of a revolutionary uprising. There was, he pointed out, a massive institutional structure of sentiment and habit by which the underlying population identifies the interests of the propertied groups with its own. "The Guardians have allowed the known facts of the case to unseat their common sense. Hence the pitiful spectacle of official hysteria and the bedlamite conspiracies in restraint of sobriety."

Along with these editorials Veblen wrote for *The Dial,* during 1918 and 1919, two series of articles. The earlier one became, in book form, *The Vested Interests and the Common Man* (1919)—a good enough popularization of his ideas on natural rights, technology, business enterprise, and nationalism, which added nothing new to them. The later series became *The Engineers and the Price System* (1921). It too was part of his journalistic phase and gave repeated references to the current scene, but it contained important fresh viewpoints. He had always been a revolutionary in overturning existing ideas; but he now spoke quite openly of a revolution in existing institutions. He still assured the Guardians that there was no danger of "a revolutionary overturn"—an assurance composed of equal parts of tongue-in-cheek playfulness, his habitual protectiveness of language, and a quite earnest belief that the hold of the possessors of power was too tenacious to be pried loose. Or at least, as he forebodingly put it—"not yet." Knowing there was no revolutionary potential among either American farmers or workers, he turned to the "engineers." They were the creative master technicians, whose brains and skill determined the state of the industrial arts, and they alone could take over the going technology without any of its pecuniary institutional encumbrances.

The book was neglected when first published, but at the end of the Hoover Administration, when economic collapse once more brought a restless social temper, it took on new life and meaning. For the first time Veblen had tried to build a research and action group around his ideas, and a number of engineers and social technicians had gathered in New York to discuss their role. But nothing came of it, except that a decade later one of them, Howard Scott, got a spell of notoriety for his Technocracy movement; and Technocracy became briefly the tail that wagged the dog of Veblen's reputation. Veblen's analysis of the revolutionary possibility of "a soviet of engineers" is still as brilliant as it was when written—and as unreal.

The Dial editorship came to an end, and Veblen was given a place on the faculty of the New School for Social Research, founded by a group of unruly spirits who had resigned from Columbia—Charles A. Beard, James Harvey Robinson, Wesley C. Mitchell. He was at the height of his intellectual influence. The liberals and radicals made much of him. Even the appearance of a volume of his earlier technical essays on economic theory, *The Place of Science in Modern Civilisation* (1919) did not frighten off the audience that read him in *The Dial* and read about him in *The Nation* and *The New Republic:* in fact, it gave his reputation the added esoteric touch that Americans seem to require. H. L. Mencken ribbed the Veblen cult in a rollicking essay in *The Smart Set*: "Veblenism," he wrote, "was shining in full brilliance. There were Veblenists, Veblen clubs, Veblen remedies for all the sorrows of the world. There were even, in Chicago, Veblen Girls—perhaps Gibson Girls grown middle-aged and despairing."

Veblen had always been a poor teacher for the common run of student, and the fact that he was in his sixties, and a sick man, did not make him less so. Each year his classes began with a large registration and dwindled to a handful. When the New School had to be reorganized, he became a costly luxury. Once more he looked about for another teaching post, but without success. He was tired and lonely. The years of intellectual and social crisis, when the World War and the Russian Revolution had ended in the restoration of the *status quo* again in Europe and America, were also years of inner tumult for Veblen. He had come out of his scholarly shell to take part in the actions and passions of his time, had watched eagerly every sign that a widespread revolutionary break of some sort was coming. "When the thing failed to come off," writes Horace Kallen, "he gave signs of a certain relaxation of will and interest, of a kind of turning toward death that seemed to grow with the years." As the bull market of the twenties unrolled, his teachings seemed again to be forgotten.

One afternoon he showed up in the office of his publisher, Ben Huebsch, with a large sheaf of manuscripts in an untidy parcel and dumped it on Huebsch's desk, saying it was something he had written but "probably not of the least interest to the publisher or anyone else." It was *Absentee Ownership* (1923), his last book. Not written with the same consistent brilliance as *The Leisure Class* or *Imperial Germany,* it nevertheless contained—especially in the series of short chapters under the heading "The Case of America"—some of his sharpest writing. It was also as a whole the maturest analysis he ever did of the American business system—of the credit structure as its foundation, of corporate finance and the corporate revolution, of "the technology of physics and chemistry" which organized American resources and of the absentee control which disposed of them. It was the work of a man who had been writing for thirty years and wanted to leave, as his final heritage, the most uncompromising assessment of business civilization in its fullest American flowering.

His strength and will were played out, and little but a mocking bitterness was left. In 1925, after several years of clash between its younger and elder members, the American Economic Association finally tendered Veblen the nomination for its presidency. He refused, saying with some asperity, "They didn't offer it to me when I needed it." The next year he went back to his mountain cabin in California. There he puttered about, read idly (he liked Aldous Huxley, Norman Douglas, and mystery stories), watched world events with a despairing irony. He died on August 3, 1929, and his body was cremated and his ashes scattered over the near-by waters of the Pacific.

—3—

One seeks a parallel for him in the history of thought and letters. Swift, Voltaire, Shaw, come most readily to mind for their satiric quality, but they were more brilliant and versatile literary craftsmen than he, and he more of a scholar than they. Marx comes to mind, who was also a scholar and a radical system-builder: but Marx was first of all a professional revolutionist, and Veblen was not. It is part of his greatness that he created his own *genre* as well as his own scheme of thought.

How can we best put the essentials of that scheme? In its negative phase it was an attack on orthodox economics, and any reassessment of Veblen must start with the sources and results of that attack. He was the terror of received truth in economics as Luther had once been the terror of received truth in religion. He riddled the notion that economic generalizations were "laws," timeless and placeless, and invested with sanctity. He contended that they were a system of apologetics for the going system of economic power. He showed, in one of the most effective series of his essays, that throughout the history of classical economics, each generation of economists had taken for granted the very things that most needed proving—the "preconceptions" they took over from the prevalent world outlook and the accepted institutions. The result was that the economists of Veblen's day assumed the existing distribution of income and power, and spent their energies on "taxonomy"—on classifying economic concepts and drawing distinctions between them, and on showing how the total income is apportioned among the factors of production according to what each deserves. Veblen scorned the moral implication of this doctrine of equivalence—that all is well in the best of all possible systems of income distribution, and that the mounting wealth and power of the rich and the grinding poverty of the poor are part of the fitness of things. He derided the psychological Never-Never Land into which it led:

> A gang of Aleutian Islanders slushing about in the wrack and surf with rakes and magical incantations for the capture of shell-fish are held, in point of taxonomic reality, to be engaged on a feat of hedonistic equilibration in rent, wages, and interest.

On the positive side, what did he propose for economics? First, that it should get an adequate psychology; second, that it should become "an evolutionary science." He wrote in one of his famous passages:

> The hedonistic conception of man is that of a lightning calculator of pleasures and pains, who oscillates like a homogeneous globule of desire of happiness under the impulse of stimuli that shift him about the area, but leave him intact. He has neither antecedent nor consequent. He is an isolated, definitive human datum, in stable equilibrium except for the buffets of the impinging forces that displace him in one direction or the other. Self-imposed in elemental space, he spins symmetrically about his own spiritual axis until the parallelogram of forces bears down upon him. . . . When the force of the impact is spent, he comes to rest, a self-contained globule of desire as before. Spiritually, the hedonistic man is not a prime mover. He is not the seat of a process of living . . .

What is to replace this hedonistic man? Veblen's answer suggests the activist psychology of which he had first heard from Peirce at Johns Hopkins and which Dewey, his colleague at Chicago, was writing about. In Veblen's words:

> It is the characteristic of man to do something, not simply to suffer pleasures and pains. . . . He is . . . a coherent structure of propensities and habits which seek realization and expression in an unfolding activity.

The crucial economic expression of the urge "to do something" was the instinct of workmanship. The "propensities and habits" became embodied in institutions. The task of economics, as Veblen saw it, was to study the origin and development of these institutions—to give

> the theory of a process of cultural growth as determined by the economic
> interest, a theory of a cumulative sequence of economic institutions stated
> in terms of the process itself . . .

that is, without bringing in any "controlling principles" from the outside, whether from capitalist apologetics or socialist ethics or Christian
theology.

One set of principles Veblen did assume: those of Darwinism. What
he took from Darwin's outlook was not what the "social Darwinians"
made up from it—the consoling thought that since life is a jungle and
the human beings merely animals in it, we need do nothing about war
and economic ruthlessness except glorify them. Veblen took from
Darwinism the basic scientific method which studied men in their
continuous adaptation to their natural and social environment, a method
which took men for what they were, and saw the conditions of their
life ceaselessly changing. For many today Darwinism has a musty
smell, but the method for studying institutional change that Veblen
derived from it is still a valid method. I shall point out later the extent
to which Veblen himself departed from it, and what his own "preconceptions" were. But, however far he may have departed from his purpose, the purpose itself was a healthy one.

—4—

Veblen's attack on the economists was only a phase of his theory of
how men behave, which in turn broadened out into a far-flung system
of social theory.

This broader system starts not with an economics but with an *anthropology*. Veblen stressed the hybrid racial composition of the human stock in the Western world. Those racial traits had become largely
settled, through natural selection, during the long period of relatively
peaceful and stable community life in neolithic times. They were the
traits that had proved most useful for human survival and effectiveness in that type of environment.

Veblen had framed for himself from his reading in archaeology and
history a *scheme of social evolution*. As he saw it, the human community in the Western world has gone through four main stages: the

economy, in which he found the origin of the related institutions of property, war, masculine prowess, and the leisure class; the handicraft economy of the pre-modern period; the machine technology. Anthropologists have since abandoned the idea of evolutionary stages in society, and prefer to study the specific history of particular civilizations. But Veblen's scheme is suggestive if not pressed too hard.

In his thinking about *human nature* Veblen held that it had developed over a long evolutionary span, but has now become relatively fixed. He took the tough minded view which regards the human animal, with his instinctive endowment, as something given that had to be reckoned with and could not be changed. But while it is tough minded, it is not a dark view. Veblen saw man as endowed with basically peaceful instincts that had been overlaid with warlike institutions; and endowed also with a horror of waste and futility, an impulse to constructive action, an instinct of workmanship. Men did not originally find labor irksome, Veblen argues in one of his early essays. It was with the institution of the leisure class that it began to seem irksome to them, by contrast with the prestige-bearing pursuits of magic and religion, war and sports.

Along with their instincts men have propensities and habits. One of their crucial propensities is that of "emulation"—the striving to outdo others in aping one's superiors in the social and economic hierarchy. This is the point at which Veblen's *theory of institutions* best fits in. He defined an institution very vaguely, as a cluster of habits and customs, ways of doing things and ways of thinking about things, both of them sanctioned by long practice and by the community's approval. I have said that Veblen laid great stress not only on instinct but also on habit. He ascribed the origin of institutions to some twist that was given to man's native endowment; but the persistence of institutions was chiefly due to the encrustation of habits of thought and action.

Veblen's thought is deeply dualist. Much of it is best stated in terms of the bitter and unending struggles that go on in the cultural arena. One struggle revolves about how men shall conceive their experience. It is the *conflict between the animistic and the matter-of-fact,* between superstition and science. The animistic bent is to attribute magical powers to spirits residing in things, so that human activity becomes a problem of propitiating the spirits. The matter-of-fact bent is to see things in terms of cause and effect, of "weight, tale, and measure." The institutions of property and war still flourish because they carry over residues of the animistic, imputing a magical power to ownership and to patriotism. The great matter-of-fact force is science, which comes from "idle curiosity" and sticks to what can be expressed in colorless terms of causation. Thus for Veblen the importance of science in modern civilization is not that it makes for progress, but that it replaces the magical by the matter-of-fact. Since the institutions that ride men and impede the functioning of their instincts are based on animism, the spread of science means the weakening of those institutions and a new chance for the release of men's native endowment. Thus science is revolutionary rather than progressive or utilitarian. Veblen had much to say against pragmatism although in the broadest sense he was part of the whole movement of social thought in America that has been called "radical positivism" because it put institutions to the test of social use.

The most revolutionary product of science is the machine. For the machine has its effects, day after day, hour after hour, upon those who work with it. This is what Veblen means by *the cultural incidence of the machine process.* What men do, how they grow accustomed to working and thinking, shapes what they become. If they work with the machine and live under the machine process, then in the end only the cause-and-effect relations will make sense to them. Magic, status, traditional and empty loyalties, religious propitiation, the waste and futility of war, property, the right to get something for nothing: these will cease to make sense. When the people realize this, the institutions are doomed.

For Veblen the shaping forces in history were economic. The main course he gave in every one of his teaching posts, from Chicago to the New School, was called "Economic Factors in Civilization." At bottom Veblen held to a *technological theory of history.* He saw the whole character of a period transformed by its technology. But not in the direct sense one might expect. A machine technology does not automatically create a system of law and politics, of education and religion, to further its goals of abundance. It creates instead a new challenge to the old institutions of law and politics, of education and religion. And the owning groups respond to the challenge—at least in the beginning—by dressing the institutions up more tightly in the old principles, and thus striving to remain masters of the technology. Thus one gets Veblen's alliance between the *vested interests* and the *vested ideas.* In the end Veblen believes that technology eats away the vested ideas and reshapes the institutions in its image. But the process takes time, and in that lag lies the area of social conflict. Thus technologies help shape the struggles of history, as well as the forms it takes in its successive phases.

This leads us to the best-known of Veblen's ideas—again a dualistic one—the classic *cleavage between industry and business,* between technology and ownership, between the industrial and pecuniary employments, between those who make goods and those who make money. It is because of this idea that Veblen has been called, by sympathetic critics like John A. Hobson, basically a socialist. Yet note that Veblen does not think in terms of the conventional Marxian class alignment of capitalists and workers, of those who own the instruments of production and those who are owned by them. He places a large segment of the propertyless—everyone in advertising, salesmanship, sports, religion, the domestic employments—in the pecuniary category. His real division is between two different kinds of disciplines—the machine process and the "pecuniary calculus." His real cleavage is between those who perform a social function and those who perform a social waste. One is reminded of R. H. Tawney's idea of a "functional society" as against "an acquisitive society."

Veblen's term for business as an institution is the *price system.* It represents the mechanism by which businessmen hold power over industrial processes to which they make no industrial contribution. It furnishes also the "cash nexus" which is at once the supreme value and the supreme symbol of a pecuniary society. It drills into the minds of businessmen (and others as well) the values of accountancy rather than production, of placing the making of profits ahead of the making of goods. Here again one finds a ceaseless struggle going on—between the effects of the price system on people's minds, and the effects of the machine process.

One consequence of Veblen's analysis is the *anti-social character of business.* The differential income that the pecuniary occupations receive is not to Veblen, as it was to the orthodox economists, a payment to the "factors of production." It is no proof that they perform any function which merits the differential, but is due mainly to the strategic fact of their position as "absentee owners." Actually, in Veblen's view, business is compelled by its basic position to a policy of "sabotage" of production. It must fight against the "inordinate productivity of the machine" by keeping prices high and supply limited.

This brings us to Veblen's *theory of business crises,* which runs in terms of the expansion of loan credit, the fall of the capitalized value of enterprises as the rates of interest rise, the destructive effect of greedily high prices in bringing lessened demand and higher costs therefore lower profits, the panic that befalls businessmen as they see profits low, interest rates high, and credit tight, the consequent toppling of the whole structure of prosperity. Thus Veblen describes crisis as an inherent part of business enterprise, growing directly out of prosperity and the cupidity and errors it engenders.

In the face of business sabotage and business depressions, why does not the "underlying population" take power into its own hands? Veblen explains this *social conservatism* by pointing out that pecuniary values exert a force which is not limited to the absentee owners or the leisure class. They cut across classes. They are powerful because of the propensity that men have to emulate the standards of value and the tastes of the dominant groups in their society, to adopt their stereotypes, and to identify their own interests and viewpoint with the interests and viewpoint of those groups. Thus Veblen's theory of power is a psychological theory of the readiness of the victim for the slaughter. He stresses the willingness of the capturable mind to be captured even more than the strategic position the captor holds.

Veblen found it unnecessary to do much in the way of the explicit formulation of a theory of politics. His ideas about political power are implicit in his ideas about social power and in his whole theory of how institutions are rooted in men's habits. More clearly than any other American thinker he has traced the way business principles ramify into law, politics, education, religion, art. His *analysis of the state* might have been a fuller one if he had not approached political power wholly by way of economic power and its psychological bolstering. As it is, the essence of the nation-state, for him, lies in its *dynastic* character. Just as every state was once a mechanism for passing power on from dynasty to dynasty, so it is now a mechanism for passing it on from one set of hands to another inside the same group of absentee holders of economic power. There are, of course, differences between states, depending on whether the cement used is that of direct authoritarianism as it was in Japan and Germany or the indirect power of the leisure class, as in England, or the power of the dynastic corporation, as in America. But for Veblen these differences seemed less important than the fact common to all states—the use of nationalist rivalries and of competitive patriotism to keep a rickety structure of war and economic predation going.

One of the reasons why he laid relatively little stress on state-forms was that he was far ahead of his time in seeing the archaic character of the nation-state. Long before Toynbee and without benefit of Spengler, Veblen had taken as the focus of his thinking not the nation-state or the political system but *the analysis of civilizations,* their strengths and weaknesses, and the riddle of their survival power. He saw "the passing of the national frontiers" by technology, science, and the price system. He noted how elements of technology are passed from one economic system to another while the other institutional traits remain rigid and unborrowed. He regarded as the common elements in western civilization the relatively stable hybrid racial type, the common instinctive endowment, and—perhaps most important—the common "state of the industrial arts," which was the possession and heritage of all classes and all nations. The test for him of whether Western civilization would survive was whether the victory would be won by instincts and technology or by the institutions that hold them in thrall.

And hold in thrall also the human personality. Veblen's thinking sheds light on the cultural pressures that beat upon the individual. He gives us in some respects a *theory of social personality:* how much of what the individual thinks and is and believes must be viewed in the shadow of institutions—his notions of prestige, his sense of respect for others and himself, his decorum and good form, his tastes, his loyalties, his willingness to kill and die, his addiction to sports and betting and his belief in luck, his politics, his attitudes toward dominance and subservience.

Veblen's system of thought is far-reaching in its scope, deep in its probings, powerful in the degree to which its parts interlock and its ends meet. It has, of course, weaknesses in it, and blind spots. There is obsessiveness with some aspects of human behavior to the neglect of others. There is overemphasis to the point of stridency. But, given all these, it is still true that Veblen has left a many-faceted heritage of thought. It has as much interest for the educator as for the economist, for the artist as for the revolutionist, for the legal theorist as for the political, for the psychologist and anthropologist as for the historian of ideas. Veblen was notable for breaking down the fences that separated the disciplines, and roaming under whatever intellectual sky and among whatever cultural pastures he chose. He was himself a locked-in personality, but one gets from his books a sense of spaciousness and of inter-relation.

—5—

Veblen was both theorist and reformer. "Where two men ride one horse," Thomas Hobbes has said, "one must ride in front." During most of Veblen's writing career—except for the last few years, after he came to New York and *The Dial*—it was the theorist who rode in front, not the reformer. Yet always he meant his writing to do something, to topple existing ideas if not existing institutions. It is worth taking a glance at Veblen the reformer.

His primary aim, to which he devoted twenty years of his hardest and most painstaking work, was the destruction of orthodox economics. He did not want economics to remain an apology for differential income inside a system of arbitrary and functionless ownership. When he called for an "evolutionary" economic science, what he really wanted was one that would be a science of collective welfare. He wanted the emphasis not on the capitalization of expected income, but upon the industrial arts as a community possession. He was interested not in the corporate dividend flowing from a differential business advantage, but in the social dividend accruing to the community as a whole from the achievements of science and the changes in the industrial arts.

Professor Joseph Schumpeter has remarked that "had Veblen been able to have his way, had his teaching not met a phalanx of competent theorists," he might have wrought in American economics the same confusion that Schmoller and the Historical school wrought in German economics. Certainly Veblen was met by a phalanx of opposition—massive, bristling, unforgiving. The punishment that the "competent theorists" inflicted on him was even more drastic than keeping him out of academic posts. It was the intellectual isolation within which he had to work. He had disciples, he had students, he had detractors. But he had no genuine critics who would approach him with sympathy but who would insist on a severe give-and-take. Veblen became a lone thinker, writing in a hostile void. So keenly did he feel the need for constructing an intellectual battering-ram to level the walls of his opposition, that he grew more and more repetitive and outlandish, and tried each time to say everything at once.

Nonetheless economics has never quite recovered from his assault.

While Veblen did not emerge the victor, neither did the system of economics which was his target. The battle is not yet over. It has not been won by the Veblenians and their "Institutional School" of economics. But it has already been lost by the classical and the marginal-utility theorists. Typically the new economics has taken the form of the "Keynesian revolution," which no longer seeks to justify God's way to the underlying population, but recognizes some of the institutional facts of life, and discusses saving and investment in terms of propensities and habits.

It has often been pointed out that Veblen had an influence on the New Deal and the New Dealers. The Great Depression broke a few months after his death, and it seemed to confirm much of what he taught. Many of the men who staffed the government agencies between 1933 and 1938 were young economists and lawyers for whom Veblen had been a legendary figure, but a perilous one, during the halcyon days of prosperity. He had written that there are no iron economic laws: there are only man-made economic institutions. In that case, why not recast the institutions by a set of new administrative controls?

For the orthodox theorists the economic order is a self-regulator. It has a mechanism by which it runs and adjusts itself, and in a free economy the decisions of businessmen take their place in that mechanism. But to Veblen, who believed that the position of the absentee corporation is arbitrary, that wealth is created by technology and that the businessman sabotages full production, the role of business is one of power rather than of function. For him the vested interests have no useful function in the economy: they have only the power to levy their tribute. Business decisions and business acts are thus primarily acts of coercion, made possible by the strategic position the corporations occupy. Even in a "free economy" the "freeness" of the economy consists in allowing the businessmen to exert their coercions without any counteracting coercions from the government. Given this theory of business enterprise, the New Dealers took a logical further step. They tried to set up a system of governmental counter-forces, to prevent the arbitrary acts of business power from wrecking the economy and making men and machines idle. They sought to construct a polity which would be the master, not the servant, of the business groups. Thus Veblenism, in essence a theory of power in the economic sphere, led to a program of power in the governmental sphere.

This is logical enough, but it is all deduced from Veblen, not explicitly stated in his books—and even less so in the New Deal. If he was one of the intellectual forerunners of the New Deal, he must not be held accountable for either its crudenesses of method or its hesitations of purpose.

As with Hegelianism, there is a Veblenism of the Right and Left. The Veblenism of the Right leads logically to a system of governmental controls which would match the coercions of business, and thus make the price system work without sabotage and without depressions. The Veblenism of the Left despairs of anything short of a complete displacement of the price system itself, and of the system of absentee owners whose vested right, as Veblen used to put it, was "the right to get something for nothing."

—6—

What about this revolutionary phase of Veblen? First of all, what relation does it have to Marxism?

Veblen was a student of Marx. His first essay after he resumed graduate work at Cornell was on "Some Neglected Points in the Theory of Socialism" (1891). His first course at Chicago was on Socialist movements. He had some things in common with the Marxists—the indictment of capitalism, the economic interpretation of history, the linking of war with property. Because of this common ground, and because he used a rapier style where Marx used a bludgeon, Veblen was hailed with delight by the American Socialists. Yet they were also bewildered. He was elusive, refused to be drawn into any Marxist movement, disclaimed any other role than that of a detached and passive observer.

The fact is that the differences between Veblen's thought and Marx's are just as striking as the common elements. The clearest confronting of those differences is found in Veblen's two essays on "The Socialist Economics of Karl Marx and his Followers," which Veblen delivered as lectures in 1906 at Harvard.

He is critical of Marx's system at every step. He dismisses the labor theory of value as an unproved assumption, which Marx takes for granted because it is an integral part of his metaphysical system. Dismissing this he dismissed also what is logically linked with it—the theory of surplus value, and the accumulation of capital out of unpaid labor value. Veblen saw that the right of the worker to the full value of the product was part of a "natural rights" philosophy. Everywhere in his writings he attacked the natural rights philosophy, because he saw it used by the absentee owners to defend the natural rights of property. Nor did he go along with the doctrine that the increasing misery of the worker would lead to proletarian revolution. "The experience of history," he wrote in a memorable passage, "teaches that abject misery carries with it deterioration and abject subjection." He ends by pointing out that in states like Germany socialism was tempering its doctrines with patriotism, and that the workers were allowing themselves to be used in dynastic adventures.

The common man was not for him the revolutionary nor heroic material that he seemed for the Marxists. Veblen had few illusions about him. He did not believe that deprivation could be turned into a drive for power. He saw the American farmer, in an occupation still immune from the machine process and its discipline, clinging to animistic ways of thought and therefore one of the mainstays of the existing order. He was contemptuous of what one of his students and colleagues, Robert F. Hoxie, called the "business unionism" of the American Federation of Labor, and saw it as simply another facet of the price system and the pecuniary calculus. He was dissatisfied with the Marxian theory of the class struggle, which assumed that the proletariat would act by a rational calculation of its class interest.

Throughout the two systems the most obvious difference is one of psychology. Marxism, like classical economics, was based on what was for Veblen the outworn and impossible psychology of Bentham, which assumes that man acts rationally to avoid pain and achieve happiness. Veblen on the other hand believed that men act from instinct and propensity, and that they often cling to habits of thought imbedded in institutions which seem sacrosanct even when they clearly run counter to their interests. Similarly Veblen did not believe, as the Marxians did, that the power of the absentee owners lies in their possession of the instruments of production, and the apparatus of the state. He saw that the real hold of the Guardians lies in the filaments that stretch between them and the minds of the underlying population.

The thinking of both Marx and Veblen was cast in the image of the nineteenth century, with its notion of life and history as process. But while in Marx's case the idea of process was derived from Hegel, in Veblen's case it was derived from Darwin. Veblen did not regard

Marx as a scientist, and pointed out that the Marxian system was completed before the Darwinian influence was felt. For Marx, as a Hegelian, history unfolded irresistibly toward a foreordained goal, through the class struggle toward a classless society. For Veblen there were no foreordained goals: only a ceaseless Darwinian process of continual adaptation, continual and cumulative change.

Having pointed out those differences I must also point out the large area of common ground between the two systems of thought. Both of them contain a basic emphasis on the economic factors in history; both stress the relation between technology, class relations, power and ideas; both are anti-capitalist in animus while they lay claim to complete scientific validity; both look forward to a revolutionary overturn of one form or another—in Marx's case proletarian, in Veblen's vaguely syndicalist.

In personal terms Veblen had none of the firebrand quality of Marx, nor could his system produce a follower like Lenin and generate world revolutionary movements. It lacked the mass appeal and the political application of Marx's writings. It could not be tailored to a crusade. Veblen himself was as far as possible from the prophets around whom cults have been built. He had an unfooled detachment from crusades and cults, and the astringency of mind which ate through the pretensions of others would not allow him to play savior to the world.

Yet it would be a serious mistake to underrate the revolutionary implications of his work. America is not a closed society of status or of sharply drawn classes, and Veblen's distinction between the pecuniary and industrial occupations is a more accurate analysis of the American situation than the class struggle is. There has been no increasing poverty and misery for American workers, but a rising standard of living and a tenacious clinging to the idea of the self-made man. Veblen's assault has therefore been on the mythology of business civilization, rather than on the theme of exploitation. The American productive plant has, despite periodic breakdowns, shown the capacity to recover and to grow steadily in power. Veblen's repeated insistence that technology is the creation of the whole people and not of the absentee owners, is the only one that undercuts the whole moral position of Big property in America. The American dream has been one of equal opportunity in political and economic life. While Veblen carefully avoids any reference to democratic ideals, he makes an analysis of corporate business power which has become the classic explanation for the betrayal of the dream. Finally, at a time when the technology of destruction makes most men aware that the next war may prove the grave of humanity, Veblen's theory that peace requires the abolition of the price system amounts to an equating of socialism with the survival of civilization.

—7—

What shall we say of the strength or weakness of Veblen's ideas for our own generation? No one has shed more light on the roots and the reach of the Great Depression, or on the cultural pattern of Germany and Japan which precipitated World War II, or on the decline of Britain as a Great Power. But there is nothing explicit in his writings to account for the Russian Revolution. The Russians had neither a highly developed price system, nor an unremitting discipline of the machine, nor a strong group of engineers and technicians. Once the Revolution occurred, Veblen was stirred by it and followed it with sympathy. At that point he began to look for signs of the spread of the revolutionary idea, but they proved illusory. He was excited by the reception Wilson got from the common people of Europe, but the character of the peace settlement was disillusioning. He thought something might come of the post-war industrial unrest in America, and believed that the common man was beginning to reach the limits of his tolerance for the price system. He was wrong. His hopes were stirred again by the British General Strike of 1926, and then let down again. All of which proves very little, except that Veblen was as wrong as most system-makers who try to apply their private time tables to immediate events in the making.

But these personal hopes and frustrations have little to do with Veblen's main doctrines. His sense of timing was bad. He had used one clock for his analysis of the instincts, the formation of habits, the growth of institutions; and he used a much smaller clock for the dissolution of the institutions, the revolt of the instincts, the erosion of the habits. He was working on a double time system, the one shaped by his scholarship, the other by his personal eagerness to see the pace of change quickened. On one level he used geologic time, on the other he used the revolutionist's calendar of a single lifetime. He was betrayed by his own all too human eagerness into forgetting—not his principles—but his perspective.

Yet there are grave weaknesses in the principles themselves when measured by the test of the major events of our time. This will be clearer if we analyze one of Veblen's key passages on the dilemma of the warlike state:

> The imperial system of dominion, state-craft, and warlike enterprise necessarily rests on the modern mechanistic science and technology. . . . Nothing short of the fullest usufruct of this technology will serve the material needs of the modern warlike state; yet the discipline incident to a sufficiently unreserved addiction to this mechanistic technology will unavoidably disintegrate the institutional foundation of such a system of personal dominion as goes to make up and carry on a dynastic state.

There are two conclusions to be drawn from this. One is that an authoritarian state like Germany, whether in Veblen's day or Hitler's, must meet its doom through inner revolution. In both cases the historic event proved to be that military defeat was the prime factor, and the disintegrating effect of the machine on personal dominion was negligible. The other conclusion is that the dynastic state is at a disadvantage in competition with a free state (also resting on a machine technology), since the free state will not be troubled by "the system of personal dominion." This is clear until, applying the analysis to the two major imperial powers of today—Russia and the United States—one asks which of them would be considered in the Veblenian scheme the free state and which the dynastic state?

For the student of Veblen the answer is not easy. A short time before he died Veblen remarked to a friend, "Naturally there will be other developments right along, but just now Communism offers the best course that I can see." Yet one wonders what he would have made of the Russian regime under Stalinism. One can, of course, apply Veblen's theory of borrowing to Russia, as he applied it to Germany and Japan. The Russians, too, borrowed the technology of industrialism from the Western world, and imposed it—as the Germans and the Japanese did—on a largely feudal tradition that had not had a chance to develop democratic ideas or parliamentary institutions. The remarkable advances in Russian economic and military power fit into the pattern that Veblen lays out in his theory of the "merits of borrowing and the penalty of taking the lead." A powerful new Russia that has elided the democratic phase of development would, by this pattern, also prove an authoritarian one. No doubt Veblen had his eye on the economics of communism, and felt that its politics was not crucial. Yet, coming back to the comparison between Russia and America, it is hard not to conclude that in Veblen's system of thought a price system without a dictatorship has more of the aspect of a dynastic state than a dictatorship without the price system.

What vitiates Veblen's thinking in this respect is that he recognizes no dynamism except the economic, and seems to care little about any values outside the technological. I have pointed out how chary he is about talking of democracy or freedom. It was partly that he disliked any tender-minded interpretation of history, partly that he preferred to focus on the economic substance rather than on the political form. But whatever the source the result was that a whole side of Veblen's thinking remained undeveloped. Granted that one cannot fight for political freedom without first leveling economic injustice, it is also true that a state which suppresses all opposition leaves even its justice at the mercy of whim, and provides no method by which the fight can be carried farther.

Veblen could have avoided this tangle if he had recognized that political values are not marginal, and that freedom too has its dynamism in history. This accounts for the feeling of inadequacy one gets in reading Veblen's memorandum on a soviet of engineers. His thesis breaks down, of course, because the engineers refused to fill the revolutionary syndicalist role he assigned them. But even had they gone through with it, what kind of society would it have meant for America? No group can take over a technology without setting it down again in a framework of political and moral values. Any revolutionary movement must come out of a context of belief that goes beyond the simple desire to have the full product of a technology.

For Veblen this would have proved an idle theme. Sometimes when students put questions like this to him, questions that seemed irrelevant, he would answer, "I don't know. I am not bothered that way." He was evidently not bothered by the kind of polity or ethos the Russian revolutionists had created, as he was not bothered by the kind of polity or ethos the engineers might create in America. For him the full social use of the machine carried along its own values. The failure to give it full scope was, in this theology, the Antichrist.

Nor can it be denied that he had a theology. For all his horror of animism, he attributed an almost animistic quality to the "discipline of the machine." It was the solvent that ate away thrones, principalities and powers, graven images and false gods. The workers and the engineers who come under the machine's full sway can no longer be unquestioning subjects of institutions of authority. Events have disproved him. The glimpses we have had into the human psyche in an era of organized evil make Veblen's thesis highly doubtful. Hitler managed to extend his sway over the workers and engineers as well as the middle class, and the men who ran the machines finally did his bidding as surely as the men who owned them. We have learned that the people whose emotional life has been dammed up by a highly mechanized culture are often exactly the people who seek release in the barbarisms of fascism and the surrender to authority. It is hard to forget that the human furnaces which reduced the Jews of Europe to ash and fertilizer were operated on the principle of the machine process.

This is not to imply that Veblen failed to size up the tragic and the stupid in our era. He had a glimpse of a cycle of war and violence when he anticipated "a substantial, though presumably temporary, impairment and arrest of western civilization at large." But however grim the view he takes, most of the grimness is visited on institutions, while the hope is focused upon the machine, and upon man himself and his instinctive endowment.

In writing about instincts, Veblen became the chronicler of a lost innocence in a Golden Age of the past. There is an excess of optimism in his belief that the central drive in man is the instinct of workmanship—the constructive bent, the hatred of futility, the solicitude for creation, and for peace in which to create. Veblen recognized that there are massive obstructions to this instinctual drive, but he found the obstructions not in man's primal and permanent endowment but in the institutions that have risen to plague him. One may doubt that man is as pristinely good and peaceful as Veblen depicts him. Or that his native endowment was necessarily stabilized, as Veblen says, in the "peaceful savage" stage of neolithic times. What we have learned about man as a political animal recently suggests that the origins of his instinctual drives may be lost in the longer and darker period of human history before the New Stone Age. The Freudian view seems juster: that there is not only a drive to love but also to aggression, not only a life instinct but also a death instinct.

Much of the key to Veblen's embittered intellectual life lies in the conflict between his essential belief in men and the desolate wasteland he saw all about. He called himself a skeptic. But he was a skeptic only about institutions, not about man himself. His faith—and it is not wholly grotesque to use such a word about him—was that the instinctive core of man is sound, and only the institutional husks are rotten. He seemed to have an almost Rousseauist belief in man's natural goodness. Like the creator of the noble savage, who believed that man is born free yet is everywhere in chains, Veblen believed that man is born peaceful yet is everywhere in turmoil, that he is born with the instinct to shape things for human ends, yet is everywhere surrounded by waste and futility. However much he wished to believe that the instincts would triumph, he was too honest an observer not to give the historical odds to the institutions:

> History [he wrote in 1914] records more frequent and more spectacular instances of the triumph of imbecile institutions over life and culture than of peoples who have by force of instinctive insight saved themselves alive out of a desperately precarious institutional situation, such, for instance, as now faces the peoples of Christendom.

What an epitaph for a Great Power world, cursed with "imbecile institutions," in an era of the most destructive violence man has ever conceived.

—8—

What remains is a word about Veblen not as theorist but as writer. He is not a graceful writer, nor is he one for the slack mind and the unwary spirit. Reading Veblen means following a sustained argument, penetrating an oblique and highly individual vocabulary, snaring overtones that may be now derisive and now indignant and now gently playful. In his less careful writing he is clumsy, wordy, repetitive. One gets the sense of endlessly chugging polysyllables, as if his sentences were a long string of freight cars rolling on forever. His greatest fault, when you read the body of his work as a whole or any one of his books all the way through, is his repetitiveness. Left so long to himself and writing in isolation, he developed a compulsion to retraverse his whole ground every time he went off on a foray or returned from one. Thus he loses rather less by excerpting than the more economical writer. Yet when all this has been said, it remains true that in the adaptation of literary form to intellectual substance and strategic intent, Veblen was a master craftsman. At his best his style must rank with the great expository and polemical styles of the English language.

There are, as I have suggested, an earlier and a later style in Veblen, as there are an earlier and a later phase of thought. The earlier style is the great one. It may be illustrated by a characteristic passage from *The Theory of the Leisure Class* (ch. x, "Modern Survivals of Prowess"), chosen almost at random:

> Addiction to athletic sports, not only in the way of direct participation, but also in the way of sentiment and moral support, is, in a more or less pronounced degree, a characteristic of the leisure class; and it is a trait which that class shares with the lower-class delinquents, and with such atavistic elements throughout the body of the community as are endowed with a dominant predaceous trend. . . . As it finds expression in the life of the barbarian, prowess manifests itself in two main directions—force and fraud. In varying degrees these two forms of expression are similarly present in modern warfare, in the pecuniary occupations, and in sports and games. . . . In all these employments strategy tends to develop into finesse and chicane. Chicane, falsehood, brow-beating, hold a well-secured place in the method of procedure of any athletic contest and in games generally. The habitual employment of an umpire, and the minute technical regulations governing the limits and details of permissible fraud and strategic advantage, sufficiently attest the fact that fraudulent practices and attempts to overreach one's opponents are not adventitious features of the game. . . . The pantomime of astuteness is commonly the first step in that assimilation to the professional sporting man which a youth undergoes after matriculation in any reputable school, of the secondary or the higher education, as the case may be. And the physiognomy of astuteness, as a decorative feature, never ceases to receive the thoughtful attention of men whose serious interest lies in athletic games, races, or other contests of a similar emulative nature. As a further indication of their spiritual kinship, it may be pointed out that the members of the lower delinquent class usually show this physiognomy of astuteness in a marked degree, and that they very commonly show the same histrionic exaggeration of it that is often seen in the young candidate for athletic honors. This, by the way, is the most legible mark of what is vulgarly called "toughness" in youthful aspirants for a bad name.

There is about this early style an air of quaintness, but it is a controlled quaintness. It never becomes eccentric or hopelessly obscure or turgid. Nor does the irony, as it tends to in the later style, become a frozen attitude of ill-humor and indignation. Veblen uses here the long probing approach, followed by the quick turn of the knife. His manner is outwardly academic, and he invests the analysis with the appearance of a deliberate and detached gravity which is intended to put the reader off his guard. Then suddenly the coupling of competitive sports with "lower-class delinquents" and "atavistic elements," and you get the juxtaposition that Kenneth Burke has well called the method of "perspective by incongruity." But Veblen is never content to achieve his effect and let it go at that. He keeps turning the knife in the wound. Affecting a sustained gravity throughout, he works out a protracted parallel between leisure-class sportsmen and lower-class delinquents, introducing a running sequence of phrases whittled down to dagger effectiveness which impale his meaning forever in the reader's memory. Then, at the end of the paragraph, the clinching sentence, with the sudden stripping away of the academic ornateness he has affected, and the introduction of a homegrown phrase from the common speech.

One might say that Veblen's literary style has exactly the qualities of "ferocity and astuteness" which he attributes to the barbarian stage of cultural evolution. His whole writing life was a war, and every book and chapter a campaign in it. Someone has said of him that he had the craft, as well as the courage, of his viking ancestors. It is true that he had mastered the arts of protective coloration when it suited his needs. He used playfulness and paradox, an over-accented analysis delivered in an under-accented language. His most effective single literary device was to take words to which heavily opprobrious connotations attached, and to use them with a wide-eyed innocence in their original precise and literal sense. Phrases like "higher learning," "devout observances," "trained incapacity," "conscientious withdrawal of efficiency," come to mind. Veblen's use of the phrases "conspicuous consumption," "conspicuous leisure," "conspicuous waste" is as good an illustration as any. Presumably he means "conspicuous" only in the sense of "open" or "manifest." Yet in his use it takes over all the emotionally loaded meaning of "ostentatious" that it has in common speech; and as a result the whole of *The Leisure Class* becomes all the more memorably an analysis of the parvenu excesses of American life in the era of the big money. Veblen as ironist is the master of the dead-pan.

It would, however, be a mistake to think of his literary artistry as restricted to the details of phrase, language, style, indirection. In one sense the whole structure of Veblen's thought was less that of a rigidly scientific theorist than of an epic novelist who took cultural history as his arena. Like some other cultural historians—Dickens or Balzac, Proust or Romains—Veblen peopled his intellectual world with well-defined symbolic types.

Consider some of these type-figures to which Veblen's writing continually reverts. There is the Peaceful Savage—a Golden (New Stone) Age figure living before property and war had corrupted his Eden, richly endowed with the instinct of workmanship. In contrast there is the Predatory Barbarian who re-appears in various guises—as a war chieftain, as a member of the priestly caste, as a gentleman of the leisure class, as a dynastic ruler. Closely related is the Captain of Industry, who started as a useful and adventurous figure in society but, when the pecuniary occupations split off from the industrial, became specialized and degenerate as the Captain of Finance. His educational offshoot, the Captain of Education, was marginal in Veblen's analysis but bitter in his memory. Equally bitter somehow was the Captain of Industry's root-type on the American scene, the Country-Town Banker or Country-Town Merchant—"reliable, conciliatory, conservative, secretive, patient and prehensile." Then there is the Modern Scientist, who transmutes "idle curiosity" into new technologies. Related to him is the Engineer, upon whom devolves the strategic chance and the historic mission of taking over the technology and establishing the industrial republic. In Veblen's later books one encounters frequently the propertyless Common Man, caught between the discipline of the machine and the lure of the values of a business civilization.

One must add that the symbol upon which Veblen lavishes his most affectionate adjectives is the Heroic Freeholder of the primitive Icelandic community—the peaceful, sturdy farmer-craftsman-citizen whose passing Veblen laments in his captivating introduction to his translation of the *Laxdaela Saga* (1925), and also earlier in his supplementary notes to *Imperial Germany*. It is this genial primitive who seems to have been the touchstone of Veblen's cultural and moral values, and who keeps cropping up in new transformations in the peaceful savage, the scientist, the common man, the engineer.

Veblen remembers getting some of the ideas for his analysis of the leisure class from boyhood talks with his father; and we may guess that back of his father's talk lay some of the ruggedness of spirit and sharpness of feeling that had been developed by generations of land-hungry Scandinavian peasants. Nor can we omit as an influence the saga literature of Veblen's ancestry, in which he read deeply. He studied Old Norse while still at college, became absorbed with William Morris's work on the sagas, and made a trip to Europe in 1896 primarily to see Morris. With its ambivalent symbols of good and evil, Veblen's work has something of the quality of the ceaseless and universal struggle of Balder and Loki. The blood-feud somehow finds its way from the society the sagas depicted into the work of a lonely American scholar describing the deep splits and tensions in western civilization.

It is interesting to observe how many of Veblen's type-figures are symbols of alienation. The peaceful savage finds himself transferred to a complex of war and waste for which his native endowment is not suited. The scientist with idle curiosity seems an outsider in a world of the pragmatic and predatory. The propertyless common man stands outside the windows of a business civilization, looking in with half-longing, half-critical gaze. The engineer holds the key to the whole structure of industrial production, but he holds the key as a hireling who has not yet learned that he can run the machine for himself and his kind rather than for his masters.

To these must be added a figure from one of Veblen's marginal, but remarkable, essays[2]—that of the Jewish intellectual whose creativeness (as Veblen saw it) flows from his being a detached observer in the larger culture of the Western world at the same time that he is a renegade from the more restricted Jewish community. In one sense this was Veblen's self-portrait. He saw the foibles of contemporary institutions with the cold clarity which only a cultural outsider can summon. Yet he was also a renegade from the narrower world of the Midwestern Norse farm-community.

He was a lone figure, the man nobody knew—not even his family and friends, not even his warmest disciples. He was a man living in a shell formed by long years of alienation and hurt, and perhaps also by the glimpses of terror he had when he probed into the nature of institutions and the course of history. As with all great satirists, there was passion underneath everything Veblen wrote. It was the passion of a man whose sense of reality was so shattering that he had to turn aside from it and fashion for himself a mask of mockery and indirection. That mask was Thorstein Veblen's style, as it was his life.

Notes

1. See the Supplementary "footnote" at the back of *Imperial Germany*, 332–40; then the longer analysis, "The Country Town" in *Absentee Ownership*.
2. "The Intellectual Pre-eminence of Jews in Modern Europe," from *Essays in Our Changing Order*.

6

Oliver Wendell Holmes, Jr.

I (1943)

—1—

The social and intellectual world into which Oliver Wendell Holmes, Jr. was born was one which had cramped many of his contemporaries. Henry Adams, who was born into the same sort of environment at roughly the same time, was to complain afterward that it was a tight and orderly little world which had almost no relation to the chaotic forces in the universe outside—and he was to translate his querulousness into great literature. But in Holmes's case the sense of security, which might have acted as an inhibition, gave his energies release and made his purposes unerring. Karl Llewellyn has remarked that Holmes should have been born an Adams. But we can find the best of the New England world more clearly exposed in him than in Henry Adams, in whom it flowered differently, with a hothouse intensity as in the gardens of Rappacini's daughter in Hawthorne's tale. In Holmes's life there is a wholeness which the New England aristocracy at its best produced.

The first essay, "Holmes: A Personal History," was originally published to introduce *The Mind and Faith of Justice Holmes: His Speeches, Essays, Letters and Judicial Opinions,* edited by Max Lerner (Boston: Little, Brown, 1943), xvii–xlviii. The second essay, "Holmes Revisited: An Afterword Essay," was originally published in a new edition of *The Mind and Faith of Justice Holmes* (New Brunswick, N.J.: Transaction Publishers, 1989), 453–72. Lerner provided commentary on Holmes's writings throughout the book.

His father, Oliver Wendell Holmes, was not only the poet, wit, and "Autocrat of the Breakfast Table," but a physician and medical researcher not without a place in the history of the fight against disease. Among Holmes's ancestors, who traced their stock back to early colonial times, the religious intensity of an earlier Calvinism had been transmuted into a sense of public service, and the concern with intellectual values led by an easy transition to a concern for intellectual freedom and civil liberties; just as in the English aristocracy the energy that earlier went into the Wars of the Roses went later into Parliament and the civil service. Holmes took a frank pride in his ancestry. "All my three names," he wrote in his autobiographical sketch for the Harvard Class Album, "designate families from which I am descended." At another point in this sketch of himself he says, "I don't believe in gushing much in these college biographies." It is important both that he felt this sentiment and that he felt also the need to repress it.

Holmes was born March 8, 1841, in Boston. His father, in a letter the next day, wrote that someone who might in the future be addressed as President of the United States was at the moment "content with scratching his face and sucking his forefinger." Boston at that time, despite a population of less than 100,000, was the commercial capital of New England and the intellectual capital of America. The New England of which it formed part had passed the peak of its preoccupation with trading, ship-building and shipping. Textile mills were springing up to which the younger people were increasingly to turn. It was a New England in which the roots of a deep religious feeling still persisted; a New England which had produced the self-reliant militancy of Emerson and Thoreau, in which Hawthorne was writing his dark guilt-laden tales, and to which Melville was soon to return to digest his South Seas odyssey. Abolitionism, feminism, transcendentalism and Fourierism were churning the consciences of men and women, reform movements jostled the genteel tradition, and the swarming wharves lay dreaming of their past side by side with the rising squalor of the new mill towns.

In this New England and this Boston young Holmes grew up. His father's rising fame as what Parrington has called "the Beacon Street wit" meant that the boy had access to some of the best table conversation in Boston—that is to say, in America. Doctor Holmes was at the heart of the salon and literary club life of Boston. Theodore Parker and Wendell Phillips, central figures in the religious and social enlightenment of the time, the secular Savonarolas of Boston, were friends of the family and without doubt influenced the boy's thinking. Ralph Waldo Emerson was also a visitor, and to the boy he was "Uncle Waldo." Holmes's father scarcely shared the radicalism of either Parker or Emerson. His strictures on his society inflicted scratches but drew no blood. His novel, *Elsie Venner,* set Boston parlors aflutter because it pricked a whole variety of reformist intellectual bubbles. He was a conservative in all his social views except religion, in which he had sharpened himself into a Unitarian knife dedicated to hollowing out the darkness of Calvinism. He blasted with his wit the millennial and crochety doctrines of the social reformers of his day. Young Holmes was thus held secure in a haven of social orthodoxy without being wholly shut off from the tumult of innovation.

But I do not mean to imply that his boyhood was overly intellectual. He was active in all the boyhood sports, learning something of the aspects of Boston which were a closed book to his elders, spending delightful vacation months in the Holmes summer house near Pittsfield, on land which once belonged to Jacob Wendell, one of his ancestors. The impression of the Lenox meadows and the Berkshire Hills was to stay with Holmes as an enduring image of New England beauty. "I love granite rocks and barberry bushes," he was to write sixty years later, "because with them were my earliest joys that reach back through the past eternity of my life." And the boy also bought himself some etching tools and as an amateur developed a taste for art which was to be one of his abiding preoccupations.

Holmes's education was that of an intellectual aristocrat. Like others of the gentility he attended Mr. Dixwell's Latin School. The skeptical mind will go back to the chapters of Thorstein Veblen's *Theory of the Leisure Class* dealing with the place of dead languages in the education of live young men. But Holmes, for all his bantering disbelief in the classics, made these languages a living instrument in his later writing, and he drew, as those earlier realists Machiavelli and Montesquieu had drawn, upon the culture from which the languages came for some of his insights into his own culture. He was to draw upon this source also for the spirit of the Roman stoics that informed him.

Following his family tradition he went to Harvard, and entered in the fall of 1857 with the class of 1861. With him at Harvard were the elite of New England, and a sprinkling of the Southern aristocracy as well. Harvard was at that time the best university in the country. It was awakening to the dawning world of American science, and it was preparing men to fill the strategic posts both in the maintenance of wealth and power in this world and the propitiation of the gods of the world beyond. The Harvard of Holmes's day stood midway between what Van Wyck Brooks has called the "flowering" of New England, and its "Indian summer." New England's flowering had taken place largely in the intellectual group outside of the college; its Indian summer was to be focused largely on the group inside the college. Between these two eras the Harvard of Holmes's time was a place through which the winds of contemporary doctrine did not blow very strongly. Holmes was interested in ideas, but except for some flurries about Abolition he had little of the radicalism of youth about contemporary issues. He had a talent for friendship, a capacity for vivid talk, and a gusto for life which made him an outstanding member of the class. He was absorbed with literature, philosophy and art. He belonged to the private clubs, the honor societies, the "liberal" Christian Union. He edited the literary magazine and wrote a prize essay on Plato. He continued with his interest in etchings, publishing in the college magazine an article on Albrecht Dürer.

But despite the placid and sheltered life he led, there were conflicts of ideas and clashes of social forces outside that were to affect him deeply, and to which to a degree he responded. Darwin published his *Origin of Species* while Holmes was in college, and his theories of the struggle for existence and the survival of the fittest were beginning to form the staple of debate. And before Darwin was Malthus, giving a similar sense of the cramped environment which, as Holmes was later to put it, pushed many lives always and inevitably down the deadline. Holmes's thought was thus early nurtured on death and conflict, and his later absorption with both may be traced to these early influences. And outside the walls of Harvard there were the growing tensions of what was being termed the "irrepressible conflict" between the North and South, between two economies and two conceptions of life. The men of Holmes's class, like those of the classes of our own decade, felt the shadow of the impending war and sought to pierce in their troubled way the darkness that stretched beyond it. Thirty years after the war, in his speech "The Soldier's Faith," Holmes thought he had caught a glimpse of its meaning—that "combat and pain still are the portion of man," that "the struggle for life is the order of the world, at which it is vain to repine."

—2—

The war came—came even before the class could graduate, so that Holmes, who like his father before him had been chosen Class Poet, had to compose his poem while training with his regiment. But since the regiment remained near Boston for a while, Holmes was able to graduate with his class. War proved to be Holmes's real college and testing ground.

It left a deep mark on him. He knew, as he later put it, that he had to "share the passion and action of his time at peril of being judged not to have lived." He learned on the battlefields of the Civil War what the realities of life were like. He enlisted in the Infantry, joining finally the Twentieth Massachusetts, a regiment which saw ample fighting through the war, with five eighths of its men either killed or wounded. Just before it moved from its training field in Massachusetts to the front, Holmes was commissioned First Lieutenant. "One day," Elizabeth Shepley Sergeant tells us, "as he was walking down Beacon Hill with Hobbes's *Leviathan* in his hand," Holmes learned of his commission. "So the young officer whom we may see in his uniform at Langdell Hall, at the Harvard Law School, with his visored cap on his knee, in one of those touching little faded photographs which were a sop to parental love—a mere lad trusting and vulnerable, like all lads who have fought all the great wars—went forth to a baptism that he has never forgotten." At the Battle of Ball's Bluff, on October 21, 1861, he received a wound in the region of the breast which at the time seemed likely to end fatally, but it proved finally to have missed both the heart and the lung. Home on leave, he is described in one of his father's letters as receiving visitors *"en grand seigneur.* I envy my white Othello with a semicircle of young Desdemonas about him listening to the often told story which they will have over again."

As soon as he was well, Holmes returned to the front. At the Battle of Antietam, on September 17, 1862, the Twentieth Infantry found itself outflanked by the Confederates and had to retreat with great casualties. Holmes, now a captain, was again wounded, this time through the neck. His father received the news by telegraph, and immediately set out to Maryland to find him. In an *Atlantic Monthly* article, "My Hunt After the Captain," he later told of how he searched along the road to Antietam which was clogged with stragglers and wounded, searched through hospitals and houses, until finally he traced him to a train leaving from Hagerstown for Philadelphia. He went through the cars until he found him, the captain, "my first-born whom I had sought through many cities." And thus for Holmes it was Boston again and another period of convalescence.

Holmes came back to the fighting in November 1862, only to be stricken with an undignified attack of dysentery. When he was well enough to be back in the ranks, he lived through the disaster of Fredericksburg under General Burnside in December 1862. On May 3, 1863, the Union forces under General Hooker fought a second battle near Fredericksburg, at Marye's Hill. There, while his company was seeking to capture a position, Holmes was struck in the heel by a piece of shrapnel, the bone splintered and the ligaments torn. The third of his wounds, it sent Holmes again to Boston, and for some time there was fear that he would lose his leg, but it healed excellently. When he returned to the army in January 1864, it was as aide-de-camp to a general; then he became a provost marshal. When he was mustered out of service on July 17, 1864, it was as Lieutenant-Colonel.

He had fought in some of the great battles of the war, although he missed Gettysburg and the battles at the close. He had seen his closest friends killed by his side. He had learned that "as long as man dwells upon the globe, his destiny is battle, and he has to take the chances of war." And with that recognition there had come a faith in the purposes, even though not fully known, for which men are called to fight, and in the strategy, even though not fully understood, that governs the campaign. Holmes never forgot these experiences. He had gone into the war a sensitive boy with nerves delicately organized and with an imagination, which does not often serve a soldier well. He had a hunger for adventure and distinction. He had had his chance at both, and at twenty-three had already "shared the incommunicable experience of war," lived through the most moving destiny that was given to his generation.

—3—

When he came back from the war, he turned to the problem of a career. His interest in philosophy was not the stuff of which professional philosophers are made. He had tried etching but did not think he was good enough. A literary career was more likely to be a by-product than a matter of direct purpose. Holmes decided that his new battleground would be the law. It was a barren ground and an unyielding one. To extract from it something great and enduring required both work and faith. Holmes was ready to offer both in full measure. It is not beyond our scope to guess that in Holmes's choice of the law rather than literature or philosophy or art, there was some buried Puritan tropism which made him turn where his strength and imagination would be most far-reachingly called upon.

The Harvard Law School, when Holmes entered it in the fall of 1864, was not yet in its great period. There were several teachers whom Holmes enjoyed. But it was not yet the day of Langdell and Ames, and the case method had not yet been introduced into Harvard. The returned soldier studied hard, so hard that his friends grew worried about him. But he knew also how to "slay the dust of pleading by certain sprinklings" which he "managed to contrive" with his friends. He took his degree in January 1866, and then set off for a visit to England armed with some letters of introduction from his father's friend John Lothrop Motley to John Stuart Mill and to Thomas Hughes, the author of the Tom Brown books. But the person he saw most of was Leslie Stephen, with whom he had already struck an acquaintance in Boston on one of those visits of recuperation from the battlefield. Holmes went on walking tours in England, joined the Alpine Club and climbed mountains in Switzerland with Stephen.

He came back to America, to be admitted to the bar in 1867. He joined a law firm and lived in a room on the top floor of his father's house on Beacon Street, overlooking the Charles River. For three years he worked hard as an apprentice in the firm, but after that his rise was rapid. His success was like an irresistible force. In 1870, before he was yet thirty, he became a lecturer in constitutional law at Harvard. In the same year, he assumed the editorship of the *American Law Journal*, which he held for three years and which gave him the chance to read widely in both the Anglo-American and Continental legal literature. Also, by compelling him to write comments on current cases, it gave his legal studies a sharpness of focus. In 1873, he edited the twelfth edition of Kent's *Commentaries on American Law,* in four volumes, with a considerable body of notes from his own pen. The year before, in 1872, Holmes married Miss Fanny Dixwell, the daughter of the principal of the Latin School he had attended, a high-spirited girl with a capacity for wit and raillery and a mind of her own. In 1874 he made a second trip to England, taking Mrs. Holmes along. There they met another recently married pair, Frederick Pollock and his wife. Both young men were interested in law and legal history, each found in the other a kinship of taste and outlook. Thus began the friendship of almost sixty years which was to be renewed by transatlantic trips and to be sustained by the now famous exchange of letters.

Holmes had to work hard for success, but he was so situated that success responded to his work. He seemed to have all the gifts the gods could offer. He had a handsome presence, a sharp and nimble mind, a great family tradition, a gift for flashing phrase, an elegance of language, a brilliant war record, a "grand tour" in Europe, a smattering of philosophy, a sense of self-sufficiency and of his own destiny, and just enough irresponsibility to set off his more substantial qualities. He taught in the classroom, he wrote editorials and articles, he read his fill of the English yearbooks, he had a chance to ponder the vistas of legal history and the relation of legal systems to their cultures.

Thus passed the decade of the '70's. It was a decade which was already under the shadow of a grasping and predatory industrialism. The onward march of American capitalist enterprise was opening up a continent and rifling as well as organizing its treasures. The legal profession was in this march a camp follower. Some of his later speeches to law students indicate that Holmes was through these years saddened at the sordid commercialism he saw, both among industrialists and among lawyers. Yet he managed to keep from being tainted by it. He had a strong enough stomach to confront it and yet the vision to look beyond to the more distant perspectives that opened up the meaning and even heroism of law.

The beginning of the '80's found Holmes moving forward in his chosen profession of legal teaching and scholarship and commentary. In 1880 he was asked to deliver a course of Lowell Lectures, and chose "The Common Law" as his topic. The lectures had ease, learning, and grace, and yet along with these there was a tough technical sense which impressed the young men who heard them as much as the delicacy of phrasing delighted them. Holmes worked hard preparing his lectures for the press, often late into the night after a day of work devoted to other duties. The book appeared in 1881 and came close to opening something of a new era in Anglo-American jurisprudence. It led to a professorship at Harvard Law School in 1882. He taught only a term, because hard on the heels of the Harvard appointment came the offer of a seat on the Supreme Judicial Court of Massachusetts. It was a dramatic moment, as Holmes tells of it in a later speech, when "Shattuck came out and told me that in one hour the Governor would submit my name to the council for a judgeship, if notified of my assent. It was a stroke of lightning which changed the whole course of my life."

Holmes could hardly have hesitated seriously between the two appointments. He had already stipulated in accepting the professorship that he should be free to accept a judgeship. After consulting with his partner, Shattuck, he took the Court. Nor had the appointment come wholly as a surprise. He had already some years earlier had his eye on judicial office, and had been fluttered by the rumor that he might get a Federal District Court judgeship, which had finally gone to another man. While legal practice and writing and teaching would have suited his ambitions well enough, he wanted to have a hand more directly in shaping law. His grandfather on his mother's side, Charles Jackson, had also been a member of the Massachusetts Supreme Judicial Court. His father was delighted with the news. "To think of it," he wrote a friend, "—my little boy a Judge and able to send me to jail if I don't behave myself."

—4—

Holmes's appointment to the Court came in December 1882, when he was forty-one. In the group pictures of the Court that have come down to us, Holmes as the most recent member sits at the extreme left, looking almost a stripling in comparison with the rest. It was a Court of rather old men, and during the decade following Holmes's appointment it had a turnover of six or seven members. Holmes had a genius for friendship and a respect for the quality of a man even when his views were greatly divergent from his own. On the deaths of his colleagues Holmes was in several instances called upon to deliver a memorial speech, which he did with both taste and insight. In fact, one suspects that one or two of these commemorative speeches may outlast the work of their subjects.

There is not much detail available, outside of the Law Reports, about the Holmes of this period. He lived at the center of a lively group of friends, and he continued his father's tradition of good talk and zestful living. But he was careful also of the judicial decencies. Owen Wister tells of Holmes's tactful but firm refusal to accompany him to a bar for a drink because "I don't somehow cotton to the notion of our judges hobnobbing in hotel bars and saloons." We get a picture of Holmes at forty-five, strikingly handsome, "lean as a race-horse," with hair turning gray, talking colorfully through an evening under the stimulus of "two brilliant listeners—handsome ladies both." He made further trips to England in 1882, 1889, 1896, 1898, and 1901. During this period, within a brief span of time, Holmes lost his mother, brother, and sister by death. His father was left alone, and the Justice and his wife moved into the old house with him, remaining as companions until his death in 1894. In 1899 the death of Chief Justice Walbridge A. Field led to the appointment of Holmes to the chief-justiceship, which he held until he went to Washington.

If Holmes's tenure on the Massachusetts Court from 1882 to 1902 is one of the least known periods of his life, it was also one of the most important. It included the two decades from the age of forty to sixty when most men have already laid down the shaping lines of their thought and done their creative work. In the nation's history these were years of industrial development, political turmoil, cultural crudeness. They were the years during which business enterprise crystallized into a structure of corporate monopoly, years of labor's awakening, of Republican domination and Populist and Socialist stirrings; years of laissez faire and of the emergence of an industrial elite; years of the "robber barons" and of the consolidation of capitalist power; years of materialist values.

Holmes was aware of some of these things, although both by inclination and judicial duty he kept shy of them. He was particularly sensitive to the coarseness of the cultural tone of the nation. In several of his Memorial Day addresses delivered during this period he speaks, with a note almost of despair, of the crass values of the men of wealth and those of the legal profession who devoted themselves to the pursuit of wealth. But Holmes saw other things as well. Unlike the liberals of the Godkin and *Nation* school he did not regard the growth of business and labor organizations as an unrelieved evil. He accepted both as part of the laws of social development.

What remedies, then, did he see for the social struggles of the day and for the slackening of the national fiber? On the whole his were the views of an aristocratic conservative who did not care much either for business values or for the talk of reformers and the millennial dreams of the humanitarians. Holmes watched Populism, trade unions, socialism as they developed and spread. He had enough curiosity to read their literature, enough good sense not to be frightened as others were by these threats to his world. As an economist he clung to the conviction that most of the reform movements were based not upon economic reasoning but upon dramatic simplification. But as a judge he thought it no business of his to interpose obstacles in the path of legislative experiments with the new ideas. Hence his famous dissenting opinions in the trade-union cases of *Vegelahn v. Guntner* and *Plant v. Woods.* Hence also his dissents from the judicial prohibition of municipal ownership of coal and wood yards and local option for women suffrage. Holmes relied ultimately on the strength of the American tradition, the self-balancing tendencies within social experiment and the competition of ideas, and the inner cogency of the qualities which he loosely called "race."

His few public utterances on these qualities and on the need for maintaining unslackened the great military tradition of the nation laid him open to attack. The *Nation* group called one of his speeches in 1895 "sentimental jingoism." Holmes's comment in his letters to Pollock was withering, but in public he said nothing. Similarly he was attacked as a "Communist" (the memory of the Paris Commune was still close enough to shape the epithet) for his dissents in the labor cases and the cases involving local autonomy. But except among the fanatics his prestige was steadily growing. Although his famous opinions were in the constitutional area, the bulk of his day-by-day work was in the fields outside of it—tort, agency, contract, criminal law. His decisions were increasingly cited by other courts. Several articles on him appeared in the legal periodicals—an unusual tribute for a judge on a state court. We do not know whether he was impatient about speaking from a restricted forum. We only know that these were years of training and discipline for him, when he tested his judicial notions and his philosophy against the hard material of the cases that came his way and against the deeply ingrained notions of his colleagues.

—5—

In 1902 Justice Horace Gray of the United States Supreme Court retired from the Court. Since Gray was a Massachusetts man, it was natural for President Theodore Roosevelt to turn to another Massachusetts man to replace him. Roosevelt at once thought of Holmes. He was attracted by the combination of the scholar with a distinguished military career, and the statesman with a literary and historical bent: after all, he found in himself the confirmation that such a blend was a good one. He was attracted also by Holmes's high reputation for legal ability and learning. And as for the dissents which Holmes had returned in the labor cases and which had brought down upon him the contumely of the men of substance, Roosevelt was not one to balk at that. In fact, he probably saw that he could turn it to advantage. The temper of the country was far more radical than any of the Republican Presidents had been able to understand. Roosevelt was getting into the swing of his trust-busting phase. He knew, deeply conservative as he was, that his social order could be preserved not by turning his back on the storm but by riding and commanding it.

The hitch lay in one speech that Holmes had made—the one on John Marshall. It was undoubtedly one of Holmes's great utterances and one of his justest judgments of a man's talent and his place in history. But to Roosevelt it seemed ominous. Roosevelt liked Marshall's broad interpretation of the national power. He saw him as the very archetype of the judge, "a constitutional statesman believing in great party principles, and willing to continue the Constitution so that the nation can develop on the broadest lines." Roosevelt knew that Holmes was a nationalist, and had long before written ecstatically to Lodge about Holmes's fervid 1895 speech celebrating the martial qualities. But his comments on the Federalist Chief Justice bothered Roosevelt. Holmes had preferred to view Marshall not so much as the single hero but rather as "a great ganglion in the nerves of society, or, to vary the figure, a strategic point in the campaign of history, and part of his greatness consists in his being *there.*"

What Roosevelt did not want on the Court, his letter to Lodge continued, was a Taney who was "a curse to our national life because he belonged to the wrong party." What he wanted was "a statesman of the national type," "a constructive statesman, constantly keeping in mind . . . his relations with his fellow statesmen who in other branches of the government are striving . . . to advance the ends of government." Roosevelt wanted assurances. "I should like to know that Judge Holmes was in entire sympathy with our views, that is with your views and mine and Judge Gray's, for instance." To select a man "who was not absolutely sane and sound on the great national policies" would be "an irreparable wrong to the nation." Roosevelt instructed Lodge to show his letter to Holmes "if it became necessary." There is no indication that he did: Lodge's answer must have been reassuring enough to appease Roosevelt's doubts. The President probably made more inquiries during the month that followed Gray's resignation. Finally, having obtained the *imprimatur* of Senator Hoar of Massachusetts, he announced Holmes's appointment in August 1902. It went to the Senate early in December, the Senate acted on it in very short order, and Holmes became a member of the United States Supreme Court on December 6, 1902.

For a while all went well between the President and his new Associate Justice. Roosevelt liked artistic and literary men around him, and made Holmes part of the group of "Roosevelt Familiars" which at one time or another included Lodge, Beveridge, John Hay, Saint-Gaudens, Owen Wister, and Jules Jusserand, with Lincoln Steffens and Finley Peter Dunne on the margin. He seems to have warmed to Holmes with his background of Civil War battles, his wit, his epigrams, his talk of books and etchings. The Holmeses, who had settled in Washington in 1903 and bought the house on I Street in which they were to live to the end, were often at the White House entertainments. But Holmes made no commitments, whether outer or inner, whether political or intellectual. The honeymoon was doomed to be short-lived and in a little more than a year it was rudely shattered. What shattered it was Holmes's dissent in Roosevelt's great trust-busting case, involving the Northern Securities Company. Despite the hopes Roosevelt pinned on him, Holmes voted against the Government, writing one of the two dissenting opinions in the case. Roosevelt was furious. "I could carve out of a banana," he is reported (perhaps apocryphally) to have cried, "a justice with more backbone than that."

He was wrong. Holmes had enough backbone to stand up against the man who had appointed him only a short while before, and who had showered on him the lavishness of his warmth and personality. Roosevelt was so single-minded in his determination to have his way in the *Northern Securities* matter that he was obtuse in his judgment of what made Holmes tick.

Nevertheless the whole Roosevelt-Holmes relationship—including the President's letter to Lodge, his doubts, his final decision to appoint Holmes, and his fury at Holmes's dissent—deserves some analysis. It involves questions that cut deep into the nature of the American governmental system and into the personality of both principles in the affair. The commentators have tended to deal too harshly with Roosevelt. The curious thing is that among those most vehement in condemning him have been the liberals. At the same time that they assert that a Peckham or a Sutherland reads his economic views into the Constitution, they condemn Roosevelt for having acted on a similar assumption. It is time that we stripped ourselves of the latent hypocrisy in this. Present-day constitutional writers pretty generally recognize that Presidents do tend to appoint justices whose thinking runs along their own grooves, and that justices cannot wholly escape reading their social views into their opinions. If both these propositions are without truth, then a quarter-century of constitutional commentary has been either wasted or misunderstood.

There were, however, extraordinary items in this instance which must qualify the propositions just stated. One was Roosevelt's brashness. He had the temerity to take the assumption on which his predecessors had acted implicitly, at least since John Adams appointed John Marshall to the Court, and to put it quite explicitly in his letter to Lodge. Roosevelt thought of himself as a good deal of an iconoclast. The man who said that he could not show J. P. Morgan or Carnegie or Hill the same regard he had for Peary the explorer, or Bury and Rhodes the historians—the man who brought cowboys and prize fighters and big-game hunters into the White House much as his kinsman-successor brings movie stars—was not a man to balk at putting down on paper the hidden assumptions on which his predecessors had acted. He was writing to Henry Cabot Lodge, as one man of the world to another. He was at that time in earnest about his antitrust crusade. He knew that there was lined up against him on the Court a minority that might easily be turned into a potential majority, and he was determined that he would not willingly appoint to the Court a judge who might consciously turn the tide against him. As Charles Beard has pointed out, Roosevelt wanted to see the harshness of corporation law tempered by a humanistic jurisprudence. Unless a President believes in government by deadlock, which he is not likely to do, he must appoint to the Court judges who are roughly of his own persuasion—not necessarily from his own political party but within the ambit of his own world-view. Only thus can he keep the various parts of his Administration moving together as an Administration. In our own time we have had a dramatic illustration of this in the New Deal constitutional crisis and in the Court appointments following it. Franklin D. Roosevelt found out that justices with a world-view reaching back decades before the era of depression and the fascist threat were able to burke the whole meaning of his Administration.

The second item was that Holmes was not the ordinary judge, any more than Theodore Roosevelt was the ordinary President. Holmes had a firmly developed judicial method to a greater degree than any other judge of that day. He had already shown this quality on the state court, as the President might easily have discovered if he had studied his opinions. He had shown an impassioned indifference to the "hydraulic pressures" that converge on "great cases," a meticulous regard for the strict legal profile of a case, an inclination to let the legislature have its way, a sophistication that prevented him from projecting his economic philosophy and calling it the Constitution—and that in an era when it would have been easy enough to identify his views with the welfare of the nation.

But this did not mean that Holmes was all compact of austerity, a god who had pierced beyond the human impulses in him. If Roosevelt had relied on Holmes to give the Sherman Act full sway because he had practiced judicial *laissez faire* toward other legislative acts, he failed to reckon with the fact that Holmes was not an Olympian but a philosopher—which is a wholly different matter. His judicial philosophy of leaving the legislature alone came from a deeper philosophy of leaving the cosmos alone. And when the strict meaning of restraint of trade at the common law coincided with this philosophy, Holmes was clad in a double armor of conviction. Roosevelt might have anticipated Holmes's *Northern Securities* dissent if he had studied Holmes's Massachusetts labor dissents. Taking into account Holmes's Darwinism and the sense of accepting the limits that the universe imposed upon him, they might well have given warning to any President hell-bent on antitrust enforcement. There was a lack of economic realism in Holmes's opinion. But it was natural for Holmes, who approached the case without a feeling for the realities of economic power involved, to accept monopolies as well as trade unions as part of the laws of the organization and the equilibrium of life. Holmes's reasoning from the history of the common-law doctrine of restraint of trade unions was learned and subtle. But the real logic of his *Northern Securities* dissent was poles apart from the logic of Justices White, Fuller, and Peckham, who made up the rest of the minority, or from the logic of Roosevelt.

These dissenting justices acted from an image of an economic universe. Roosevelt acted from an image of a political universe. Holmes acted from the image of a philosophic universe. And because he had so firm a nucleus of conviction, he was unperturbed by Roosevelt's lashings and his concentrated fury.

The appointment to the United States Supreme Court was for Holmes the culminating opportunity in a career of thought and effort. Behind him was a long row of cases—thousands of them; before him stretched thousands more. Each case required courage of heart, sharpness of mind, wisdom of judgment, cunning of hand in contriving the right words.

It was because Holmes felt thus that he was troubled at the comments in the press that greeted his appointment. The appointment itself went through the Senate smoothly enough. But when Holmes's name was first announced, he was irritated at the quality of the "stacks of notices." "The immense majority of them," he wrote to Pollock, "seem devoid of personal discrimination or courage. They are so favorable that they make my nomination a popular success but they have the flabbiness of American ignorance." They generally mentioned Holmes's *Vegelahn* dissent, and insinuated that its author "has partial views, is brilliant but not very sound." And then there follows in Holmes's letter one of the rare instances of a *cri du coeur*: "It makes one sick when he has broken his heart in trying to make every word living and real to see a lot of duffers . . . talking with the sanctity of print in a way that at once discloses to the knowing eye that literally they don't know anything about it." Thus Holmes had his taste of running the gantlet of lay opinion on a national scale. It was not a severe ordeal as such things go. Chief Justice Taney before him went through a far worse one when his nomination came to the Senate and an outcry arose that he had been Andrew Jackson's "pliant instrument" in the Bank controversy. Justice Brandeis was to have an even bitterer cup to drink when the corporate powers and their spokesmen in the Bar Association sought in a protracted Senate fight in 1916 to block his appointment. For Holmes's sensitive spirit either of these major attacks would have been a catastrophe, but his own minor one was sufficiently galling.

Holmes was not a young man when he took his place on the Court.

He was sixty-one. Two members of the Court, Justices White and McKenna, were younger than he. Of the rest, there was no one as much as ten years his senior. It was not a brilliant Court nor an enlightened one. The two great justices who had made judicial history in the last decade of the century—Justices Miller and Field—were both gone. Those who were left were not even half-gods. Chief Justice Fuller was a nonentity. Of the rest, only Justices White, Harlan, H. B. Brown, and McKenna had more than average ability, and of these only White and Harlan had real stature. All of them, with the exception of Harlan, were deeply conservative, if not reactionary in their social outlook. The main outlines of judicial strategy had already been laid down—first, in the battle over the interpretation of "due process" between the cohorts led by Field and those led by Miller up to the middle of the 1880's, and then by the sequence of decisions in the 1890's breathing a bleak laissez-faire philosophy. It was clear that the whole duty of a Supreme Court Justice lay in filling in the outlines of these decisions and in using constitutional law as a way of entrenching the system of economic power.

Holmes refused to live up to the rules of the game so conceived. He had no intention of conscripting the legal Constitution as he saw it to the uses of the economic Constitution, any more than he would conscript it to the uses of a political program. If he disappointed President Roosevelt in the *Northern Securities* case, he had many more disappointments in store for those on the other side of the fence. His first opinion in 1903 (*Otis v. Parker*) showed clearly his intention to give state legislative action a broad margin of tolerance, even if it implied a system of state regulation of economic activity. But it was not until 1905, in the *Lochner* case, that Holmes found his real stride on the Supreme Court.

—7—

There were three important turning points in Holmes's career on the Supreme Court. One was the *Lochner* dissent in 1905, the second was the coming of Justice Brandeis to the Court in 1916, the third was America's entrance into the war soon after, bringing in its wake a group of civil liberties cases which were to occupy Holmes from 1917 for almost a decade. Each of these is worth more than passing mention.

With the *Lochner* case Holmes really began firing his big judicial guns. Up to that time no really great issue had arisen, although Holmes had given distress to the camp followers of both sides. The *Lochner* dissent marked a turning point. It had every index of having been painfully thought out. It had the clarity of a trumpet call after which there could be no retreat. There have been those who have read Holmes's dissent as mainly an exercise in satire. Charles Beard, for example, speaks of Holmes "allowing his genial wit to melt the frosty verbalism of the law." "Genial" is a curious adjective to apply in this case. Similarly when Thorstein Veblen a few years earlier published his *Theory of the Leisure Class* the critics viewed it as an elaborate literary satire. Like Veblen, but in his very different way, Holmes was very much in earnest. He had not entirely forgotten the military strategy of his Civil War experience. He knew that the thrust at the enemy must be sudden and sharp, with all your might. "When you strike at a king," Emerson had told him long before, "you must kill him." Holmes was striking not only at Justice Peckham's majority opinion in the *Lochner* case but at the whole dark and intolerant judicial tradition which Peckham was expressing.

While Holmes's motivations were those of a legal craftsman determined not to see his craft distorted, the consequences of his opinions reached to the living standards of the common man and his struggles for dignity. The *Lochner* dissent did not stand alone. In the quarter-century of judicial labors that remained to him, Holmes fought for the right of the legislature to promote equality of bargaining power for workers, for the right of social experiment, for state and federal social legislation, for the right of the people to develop an effective tax administration, for adequate governmental power in peace and war. He fought with courage and with subtlety. Where by yielding ground slightly he could get the rest of the Court to go along with him, he did so. But where no compromise was possible, he continued to speak forth, with a magisterial manner and a summary brevity which infuriated his opponents just as much as it delighted his followers.

And followers he did have. For the young lawyers and the students still in the law schools, looking about them for some figure who rose above the deadening plains of legal commercialism and judicial complacency, some veteran who could give them hope that they would not become the mercenaries of a corporate economy, Holmes became a symbol. His opinions were caught up by the law journals, which were just becoming a force. Those who fought to temper the harshness of corporate power and those who, whatever their views, sought in law a vitality that he restored to it, combined in homage to him. They read him avidly, they quoted the Holmesian nuggets they discovered, they wrote about him. Holmes was deeply pleased and yet he was basically unmoved. The real motivation came from deep within, from his craftsman's conception of the judicial power, his philosophy of its place in a limited universe, his unflagging sense of being part of a long campaign of history.

—8—

But it was a lonely fight. For a decade and a half, aside from occasional support from Harlan and then from Charles Evans Hughes, Holmes stood pretty much alone. But in 1916 with the appointment of Louis D. Brandeis to the Court, this was changed.

The relationship between Holmes and Brandeis was a complex one. Brandeis brought to the Court a first-rate legal mind, an arduous education in social realities, and a fund of economic knowledge. He brought a seriousness of intent and an unwavering will. While there can be no question that Brandeis exercised a substantial influence over Holmes, we must remember that not only the contours of Holmes's mind but also its basic propulsions had already become fixed by the time Brandeis came to the Court. The influence was vastly overestimated by men like Chief Justice Taft, who allowed his judgment to be swayed by his fear and prejudice. When he said in a letter that Holmes enabled Brandeis to cast two votes instead of one, it was a peevish utterance and he was unjust to both men.

They had known each other in Boston when Brandeis was a young lawyer just out of Harvard, and Holmes a state court judge interested in the affairs of the school and its graduates. But after that, except for Brandeis' appearances before the Court in Washington as a counsel, they had little contact until Brandeis became a colleague. There can be no question that Holmes was struck by Brandeis' complete integrity as well as by his vast knowledge, by his ethical sense, by his almost agonizing determination to do the right thing. "There goes a *good* man," he would say to Mrs. Holmes when Brandeis left their home. But the differences between the two were profound. Brandeis was an economist where Holmes was a philosopher. He was austere where Holmes,

except when he was deeply aroused, tended to be whimsical, para-
doxical and gay. Holmes was the author of *The Common Law*, "The
Soldier's Faith," and numerous delightful and discursive letters to Pollock and others. Brandeis was the author of *Other People's Money*, and
when he wrote letters they were like communiqués from a battlefield,
with the rattle of artillery sounding in their one-two-three memorandum
sequence. Holmes thought in terms of a finite universe of which man
was only an infinitesimal part, and was skeptical of any sort of moral
imperialism, including social reform. Brandeis saw the emergence of a
concentrated corporate power within the commonwealth, of a state
within a state, and bent every effort toward making real his dream of a
Periclean democracy on the American plains. Brandeis was Holmes's
conscience, and Holmes still had enough of the Puritan in him to have
a slumbering conscience that could be awakened and fortified. But
while Brandeis, as a conscience, bolstered Holmes's legal views and
strengthened his more liberal impulses, he could not change Holmes in
essentials. Despite all his proddings, Holmes could never read any of
the economic treatises Brandeis urged on him. They were "improv-
ing"—an epithet Holmes applied to anything that disturbed his sense
of a limited universe. Brandeis he considered one of the "onward and
upward" fellows. The tastes of his friend, Sir Frederick Pollock, although not nearly so deep a person as Brandeis, were nearer his own.

—9—

With the outbreak of the World War, the Court was confronted by
new problems. Holmes had never been an anti-militarist. He had always seen peace as "a little space of calm in the midst of the tempestu-
ous untamed streaming of the world." "High and dangerous action,"
he had said, "teaches us to believe as right beyond dispute things for
which our doubting minds are slow to find words of proof." If Holmes
had been less of a philosopher, he would have come close to being
something of a fire-eater. He had been increasingly troubled by noting
among the young secretaries who came to him from the Harvard Law
School, part of whose job was to read aloud to him and with whom he
discussed life as well as law, an increasing skepticism of patriotic
values. He had scant belief in this "experimenting in negations." And
yet it is characteristic of him that while with the outbreak of the war
he had far fewer words to eat and fewer attitudes to erase than anyone

else, he did not go as far as others in uncritical glorifications of the war. This was partly because his whole method was to proceed by continuities rather than by mutations, partly because his critical mind sought always to balance the excesses he saw around him. It was also characteristic of Holmes that one who all his life had had a fighting faith should now be so moderate in trumpeting it and so wary of its abuse.

He had always liked the English without being an Anglophile. In England's moments of greatest danger during the war Holmes in his letters to Pollock rejoiced with the English victories, expressed concern at the reverses and the bombing raids on London, shared Pollock's impatience with President Wilson's conduct of foreign affairs in the years before America's entrance into the war, and would probably have preferred his former colleague Hughes in the Presidency after 1916. He was, to be sure, civilized enough not to let the war wipe out his feeling of esteem for the German legal scholars and historians whom he had known. But when the hour of decision came for America, Holmes had no hesitation. "Between two groups that want to make inconsistent kinds of a world, I see no remedy except force."

Holmes did not idealize the actual experience of war. He had learned what it was like. But he knew long before our own discovery of it the slackness of individual social will out of which the pacifist impulses grow. Philosophically he accepted war as part of his universe. He had, moreover, a belief in the toughening effect of warlike sports and pursuits ("a price well paid for the breeding of a race fit for leadership and command"). To most of us today such words will seem dangerously close to imperialism. But Holmes was more concerned with national cohesion than with conquest. He thought that the war experience gave the individual once more a sense of being part of "an unimaginable whole." If this is mysticism it is the sort that the recent experiences of Britain, Russia, and America tend to validate. These quotations have been from the Holmes of the 1890's. But as late as 1913, in his speech on "Law and the Court," he expressed "an old man's apprehension" that "competition from new races will cut deeper than working men's disputes and will test whether we can hang together or can fight."

Because of these convictions the war, when it came to the Supreme Court, did not catch Holmes intellectually unprepared. As a judge there were two principal problems he would have to face. The first was the question of the positive powers of a wartime democracy. For all his relativism, Holmes saw the war as a struggle on our side for our conception of civilized values. He could not see, therefore, how the network of government regulation of industry and the daily lives of people fell outside the Constitution or was a prohibitive price to pay for the survival of these values. The opinion which best expresses this belief is in *Missouri v. Holland,* the migratory bird treaty case, and in *Block v. Hirsh,* the leading Emergency Rent Law case. That Holmes would have extended the same logic from the Congressional power to the Presidential war power follows from the analogy of his reasoning about the governor's power in *Moyer v. Peabody.* And it is likely that the present Supreme Court will similarly uphold the current working conception of adequate war powers in a democracy.

A more difficult problem that came before Holmes and the Court was that of civil liberties in wartime. As a Massachusetts judge, Holmes had dealt with the regular run of civil liberties cases and in one, *Commonwealth v. Davis,* had written a legal opinion which was much cited later by those wishing to restrict by municipal ordinance the right to use public property as a forum for discussion. It was by no means a foregone conclusion, therefore, that Holmes would, with the World War cases, become a champion of civil liberties.

That he did may be traced to several strands of influence. One was Holmes's sense of critical balance and his dislike for the excesses committed by wartime patrioteers. A second was his admiration for the civil liberties of the English tradition, and for the temperate manner in which they handled problems of intellectual freedom. A third was the influence of Brandeis, who brought to the Court a fierce determination that nothing should destroy the right of criticism upon which democratic change depends. One may guess that in this association Brandeis helped enrich Holmes's grasp of the social values of the problem, and Holmes's contribution was to give the conception sharpness of legal contour and his unique gift of form. And finally there was Holmes's growing sense that men could do little by repression to divert the movement of events. This comes out most sharply in 1925 in the closing paragraph of his dissent in *Gitlow v. New York:* "If in the long run the beliefs expressed in proletarian dictatorship are destined to be accepted by the dominant forces of the community, the only meaning of free speech is that they should be given their chance and have their way." Here he sees free speech as the core of the succession of political power in a democracy, and the larger function of government to give expression to the struggle of life.

To these factors must be added Holmes's sense of legal craftsman-ship and his devotion to legal values. That this was a real devotion is clear not only from the great personal reluctance he felt about his opinion in the *Debs* case, but even more from his brief memorandum on refusing a stay of execution for Sacco and Vanzetti in 1927. There is very little that Holmes added to the philosophical conception of intellectual freedom in a democracy, although he gave it a literary sharpness. His creative work lay in reducing the nebulousness of philosophical concepts to usable legal standards. In the *Schenck* case, and after that in the *Abrams* and *Gitlow* dissents, Holmes worked out the tests of clear and present danger and of actual intent which may serve as a point of departure for Supreme Court action in this area.

The philosophical concepts of intellectual freedom have been rela-tively constant from Milton to Mill, and from Bagehot to Holmes and Brandeis. The legal concepts have been given greater precision. But the social framework within which these philosophical and legal crite-ria are to be applied has changed drastically from the England of Milton's day to the America of our own, from the licensing acts which represented the dangers to intellectual freedom in the time of the Stuarts to the obscene scribblings of Coughlin and Pelley or the divisionist articles in the Chicago *Tribune* which represent the danger in the time of the Nazi thrust for world empire. Rarely have the contours of an intellectual and political problem shifted so drastically as in the de-cades between the prosecutions of Debs and Pelley, between the Post Office order against Berger's Milwaukee *Leader* and that against Coughlin's *Social Justice.* Neither the national sedition laws nor the state criminal syndicalism laws, which were chiefly relied on in the period of the first World War, seem adapted to the present social situation. Professor Herbert Wechsler has expressed this change with remarkable incisiveness: "The enemies of American democracy, who-ever they are, are not advocating its violent overthrow. In the field of speech, they are talking about the vices of England, or of the Jews, or the folly of war or the advantages of trading with a victorious Germany. In the field of action, their eye is not on the overthrow of the government but on retarding production for defense. . . . The legislation which speaks in terms of advocacy of violent overthrow . . . represents an uncritical acceptance of a formula devised during the days when the Communist manifesto represented the technique of revolution; when revolutionaries operated by declaring rather than disguising their principles." And

Dean Mark Howe has re-enforced this viewpoint in a notable review of Chafee's *Free Speech in the United States.*

But all this has to do not so much with Holmes's own position as with the controversy over the present-day applications of it. It is a tribute to the mark that Holmes has left on us that in much of the current controversy over free speech in wartime the fires of doctrine should rage over how Holmes would have interpreted the problem and what he would say if he were alive today.

As he grew older, Holmes liked to joke about his being an old man. Yet behind the jest there was a serious concern lest he outstay his competence on the Court, as others before him had done. To the end of his tenure, however, there was no sign of declining powers. He had, of course, increasingly to conserve his strength, particularly after a major operation he had to undergo in 1922. In 1929 his wife died. Life was drawing to a close for him. In 1931, on the occasion of his ninetieth birthday, honors and tributes were heaped upon him from all sides. On January 12, 1932, he retired from the Court. He felt like a schoolboy released from his duties. He could no longer write letters by his own hand, but he continued with the aid of his secretary to read and keep in touch with the new figures on the intellectual horizon. With his zest for life scarcely diminished, he waited serenely for death. It came on March 6, 1935. Two days later he would have been ninety-four.

—10—

Is the influence he left a transitory one? And are we in danger of accepting him too uncritically? We have had warnings lately, from Walton Hamilton and others, against the development of a Holmes cult. And yet, if the materials for a cult are there, the warnings will do little good. Despite the strictures on Holmes and the skepticism about him from skeptical minds, there will be in every generation young men to read Holmes's words who will not read the words of warning about him. And their minds will be captured not alone by the words but by the personal image of Holmes that emerges from them. What is this image? Borrowing the notion of a guardian genius, one might say that Holmes was watched over by one of those grave-gay deities of the Greeks with his Apollonian serenity and his irrepressible high spirits. What disappoints many about Holmes is the absence of passion and of a feeling of dedication, the lack of the pattern of torture and complexity such as the generations following Dostoevski and Nietzsche have come to expect of the modern hero. To use Nietzsche's dualism, there was very much of the Apollonian in Holmes and very little of the darker urges of the Dionysian.

He had a serenity even in his moments of anger or near-despair, an assurance even in the midst of skepticism. It is a chastening thing to read his writings over the span of his life—to see how slow has been the movement toward a workable democracy, how many obstructions have been placed in its path, how unmalleable have been the interpretations placed on the fundamental laws by the dominant judicial caste, how spirit-breaking the efforts to fight against complacency and blindness. But if it is chastening, it is also heartening, particularly today when the young men need to be heartened about the future of a militant democracy: heartening to see how at the high tide of capitalist materialism there were still those who stood by their faith in social reason and in the competition of ideas, their belief in the steady, if slow, march of social progress. Holmes was one of these. He was at once buoyant and unfooled. The most striking thing about him was that he refused to live in a closed universe. He was a great spokesman of our Constitutional tradition because he was a great enough conservative to stretch the framework of the past to accommodate at least some of the needs of the present. He saw himself as part of the army of historic movement, whose "black spearheads" he saw "stretching away against the unattainable sky."

That is different, however, from saying that he was a conscious militant in the armies of social change. To lay violent siege to history was as little in his temperament as to shake his fist at the cosmos. He accepted the limits both of history and of nature and within those limits he found his freedom in a free world. He was part of no movement. What he said and wrote did not grow out of the current social experience or the emerging cultural forces. They were rather the reaping of past experience and the extraction of its full implications by a man who was content enough with life, but who did not feel God enough to hem in those whose passion for change was greater than his.

In every culture the core of its existence has been a poetic attitude toward the world. This attitude has often been better expressed by the symbols of literature and art than by the urgencies of political or economic doctrine. For the poet can often distill into his symbols even the experiences of which he has not been a direct part, particularly if he have in him a sense of the past and a sensitiveness to the mood around him. Many have wondered how an aristocrat like Holmes, who lived the life almost of a recluse, who would have nothing to do with the mechanical gadgets of American life, who refused to read the newspapers and identified himself with none of the political or economic movements of his time, was nevertheless able to distill into his writings the sense of American libertarian democracy. One may as well ask how John Keats, despite his limited experience, was able to put into his poetry both the power and pain of his Europe. I venture the belief that the son of Dr. Holmes turned out to be more of a poet than his father, if by poet we mean someone who pierces the appearances of life and expresses his vision in moving symbols. And if this sheds some light on Holmes, it should be not without meaning for his age that one of its poets should have had to work in the intractable material of legal technics.

Despite this—better, because of this—Holmes has had a great impact on our Constitutional development and national history. For a time it seemed that his work, however gallant, would prove frustrate. The Supreme Court majority continued to show a glacial hostility to his basic constitutional attitudes, and the country as a whole showed an indifference to his fighting faith. If Holmes had to wait for his vindication on the latter until Dunkirk and Pearl Harbor, his victory with respect to the former came earlier, only a year or two after his death. The constitutional crisis of the New Deal and the struggle over the Court reorganization plan of another Roosevelt cleared the way for the complete adoption of Holmes's views on constitutional law. The new doctrinal directions of the present Supreme Court spell more than anything else a return to Holmes. Chief Justice Stone was his faithful companion in dissents, Justice Frankfurter his devoted disciple, and all but one or two of the others have studied him and caught his spirit. While they may disagree as to what Holmes's meaning is for today, they carry on much of their work in his shadow.

Thus Holmes has created the means for his vindication. But his vindication in turn will tend to reduce that sense of wonder upon which a man's *éclat* in history depends. Holmes wrote in his essay on Montesquieu that "because his book was a work of science and epochmaking, it is as dead as the classics." Similarly in some of his letters to Pollock on the difficulty today of reading the classics, he points out that what has been borrowed from them and built into the structure of our own thought, strips them of the sense of newness and surprise. That may well happen to Holmes in the next few generations. And yet, despite what familiarity may do to his thought, there is beyond the thought the imprint of a unique personality and of a poetic image.

There are those who compare Holmes with John Marshall. The comparison is unjust to both men. Unlike Marshall, Holmes is a great man regardless of whether he was a great justice. He will probably leave a greater effect on English style and on what the young men dream and want than upon American constitutional law. Marshall's reputation stands or falls with the vested interests he defended and with the viability of the system of economic relations that leans heavily on his constitutional interpretations. The greatness of Holmes will survive the vested interests and their constitutional bolstering. It will stand up as long as the English language stands up, as long as men find life complex and exciting, and law a part of life, and the sharp blade of thought powerful to cleave both.

II (1989)

—1—

An author is lucky to have the chance to revisit as early a book as this one, and to get his licks in once again. I gathered these utterances of Justice Holmes and wrote prefaces for them half a lifetime ago when I was instructing the young at Williams College in constitutional history. At forty, in 1943, I was already a veteran of the passions and actions of the New Deal constitutional wars. Whatever impulse incited me to these labors, I recall the excitement that sustained me in grappling with the character and thinking of so enigmatic a figure.

The original version of one's work—if it amounts to anything—is always a hard act to follow. As I reread the book the thing of wonder to me is my youthful brashness in daring to plan a venture a third of whose pages comprised my comments on the two-thirds that were Holmes's. Given his magisterial brevity, my prefaces to his opinions were often longer than what they prefaced. It was, I fear, a case of the context swallowing the text. What saw me through it was the effort to present a total rather than a specialized view of Holmes—to integrate the personal journey with the professional and intellectual, the mind and character with the style, the strengths and vulnerabilities of a thinker with his impact on history.

Happily the book had a sturdy life over the years, enduring the constitutional tumults that tested its viability. The occasion for republishing it is also an occasion for reviewing the scholarship of the intervening years, taking the measure of Holmes again, charting afresh the stages of his constitutional journey and the trajectory of his reputation, rethinking his relevance for an America almost a half-century after his death.

In the case of a federal judge his constitutional journey[1] starts well before his actual decisions, with the early history and the turning points in the ideas that bear directly on them. Slow step-by-step growth may be part of the story, but also the creative leaps—mutations, as it were—which are at times all but inexplicable.

The seminal period for Holmes was the triad of the Civil War, the law school student years, and the long days and nights spent writing his formative essays for the *American Law Review*. They were the source from which the river of legal history began its strong flow for him. Holmes was twenty-one when he was first wounded at Ball's Bluff. He was in his late thirties when he began to write *The Common Law*—unillusioned, skeptical, stoic, yet with a deep fire of insight and purpose.

During his years of intense study he shaped the leading ideas he put together in the *Common Law* lectures—the anthropology, history, economics, psychology, the deep experiential and pragmatic thrust, the epigrammatic style, the shying away from certitudes and absolutes, the legal philosophy that he saw (in Voltaire's phrase) as "history teaching by example."[2]

We have the sense in reading his letters to Pollock and Laski that Holmes did everything with an easy grace. Yet his years of early labor suggest that it was a hard-won grace. He spoke later of the "icy night" that enveloped him in the harsh law school years, which must have seemed a continuance of the Civil War traumas, on other battlefields, with other enemies. Holmes had in those years something like Yeats's knotty "fascination with what's difficult." He later gave the impression of a conjurer's capacity to untie the knots, presto, or to cut through them with a swift decisiveness. But he had prepared the ground in his years of ordeal. Compared with the disciplined mastery he had to achieve early, everything after that was made to seem easy.

The Common Law which he completed at age forty, was thus the deftly prepared turning point that made everyone take him seriously as a comer. It forked off into two roads that were swiftly opened to him—as legal scholar and professor and as State Supreme Court judge. Like Robert Frost, another Yankee of ribbed words, Holmes could not take both. He chose the second, I suspect, because it enabled him "to think for action upon which great interests depend." It is tantalizing to speculate about where the road not taken might have led.

Holmes never wrote another book. Yet in his two Court tenures, of twenty and thirty years, he wrote a sheaf of opinions that led to his becoming in time a kind of judicial Philosopher-King, somewhat disdainful of the crown he wore with an amused tilt—but he nonetheless wore it.

—2—

In my commentary on the State Court opinions I drew a distinction between the Holmes of private and of public law. I might have made it sharper. His public law opinions formed a transition to his Supreme Court views, especially in his deference as a judge to majoritarian decisions of legislative bodies. But the reputation he achieved on both courts thrust his earlier importance for private law into the shadow. We all worked and wrote in that shadow.

What we missed was the shift in Holmes's private law thinking under the nitty-gritty testing of his State Court duties. As a scholar he had been an intellectual radical, like his friends in the "Metaphysical Club," and was influenced by the positivist science of the time. It added a strong conceptual strain to his pragmatic inclinations. It didn't negate his recoil from formalism and from the heavy constrictions of philosophical idealism. But it made him willing to apply standards and strike principled approximations to resolve the hardest problems of legal thinking.

If the conceptual Holmes survived the State Court experience it was in a considerably altered state. He still aimed at clear principles and an "external standard," whether in torts, contracts, or property law. But the dividing line between the clashing sets of social desires was more blurred in action than it had been in the scholarly cloister. He couldn't fall back on the "not unreasonable" legislative bodies, as he did in public law. Nor was he willing to rely on the judgment of juries beyond their findings of fact. He saw no certainties in the competing social interests that clustered around every case. He saw instead a shadowy continuum that led to something like an "uncertainty" principle. He had to draw a line somewhere, however, make a choice between "irreconcilable desires"—and thereby play something of an activist role in "making law."

It must have been a chastening experience for him, but also a growth experience. It was in these years that he moved decisively from the law as a set of rules linked with "rights" or "duties" or moral imperatives to the law as a prediction of what the courts will operatively do. This led him inevitably into the depths where certainties as well as logics dissolved and where at times arbitrary choices had to be made. A half-century later (as G. Edward White notes) the efforts to dig into Holmes's importance as a private law thinker led to "a larger rediscovery of the history of private law."

Meanwhile Holmes led a relaxed life, took vacations in Europe, read French novels, corresponded widely—and waited for the Godot of the coveted prize. We tend to see a kind of inevitability in his progression to the summit. Yet it was a near thing, hanging on the hairbreadth of Henry Cabot Lodge's reassuring response to Theodore Roosevelt's anxiety. Holmes had become Chief Justice of the Massachusetts Court by the 1900 term and was attracting national attention. But he was already sixty-one when the choice was made, and he wouldn't have been *papabile* much longer. A lot of history would have come out differently if T.R. had insisted on a "safer" man.

—3—

This emphasis on law as what the courts will actually do led ineluctably to a focus on the judge himself and the workings of his mind—articulate or not, conscious or unconscious. There are hints of this in his State Court opinions—this journey into the interior of a judge's mind—but the flowering came soon after he reached the Supreme Court.

It is clearest in his *Lochner v. N.Y.* dissent (1905), which created a new jurisprudence—one of self-awareness of a judge's unstated philosophical premises and his social priorities. It led to the recognition of the need to come to terms with this underlying set of personal premises, at the peril of "playing God" with judicial lawmaking.

It was a turning point in Holmes's intellectual journey but also in that of successive generations of students. I read the dissent as a graduate student in the mid-1920s, as did my generation. It created a school of "legal realism" in the law school culture later in the 1930s. Yet little note has been taken of its strategic aspect from 1905 to the New Deal attacks on the Court in the mid-1930s.

Holmes was on polite terms with his Court brethren, but their succession of rigid decisions furnished the laboratory in which he developed his strategy for meeting and overcoming them. He was a solitary fighter, and had no one to talk with until Brandeis came to the Court in 1916. Brandeis brought a sociological jurisprudence with him from his

Populist progressive years, and he documented the new "felt necessities" of the time. But Holmes dug deeper, into the hidden logic of the "unarticulated major premise" that underlay the conservative lawmaking, and also into the fears and commitments that shaped the priorities of judges like the formidable Justice Peckham who wrote the Court opinion in *Lochner*.

This led Holmes to his doctrine of "judicial deference." The important fact about it was that it brought all of Holmes's insights together and served as a strategic weapon in the doctrinal wars for generations. I don't say it was all calculated. I do say that without Holmes's shrewd conceptualizing capacity it would not have happened that way or that soon.

In his address on John Marshall, with its guarded praise, Holmes asserted that his influence lay in being *there* at a strategic point in the campaign of history. We can turn his remark about and see that it was true of Holmes as well. He was *there*, exactly when a Court of resourceful conservatives was creating a set of doctrines—notably "liberty of contract" and "due process of law"—to protect an archaic property system against its challengers.

We all declaimed and wrung our hands over these indignities. Yet it devolved on Holmes to bear the burden of contriving an equally resourceful doctrinal strategy to counter them. He achieved it with the concept of judicial deference to reasonable legislative majorities. By the mid-1930s and their constitutional battles we were calling it "judicial restraint" and using it against the "judicial supremacy" of the conservative Court majority.

In Holmes's relations with the liberal law school professors the ardor was all on their side, and it increased with his decisions and dissents on free trade in ideas. He saw these opinions of his as meditations on how to reconcile the clashing imperatives of speech—of a nation seeking to guard its very existence and of the same nation striving to retain its soul by refusing to quench the fires of competing ideas.

Holmes was not one of the "First Amendment voluptuaries" (as Alexander Bickel has dubbed them), drunk with an absolutism that sees only one of the imperatives. Holmes saw both and picked his way warily between them. To have moved in a brief period from the majority "clear and present danger" test of *Schenck v. U.S.*, to the majority opinion upholding the *Debs v. U.S.* conviction, to the ringing *Abrams v*

U.S. dissent was in itself a daring and scrupulous journey. Holmes performed his conceptual differentiations between them with a scalpel-like precision and couched them in quicksilver phrases that still dance and live in the memory of every constitutional scholar. The final product was his own, yet this was one phase of his journey where a notable dialogue took place, involving exchanges with (among others) Brandeis, Laski, and especially Learned Hand.[3]

—4—

Much has been written on the "apotheosis" of Holmes by the "legal realists" of the 1930s and more generally by the New Deal liberals. As an unchartered member of both groups I can bear witness that the charge of our "hero worship" and "mythmaking" is overdone. I had few illusions, either in the book or the *Nation* and Law Review articles that preceded it, about Holmes as a liberal. We knew that he was an economic, social, and neo-Darwinian conservative and that his judicial doctrine—however powerful a strategic weapon it proved—was based on an intellectual austerity that few of us as combatants in the liberal wars could muster. Holmes never walked on water for us. There was no liberal canonizing of him as there was of Brandeis and supremely of Franklin Roosevelt.

Of the principal "Realists," Karl Llewellyn was poetic about Holmes because that was his style, but he was also sophisticated in his insights; Walton Hamilton saw his importance, but he was astringent about "dating Holmes"; and Thurmond Arnold was caustic about everyone, not excluding Holmes. Only Jerome Frank was a bit excessive in his often quoted final chapter (in *Law and the Modern Mind)* about Holmes as a paradigm of a "mature man."

For a time the Realists were fascinated by Holmes. They needed him more than he needed them. He was the symbol that gave cohesion to them as a "school." It was a passing phase. They have regrouped since, found other symbols, rallied behind more exotic causes, under other banners.[4] Even when they marched to the same drum, neither Holmes nor they allowed themselves to be diverted from their own campaign of history.

Holmes left the Supreme Court just as the New Deal entered history. They barely bowed to each other in passing, although the White House and many of the new agencies were staffed by Holmesians. It was well that Holmes was no longer on the Court during FDR's attacks on the "Nine Old Men": had he stayed he would have been the oldest—and the wisest. The Court-packing plan would doubtless have been anathema to him, as it was to Brandeis and Hughes. Yet Holmes's opinions not only laid a base for attacking judicial supremacy; they also furnished a rationale for accepting legislative social experiments like the New Deal and validating an executive power adequate to the nation's survival.

Holmes could not have known—nor could I—that the Roosevelt constitutional revolution of the 1930s would first enshrine and then undermine his reputation. The trajectory of the rise and fall—and rise again—of the Holmes heritage is a richly theatrical chapter in the history of ideas. It has had echoes in the legal scholarship and is worth tracing for its ironies and paradoxes.

Broadly put, the Holmes legacy flourished in the 1930s, tottered in the 1940s and 1950s, collapsed in the 1960s and early 1970s, and revived in the later 1970s and 1980s. These vagaries of his reputation, curiously, had less to do with his constitutional doctrines than with his larger philosophy and indeed with the perceptions of his character. Most of all they were governed by what was happening in the law school culture as it watched the Roosevelt Court and its successors and responded to the pressures of the larger political culture. Holmes became part of history, and the story of his reputation is a story of the ways in which a dominant legal elite deploys the uses of history.

—5—

In retrospect the most radical thing about my book was its title and therefore its central theme—that Holmes possessed not only a striking mind but a unique faith. This was heresy at the time and became even greater heresy during the decades when he was under attack. Is it possible (his critics asked) that this agnostic, skeptic, Darwinian had a faith? Yet the faith informs his thinking, which cannot be studied without it.

We must not forget that his core experience was the near encounters with death in the Civil War when brother fought and killed brother, each convinced of the rightness of his cause—a conviction that Holmes came to call a "fighting faith." He knew that time withers every faith but also knew that we need it as a symbolic mode of giving meaning to life in an uncaring universe. His "can't helps" represented a way of coming to terms with the urgency of ultimate and absolute truths. It was as far as he was willing to go toward universal as well as unique patterns, and he made them personal, not general.

The liberals came to see Holmes as a disembodied mind, lacking compassion for the welfare of his fellows, unwilling to use his judicial gifts to elevate their condition. Yet to see him thus is to miss the point of the Holmes enigma. Compassion was not one of his prime values, but neither was force—certainly not the force of the state. Competition and struggle were the essence of life, death was its sanction, and faith transcended both.

Hence the "dark" quality that many have seen in Holmes. The attack was only in part on doctrinal grounds. It was largely characterological. Paradoxically it united the liberal Left, which dominated the legal culture, with the Catholic and traditionalist Right, which had its own agenda of opposition to Holmes—the doctrine of "natural rights." For a time both Left and Right found common ground in seeing Holmes as a strange creature—the Left depicting his as a cold, uncaring spectator, the Right as a savage pre-Hitler totalitarian.

There is little question that there was in fact a side of Holmes that was extraordinarily detached from the everyday pressures and urgencies of life. Only a warrior who had been through the battles and had experienced death as closely as Holmes could be so consistently "above the battle." There was an archetypal Jungian "shadow" in Holmes that not only furnished his dark side, but also gave him his rocklike strength of character and his steadiness of vision.

True, his death experiences also left a scar on his life perception, making him less open to humanist thinking, so that he made short shrift of any liberalisms other than free trade in ideas, and wrote too much off as "uplift." Edmund Wilson, writing in the early 1960s, spoke of "the carapace of impregnable indifference to current pressures and public opinion" that marked Holmes. G. Edward White, in 1971, wrote of his "articulated refusal to take pride in being human," which made him "the least heroic of America's heroes."

Had Holmes lived longer, all this would have thoroughly disqualified him from membership in the Warren Court. It kept Holmes from being proudly and generously accepted, even during the recent decades of his "revival." But to ask for a Holmes with these added "enlightened" and "progressive" qualities would miss the point of the total Holmes and how his critical life experiences had made him what he was. They account for the flaws in his thinking but account also in part for the strength both of his mind and faith.

One gets in Holmes the sense of life and death entangled with each other in an *agon* without end. He didn't use Eros and Thanatos as his symbols for it, unlike Freud, who wrote after another war as he came to recognize the role of death. Both men, strikingly, went through a similar experience of starting with a positivist belief in the science of their day, getting fascinated by the hidden agenda of the mind, and moving ever closer to the dark imperatives of the instinctual drives expressed in life and death.

—6—

If Holmes fell from grace as an idol of the liberal Left, he was anything but a darling of the conservative, traditionalist, and moralist Right. How could they not oppose him? His positivism and realism enabled him to define law operatively without recourse to the dimension of "ought" that conservative as well as liberal moralists have found indispensable. In bringing the "bad man" into his theory of law Holmes used the adjective almost wryly to mean, matter-of-factly, whatever got him entangled with the law's sanctions. As a young editor he read all the Continental theorists of "natural law" and "natural rights," including the windy ones—and rejected them. Natural law was too static and absolute for an evolutionary thinker who knew how the conception of "nature" had changed over the ages. The breezy authority with which Holmes dismissed a whole phalanx of weighty scholars made him all the more exasperating.

I had to confess myself somewhat troubled, in my original prefaces, by the gap I found in Holmes's thinking: "Holmes did not adequately bridge the gap between [his] two worlds. There was in him a deep conflict between scepticism and belief, between mind and faith, between a recognition that men act in terms of a cold calculation of interests, and a recognition also that they are moved by symbols..." I added that his effort "to take account of both strains...was not wholly successful," but that it stretched him into becoming "a full-statured person," more than he would have been if he had restricted his energies "to the narrow confines of one or the other partial view."

I still hold this a viable view, although I shall add some further reflections below on the "natural rights" (rather than "natural law") philosophy of both Left and Right."

When Holmes left the bench, in 1932, it was not yet clear how any coalition war effort against Hitler might fare. There had been premonitory scholarly articles, from 1941 to 1943, mostly by Jesuit legal thinkers, on Holmes as forerunner of the ideas of Hitler, Göring, Goebbels, and Himmler, but it was left to Ben Palmer, in the year the war ended (1945), to put the same thesis in a popularized form, yielding to the alliterative seduction of his title, "Hobbes, Holmes and Hitler.'' Admitting that Holmes "did not go around like a storm trooper, knocking people down," he nevertheless saw Holmes as a source of "totalitarian" philosophy.

The controversy raged through the rest of the 1940s and the 1950s, engaging more time and verbiage than it deserved. It also evoked some necessary reassessments of Holmes's evolutionary approach to legal philosophy, which he had always put more nakedly—almost perversely—than he had to. What happened to Holmes's legacy, starting a decade after his death, came with a fantastic irrelevance out of the full revelation of the Holocaust, which would have been as alien to him as he to it.

We see the roots of Nazism more clearly now. They had nothing to do with the Hobbesian doctrine of sovereignty nor with Holmes's legal pragmatism. They shed a cruel light on the German intellectual tradition of a Europe in which Nazism emerged and flourished. One has to ask what good the centuries of French Enlightenment and German "natural law" thinking did when it came to confront the radical evil of Hitler. Holmes never had a love affair with either of them. Nor has Hannah Arendt's foray into the Enlightenment thinkers, on the intellectual origins of totalitarianism, tempered the continuing criticism of Holmes. The critics have not taken adequate account of the role of "social engineering" strategies and fantasies, both Right and Left, in the genocides of Hitler and Stalin.

There is a key passage in Holmes in which he concludes that he is "in the universe," not the universe in him—that he is therefore not God in it and disdains to "play God" in shaping the destinies of others in the same universe. In a deep sense, his working theory of judging was grounded on this metaphysic.

The liberals who found Holmes and his gnomic language so engaging in the 1920s and 1930s did so not because they liked all his judicial outcomes and his philosophy, and certainly not because of his metaphysic. They were willing to overlook his departures from their liberal ideal in his *Schenck* and *Debs* opinions because they fixed on *Abrams, Gitlow,* and *Schwimmer.* They too lived by symbols, and Holmes was for them a symbol of resistance to the reactionary Court majority, a symbol also of enlightenment on the Bill of Rights, and— in the case of the Realists—a symbol of a down-to-earth willingness to reckon with the here and now that they equated with a kind of liberal modernism. As with love and marriage, their disillusionment with him came out of their initial illusions. When they looked closer and found that this wasn't the love object that had once enchanted them, they recoiled more strongly.

As it happened, their recoil (like that of the "natural law" conservatives) came at the war's end, in the mid-1940s. It lasted for some thirty years, mounting during the Warren 1960s. The dynamics of the recoil are not analyzed clearly in the accounts of it in the legal literature. In the 1940s and after, a series of generations came into the law schools sharply different from the constitutional generation I knew in the 1920s and 1930s. The true key to their change was the succession of activist Supreme Courts, starting with a Court appointed almost entirely by Franklin Roosevelt. Behind this in turn is the story of the political cultures that we call the New Deal, the Fair Deal, the New Frontier, and the Great Society, and their impact at once on the Supreme Court members and on the law school culture that served as their support system.

Despite Holmes's half-century of judging, including thirty years on the Supreme Court, his impact on constitutional law proved narrower than seemed likely in the early 1940s. The *Holmesian moment*—if we may call it that—was his burst of creative fire between *Lochner* in 1905 and the free-speech cases in the early 1920s. The fact that many of his great opinions in this period were dissents is witness to Holmes's fate in having to spend his best years on a Court whose majority saw him as marginal to the judicial culture of the time. In fact, this brief spell saw the mature harvest of the great sowings in his hungry young years and the years of manhood on the State Court.

Aside from the force of his basic decisional philosophy, Holmes's doctrinal resourcefulness in sheer constitutional terms was not great. On that score it didn't match Justice Hugo Black's on the Roosevelt Court or the doctrinal fertility of the later Warren group. The reason is clear enough. The burden of Holmesian thinking was to define the judicial power narrowly and set limits to it. The burden of the later activist thinking of the Roosevelt and Warren Courts was to expand the judicial power, and to that end a doctrinal fertility was an imperative.

After Holmes's retirement in 1932 the Holmesian moment continued its brief triumph, in "a little finishing canter before coming to a standstill"—the horserace metaphor he used in his ninetieth birthday. It lasted as long as his strategic legacy was useful in helping to fight the anti-New Deal decisions and later to validate the New Deal legislation. But with the first Roosevelt appointments to the Supreme Court in the closing 1930s the new masters of the Court no longer needed the Holmesian doctrine. After that it stayed alive until the Warren Court, but only as an element of contention in the great feud between two Court factions. The impetus of the new *Zeitgeist* succeeded in ending the Holmesian moment.

—7—

The nature of this *Zeitgeist* is worth some probing for the light it sheds on what happened to the Holmes legacy and why. The episode of Holmes's meeting with Franklin Roosevelt has a symbolic importance. Flanked by FDR's intimate, Felix Frankfurter, and Holmes's former law clerk, Tom Corcoran, the President-elect visited the ancient Justice. Asked later what he thought of his visitor, Holmes replied, "A first-rate temperament, a second-rate mind." Whether Holmes was right or not, the episode was premonitory of the collision between the Holmes legacy and the New Deal. Holmes was wide of the mark in one respect. This "second-rate mind" was resourceful enough to use Holmes's judicial strategy, and then became impatient of it and exploded in the militancy of the "Court-packing"[5] plan. Roosevelt ended by appointing a Supreme Court that fused the expanded executive power with a new liberal judicial activism.

There were powerful minds and personalities on the Roosevelt Court, clearly the ablest in American Constitutional history. No one's *epigoni*, they were masterful men in their own right. The most talented of them came out of the assertive New Deal political culture. They were *novi homines*, a new, aggressive breed of political men: an Alabama redneck from Clay County who became a brilliant lawyer and Senate militant;

a Jewish immigrant from Austria who worked with FDR in World War I and whose law students planned and staffed half the New Deal administrative agencies; a farm boy from Yakima, Washington, who became a law professor and ran the Security Exchange Commission; a Buffalo lawyer who skipped law school and became FDR's creative Attorney-General.

These four men, forming as vivid a core for a Court as any we have seen, became involved in a doctrinal feud that continued into the Warren Court. Hugo L. Black and William O. Douglas found the Holmes legacy both irrelevant and obstructive to their aims, while Felix Frankfurter and Robert H. Jackson used it still as a strong, shaping, decisional force.[6]

They all strove to be resourceful tacticians in their doctrinal maneuvers. Of the first pair, Douglas had the less original mind, distracted by sprawling interests that went beyond law to a liberated philosophy of life, both private and public. He tended to follow Black's doctrinal leads, combining them with an adherence to Brandeisian concepts, including notably the "right of privacy," which was to prove expansive in later Courts.

Next to Holmes, Hugo Black may prove to be the strongest, most original judicial mind since Holmes. His aim was to translate the New Deal revolution into constitutional law, and he succeeded. Largely an autodidact, he used historical excursions (not always accurate) to discover the original intent of the Fourteenth Amendment in order to enlarge its impact. He built a bridge between a literalist absolutism on civil liberties and an expansionism of social protections, using historicism, the "incorporation" doctrine, "equal protection," and the Establishment clause. His writing had a crude power in place of style but he was a constitutional warrior in the Roosevelt, Vinson, and Warren Courts, with an unmatched doctrinal creativeness.

Felix Frankfurter had a richer, more intricate, more complex mind than Black or any Justice since, and his style reflected it. His problem was that he was over-prepared for his Court role. He had lived too many lives when Roosevelt named him to the Court—as reformer and professor at Cambridge, as Brandeis's alter ego, as Holmes's most fervent adherent, as FDR's close friend and adviser on every issue of state. He was Faustian, reaching out to all his competing hungers, while Holmes was Lucretian, with a long view of how the evolutionary gods play with human destinies.

In terms of internal mental struggle Frankfurter was the central dramatic figure of the Court's history—a neo-Holmesian at heart, striving to reconcile the Holmes legacy of a constrained judicial doctrine with his commitment to a strange mixture of Brandeisian and New Deal social progressivism. It made for great intellectual theater and resulted in some remarkable (if unpopular) opinions in which he balanced the conflicting pulls on a perilous edge of decision. Yet it couldn't overcome the thrust of social forces that sustained Black's views. In the end, in his historic meeting of minds with Chief Justice Warren in *Brown* (1952), Frankfurter achieved his ultimate ideal of judicial statesmanship, moving beyond the Holmes doctrine in a time and area so fraught with the clear and present danger of ethnic divisiveness that Holmes might well have reached the same result. For Holmes didn't like a vacuum of action and *Brown* filled a great one.

Robert H. Jackson went along with Frankfurter and Warren on *Brown*, although more reluctantly than any of the others. He had an asperity of thought and word that made him the best stylist of the group. He wrote eloquently against judicial supremacy in any form and was quick to note the twistings and turnings of his liberal brethren in trying to avoid the charge. But he too suffered, as Frankfurter did, from the constraints of a decisional method that left most of the juicy doctrinal inventiveness to the opposing camp.

From FDR's appointments through Truman's and Eisenhower's the constitutional wars raged, with varying results. But the long trend line of the political and legal cultures was liberal-activist, and the Holmes heritage seemed distasteful, even repugnant, to generations of the young. The impact of this era on his reputation can scarcely have come as much of a surprise. The dominant liberal group didn't like either the austerities of Holmes or his doctrine of judicial deference. Quite naturally they honed in on their own philosophy of judicial activism, social engineering, and doctrinal inventiveness—all of which had been alien to Holmes. The Eisenhower appointees, Warren and Brennan (paradoxically liberals), fed the fires of the Court generation that went by Warrren's name, while the Johnson appointees renewed and sustained them. It was the apogee of constitutional activism, which makes some sense of the fact that the Holmes legacy reached its nadir during the Warren 1960s.

The perceptions of Holmes by the Law School culture were too narrow. While Holmes was the source and father of judicial deference, it was only one of the principles he judged by. Since he was wary of "general propositions" and shied from making an absolute of any, he made no absolute of this doctrine either. It was a star to steer by, but no chart for rough waters. He saw it as useful for a time in keeping the reactionary activism of his brothers from seizing a new America that was coming to birth and holding it unconstitutional. He also saw his deference doctrine as a way of keeping the contending powers of a democracy in balance, giving leeway to the majoritarian principle in legislative bodies—except when the threatened rights were basic to the competition of ideas and of values systems that underlies all social change.

Yet Holmes never turned his doctrine rigid, never carried it into historical excursions in search of "original intent," never read the Constitution with a literalism that would leach out its meaning, any more than he read it with an expansionism that would bloat it beyond coherence. He recognized that the Constitution is a changing organism, as the nation is. Yet he also saw that both Constitution and nation need power to make them effective.

He refused to turn any of the three powers—executive, legislative, judicial—into an eidolon. Each had its functions. But when confronted by an aggressive expansion from any of the others, the deepest power of the judiciary was to establish a principle and draw a line of separation. "A line there must be" was Holmes's constant imperative from the time of his early State Court decisions to his great national organismic ones on the executive and taxing powers.

—8—

Two current schools of constitutional thought present the strongest challenge to the Holmes legacy. One from the Left, the other from the Right, both strike at the vulnerable point the Holmes legacy presents in terms of finding firm criteria for confronting a constantly transforming world with a document two centuries old. Law is not like literature, art, and philosophy, which can be distanced from the daily immediacies. It is caught in their whorl. When the immediacies change, in the form of instant media, "Artificial Intelligence," global money markets, missile systems in space, biotechnics, born-again faiths, drug addictions, terrorisms, and AIDS, we spot the archaisms in the document and demand new judgments and constitutional relationships that will meet the current discontents.

The Holmes answer was that there is a plenitude of power in the total constitutional system, and the Courts must draw a line between its claimants, but not to the enhancement of the judicial power when others have acted or can act. This didn't satisfy the challengers from the Left, from Black and Douglas through Warren, Fortas, and Brennan.

If I call them the "Warrenites" for convenience, I refer to the Warren Court as symbol. I mean also to include their philosophical support system in the universities and law schools, those who feel that too many "rights," of individuals and groups, will slip through the crevices of the Holmesian doctrine, leaving them unprotected unless the Courts act to do the protecting—whence the need for their activism. Ronald Dworkin found a phrase, "taking rights seriously," that summed up their concern.

The Holmes legacy was vulnerable to this concern. It failed to meet the fear that in the absence of judicial action—given prejudiced, fearful, or apathetic legislatures and executives—the cases of voting reapportionment, desegregated schools, the right to counsel, the *Miranda* warnings, affirmative action, the access to abortions, and the protections against sexual harassment would all have failed to be taken seriously enough to fill the social void or meet the social injustice. More than anything it was this fear and the failure to meet it that turned the courts and law school culture away from Holmes for so long. His "felt necessities" applied to the shaping of the common law, but failed to still the clamant social urgencies that besieged constitutional law.

The trouble was of course that the expanding universe of liberal activism had no moral philosophy of its own to set limits to its rising entitlements and the interest-group incitements they provoked. The embrace of an unlimited rights dynamic within such a society heightens the centrifugal forces in it, diminishes the centripetal ones, and makes it all but impossible to govern from a center that will hold. It was the growing awareness of this, since the early 1970s, that reached the electorates and courts, undercut the liberal legal culture, and sent Holmes's reputation into an upward arc.

While the liberal aversion to Holmes came from his deflating of all utopianisms, the conservative attack focuses on his pragmatism and his values relativism. Unlike the liberals who read selective "rights" into the Constitution through the "penumbra" around them, the traditionalists make the stronger case against Holmes from their "natural right" base, with a firm belief that the essential nature of man can be used to ground a good society and keep it from the ravages both of a grandiose activism and a laissez-faire particularism.

It is an insight that has given the Straussians (if I may use them as a counter to the Warrenites) a considerable entrance into constitutional history and law.[7] If they have a strong case to make against Holmes it is not because they are right about their version of "natural right" and Holmes wrong in his scepticism of all such philosophies. It is rather because the fault line between his pragmatism and his evolutionism kept him from offering a principle of cohesion to keep a postmodern society from disintegrating under its centrifugal pressures.

The problem of the Warrenites was their failure to set limits. The problem of the Straussians is that their flight from relativism and their quest of the single "truth" expose them to the enticement of absolute thinking. No movement of thought has yet succeeded in finding the common ground of truths and values in the history of human experience on which an absolute "natural right" can be based. Yet the anthropological approach, which the young Holmes used in his researches on *the Common Law,* might still yield a cluster of intersecting values that would be useful for constitutional thinkers as well. This might give judges a direction for meeting the strong social urgencies of the time, and for adding a measure of statesmanship to the Holmes legacy of judicial deference.

—9—

A word about the Holmes style. Almost every attack on him pays tribute to it, but only as a kind of adornment, even an excrescence, which obscures the "savagery" or "bleakness" of his doctrine. It makes no sense. however, to garland Holmes for being an artificer of beautiful passages while dismissing him for being wrong-headed. There are in fact some flowery passages in Holmes, especially in his perorations, and over the years he repeated favorite expressions in his speeches and correspondence. Yet in the judicial opinions themselves there is hardly ever a surplus word, a self-indulgent adjective, an unnecessary phrase. It is style that cuts to the marrow of the issue at hand.

"A word is the skin of a thought," he wrote. It is more than an epigram; it is a thought that sheds light on his style. Holmes became a jurist but never ceased to be what he had all along dreamt of being, long before his law school years—a philosophical writer. There is no separation in him between style and substance; they are one. The word encloses and illumines the thought, which gives content and meaning to the word. Both his word and thought have the same crispness, economy, cutting edge, the same sparkling sense of playfulness, the same perversity in the face of fashions, the same unerring aim at the jugular—the same essence and permanence.

I add a personal note about my own perception of Holmes. Several years before the book's publication, Walton Hamilton, then at Yale Law School, wrote an influential *Law Review* article, "On Dating Mr. Justice Holmes." It said in effect that Holmes had come to seem both timeless and dateless, yet he was in fact a creature of his time and needed to be dated. As it happens, Hamilton was my teacher at the Robert Brookings Graduate School, where I learned some constitutional law in 1925 and first encountered the great Holmes decisions. One thing Hamilton taught us was to "place" a thinker in time and in social and personal circumstance. I sought to do it in this book, especially in the introductory essay on Holmes's "personal history."

Where the critics of Holmes (including Hamilton) had it wrong was in believing that the act of placing a thinker or artist in time strips him of what timelessness he has achieved. This has not proved true of Emerson, Whitman, O'Neill, and Faulkner, or of either William or Henry James who were of Holmes's generation and social circle. Like them all Holmes was a creature of his time and circumstance, but—also like them—he reached beyond it to universals. In his case the universals involved the process of judging, including the complex and intrusive role of the judge himself.

Because judicial review is the greatest American achievement in the arts of the polity, we have needed thinkers with insights that start with particulars and reach to the universal. It cannot be said of Holmes that he was free of the judgment of successive generations. Yet, however savaged, he has survived and somehow prevailed. Of all the American judges in time and circumstance there is a quality of *gravitas* in Holmes that gives him a measure of this timelessness.

There have been a number of attempts to write Holmes's life, but all have been partial or truncated. He is a hard subject to seize. Grant

Gilmore, the custodian of the Holmes papers after the death of his biographer, Mark DeWolfe Howe, saw more "darkness" in Holmes than he could handle and gave up. Yet he stated: "To the extent that I can follow the dark outlines of his thought Holmes was both a greater man and a more profound thinker than the mythical Holmes ever was."

I never took either of the Holmes myths as final—the mythologizing of the 1920s and 1930s or the counter-mythologizing of the mid-1940s to the mid-1970s. Holmes is indeed a mythic figure, but in a different sense from myth seen as unreality. He has become mythic in the sense that his constitutional journey has become part of the journey taken in each generation—including the journey of those who resisted and attacked him.

Nor do I take the Holmes "revival" of the past decade as decisive or final. His critics made law school reputations by him, only to be dismayed by the refusal of his reputation to lie down and die. The faithful on the Burger and Rehnquist Courts in the 1980s picked only a single strand of Holmes for their fealty—judicial restraint—but they turned it into a historicism of "original intent" that attenuated what he meant and missed the richness of his range.

There will be other dips and rises in his reputation. A figure like Holmes becomes a way of looking into the mirror of ourselves and our time. He will rise and fall with the "felt necessities" of time and selfhood, with attitudes toward civilizational change and continuity, with perceptions of the life and death principles, and with the imperatives of the most difficult of all arts of governing—the art of adjudication.

This is especially true in an America that has suffered convulsive changes since Holmes's death, becoming not only a nation of competing pluralisms but a kingpin of the Western imperium, in a world of terrorism but also of an emerging community of law. Holmes couldn't have foreseen it, yet it is wholly compatible with his long perspectives. In such an America of changes and chances there is—more than anything else—a need for cohesion through permanences. I say "permanences," not "absolutes." "Continuity with the past," Holmes noted, "is not a duty. It is only a necessity."

Holmes didn't think much of engineered changes in which politically minded judges decide what is good for others. He did very much believe in broad evolutionary change and wanted judges to be part of it and to help set its channels and limits. With such a philosophy he defined the judicial tasks of his own age—and of ours—more trenchantly than any of his assailers or followers. This is his relevance for today and tomorrow.

Notes

1. For a discussion of this concept, see Max Lerner, *Nine Scorpions in a Bottle: Adventures in Supreme Court History and Politics*, ed. Richard Cummings (New York: Arcade Publishing, 1994), which deals with Holmes along with other constitutional "greats."
2. For additional research and scholarship since I wrote, see the first two volumes of Mark DeWolfe Howe's great unfinished biography, *Justice Oliver Wendell Holmes: The Shaping Years* (1957) and *The Proving Years* (1963), Edmund Wilson's shrewd and quirky essay in *Patriotic Gore* (1962), and the two volumes of Holmes-Laski correspondence (1953).
3. Hand held out for a more absolute First Amendment standard of "direct incitement" before state intervention would be warranted. The Brandeis test was whether there is still time for "education." On the *Abrams* case see Richard Polenberg, *Fighting Faiths* (1987). For the Hand incident see Frederic R. Kellogg, "Learned Hand and the Great Train Ride," *American Scholar* (1987), 471–86, drawing on letters in a biography of Hand by Gerald Gunther, *Learned Hand: The Man and the Judge* (New York: Alfred A. Knopf, 1994).
4. Their more extreme descendants now known as the Critical Legal School ("Crits"), have merged some extensions of "Realist" thinking with residues of the "Critical" Frankfurt School, along with Deconstructionism. It is a far cry from Holmes, yet it suggests how he anticipated a century ago much that is now seen as radical and strangely new.
5. I can bear witness to the way the angry young New Deal militants felt, since I backed the Court plan as an expression of a daring executive supremacy to counter the judicial. See my *It Is Later Than You Think* (1938), in a new edition with a new afterword essay (New Brunswick, N.J.: Transaction Publishers, 1989).
6. For some writings of mine on all four see *Nine Scorpions in a Bottle*.
7. For a discussion of the impact of Leo Strauss and the "Chicago School" upon American constitutional history and law see Gordon Wood, "The Fundamentalists and the Constitution," 35 *New York Review of Books*, (18 February 1988): 33ff.

Index